William Greenough Thayer Shedd

A History of Christian Doctrine

Vol. I

William Greenough Thayer Shedd

A History of Christian Doctrine
Vol. I

ISBN/EAN: 9783337027919

Printed in Europe, USA, Canada, Australia, Japan

Cover: Foto ©Lupo / pixelio.de

More available books at **www.hansebooks.com**

A HISTORY

OF

CHRISTIAN DOCTRINE.

BY

WILLIAM G. T. SHEDD, D.D.

PROFESSOR OF BIBLICAL LITERATURE IN UNION THEOLOGICAL SEMINARY,
NEW YORK.

IN TWO VOLUMES.

VOL. I.

THIRD EDITION.

NEW YORK:
CHARLES SCRIBNER'S SONS,
743 AND 745 BROADWAY.

Entered, according to Act of Congress, in the year 1868, by
CHARLES SCRIBNER,
In the Clerk's Office of the District Court of the United States for the Southern District of New York.

Trow's
Printing and Bookbinding Co.,
PRINTERS AND BOOKBINDERS,
205-213 *East 12th St.*,
NEW YORK.

PREFACE.

The History of Christian Doctrine here given to the public is the result of several years of investigation, while the author held the professorship of Ecclesiastical History in the Theological Seminary at Andover, Massachusetts. As this is the first attempt of the kind in English literature, to write an account of the gradual construction of all the doctrines of the Christian religion, he had no models before him, and was compelled to originate his own method. Upon a survey of the vast field, it appeared to be the most simple and perspicuous plan to investigate each of the principal subjects by itself, starting from the first beginnings of scientific reflection upon it, and going down to the latest and most complete forms of statement. This method, though not without some disadvantages, recommends itself by reason of the opportunity it affords for continuous investigation, each part flowing out of the preceding and preparing for what follows, and the whole making a single and strong impression. Such a method is in harmony with the nature of history itself. The reader follows a single stream from its rise in its head-waters through all its windings, until it discharges itself, *immenso ore*, into the sea.

The history of Christian doctrine thus conceived and composed is one of the strongest of all defences of the Christian faith. It is a common remark, that a powerful statement is a powerful argument. This is true of the dogmas of Christianity. But there is no statement of revealed truth more clear, connected, and convincing, than that which it obtains in the gradual and sequacious constructions of the Church, from century to century. Let any one trace the course of thinking by the theological mind, upon the doctrine of the Trinity, e. g., and perceive how link follows link by necessary consequence; how the objections of the heretic or the latitudinarian only elicit a more exhaustive, and at the same time more guarded, statement, which carries the Church still nearer to the substance of revelation, and the heart of the mystery; how, in short, the trinitarian dogma, like the Christian life itself as described by the apostle, "being fitly joined together, and compacted by that which every joint supplieth, maketh increase unto the edifying of itself" into a grand architectural structure,—let this process from beginning to end pass before a thinking and logical mind, and it will be difficult for it to resist the conviction that here is science, here is self-consistent and absolute truth. It cannot be that the earnest reflection of all the Christian centuries should thus have spent itself upon a fiction and figment. The symbol in which this thinking embodied itself must be the exponent of a reality. Such is the impression made, and such is the unavoidable inference.

Christianity is, ultimately, its own best defence. The argument of a holy and beautiful life, it is universally conceded, is unanswerable; and so is the argument of a profound and homogeneous system. At a time when the divine origin and authority of the Christian religion are disputed and combatted with more than ordinary violence, it is seasonable to introduce the opponent to the Christian dogmas themselves, in the very act and process of their scientific construction. If he is capable of connected thinking himself, and his mind is at all accustomed to high problems, before he is aware he will be caught in the intellectual process, and whether he accept the conclusions of the ecclesiastical mind or not, he cannot but respect the mental acumen and energy which are exhibited. The history of such a mind as that of Ferdinand Christian Baur exemplifies this. To what degree that remarkable scholar and thinker was practically affected by the studies of many years, in the mines of Christian doctrine, is known only to the Searcher of hearts; but no one can peruse a page of any of his dogmatico-historical works without perceiving, that contempt for that great system which the oecumenical mind has built up out of the living stones of revelation was no feeling of his. The system was too vast in its reach, too comprehensive in its scope, too high and too deep in its aims, to provoke either ridicule or scorn. It might be a failure, but it was a splendid failure.

Respecting the sources whence this history is derived, the authors mentioned under the head of "Literature," at the beginning of each book, will indicate the works that have been most drawn upon. The writings of Athanasius, Augustine, and

Anselm, have yielded much solid and germinant material. To the dogmatic historians of Germany of the present century, I am greatly indebted; and not less so to the great lights of the English Church in the preceding centuries. These latter have been unduly overlooked, amidst the recent fertility of the Teutonic mind. Though comprising no continuous and entire history of Christian doctrine, and even when investigating a particular subject oftentimes doing it incidentally, the labors of Hooker and Bull, of Pearson and Waterland, are every way worthy to be placed beside those of Baur and Dorner. The learning is as ample and accurate, the logical grasp is as powerful, and the judgment more than equal. To these must be added the two manuals of Baumgarten-Crusius and Hagenbach, which have to some extent furnished the rubric under which the generalizations have been made, as well as considerable material itself.

But while the leading ancient, mediaeval, and modern authorities have been used, it has been my endeavor to fuse everything in my own mind. Perhaps the chief criticism that may be made upon the work is, that it betokens subjective qualities unduly for a historical production. That the work pays more attention to the orthodox than to the latitudinarian drift of thought, is plain. It is impossible for any one author to compose an encyclopaedic history. Every work of this kind must be stronger in some directions, than in others. I have felt a profound interest in the Nicene trinitarianism, the Augustinian anthropology, and the Anselmic soteriology, and from these centres have taken my departures. To what degree I have succeeded in fairly stating the variant or opposing theories, must be left to the judgment of each reader.

The work has been put to press amidst the pressure of engagements incident to a large pastoral charge. More leisure would have improved it. But it is committed, with all its imperfections, to the common current, with the hope, and aspiration, that it may contribute something towards that victory and triumph to which Christian science is destined in the earth.

NEW YORK, *Nov. 4th*, 1863.

CONTENTS

OF THE FIRST VOLUME.

INTRODUCTION.

	PAGE
§ 1. Methodology,	1
§ 2. Idea and definition of History,	7
§ 3. Development discriminated from creation,	11
§ 4. Development discriminated from improvement,	15
§ 5. Distinction between Sacred and Secular History,	18
§ 6. Uses of these definitions and distinctions,	23
§ 7. Relation of doctrinal to external history,	25
§ 8. Specification of the method adopted,	28

BOOK FIRST.

INFLUENCE OF PHILOSOPHICAL SYSTEMS UPON THE CONSTRUCTION OF CHRISTIAN DOCTRINE.

CHAPTER I.

Philosophical influences in the Ancient Church: A. D. 1–730.

§ 1. General features of Platonism and Aristotelianism,	51
§ 2. Philosophy at the time of the Advent,	60
§ 3. Philosophy in the Apologetic Period: A. D. 70–254,	62
§ 4. Philosophy in the Polemic Period: A. D. 254–730,	68

CHAPTER II.

Philosophical Influences in the Mediaeval Church: A.D. 730-1517.

§ 1. Platonism of the Mystic Theologians, . . . 75
§ 2. Aristotelianism of the Scholastic Theologians, . . 81
§ 3. Reaction against extreme Aristotelianism from the Later Mystics, and the revival of Greek Literature, . 85

CHAPTER III.

Philosophical Influences in the Modern Church: A. D. 1517-1850.

§ 1. Philosophy of the Reformers, ... 89
§ 2. Philosophy of the English and Anglo-American Churches, . 92
§ 3. Philosophy in the German Church, . . . 95

BOOK SECOND.

HISTORY OF APOLOGIES.

CHAPTER I.

Defences of Christianity in the Apologetic Period: A. D. 70-254.

§ 1. Preliminary Statements, ... 103
§ 2. Ebionite Skepticism and Christian replies, . . 106
§ 3. Gnostic Skepticism and Christian replies, . . . 113
§ 4. Pagan Skepticism and Christian replies, . . 117
§ 5. Recapitulatory Survey, ... 131

CHAPTER II.

Defences of Christianity in the Polemic Period: A. D. 254-730.

§ 1. Preliminary Statements, ... 133
§ 2. Mutual relations of Revelation and Reason, . . . 135
§ 3. Mutual relations of Faith and Science, . . . 154
§ 4. Mutual relations of the Supernatural and the Natural, . 164
§ 5. Recapitulatory Survey, ... 170

CHAPTER III.

Mediaeval Defences of Christianity: A. D. 730–1517.

§ 1. Preliminary Statements, ... 177
§ 2. Apologetics of Anselm, Aquinas, and Bernard, . . 179
§ 3. Apologetics of Abelard, ... 186

CHAPTER IV.

Modern Defences of Christianity: A. D. 1517–1850.

§ 1. Preliminary Statements, ... 190
§ 2. Intellectual Deism of Herbert of Cherbury, . . 192
§ 3. Materialistic and sensual Deism, . . . 196
§ 4. Replies to English Deism, ... 203
§ 5. French Encyclopædaism and German Rationalism, . 216

BOOK THIRD.

HISTORY OF THEOLOGY (TRINITARIANISM) AND CHRISTOLOGY.

CHAPTER I.

General Doctrine of the Divine Existence.

§ 1. Name of the deity, ... 223
§ 2. Pantheism and dualism in the Church, . . . 225
§ 3. Evidences of the Divine Existence, ... 229
§ 4. Divine Attributes, ... 240
§ 5. The Pagan Trinity, ... 243

CHAPTER II.

Ante-Nicene Trinitarianism.

§ 1. Preliminary Statements, ... 246
§ 2. Classes of Anti-Trinitarians, ... 253
§ 3. Trinitarianism of the Apostolic and Primitive Fathers, . 261
§ 4. Origen's Trinitarianism, ... 288

CHAPTER III.

Nicene Trinitarianism.

§ 1. Preliminary Statements,	306
§ 2. Problem before the Nicene Council,	308
§ 3. Nicene doctrine of Eternal Generation,	315
§ 4. Nicene doctrine of the Holy Ghost,	355
§ 5. Terminology of Nicene Trinitarianism,	362
§ 6. Critical estimate of the Nicene controversy,	372

CHAPTER IV.

Post-Nicene Trinitarianism.

§ 1. Mediaeval Trinitarianism,	376
§ 2. Trinitarianism of the Continental and English Reformers,	378
§ 3. Unitarianism,	383
§ 4. Latitudinarian Trinitarianism in the English and German Churches,	385

CHAPTER V.

Doctrine of the Person of Christ.

§ 1. Principal Heresies in Christology,	392
§ 2. The Chalcedon Christology,	309

CHAPTER III.

Mediaeval Defences of Christianity: A. D. 730–1517.

	PAGE
§ 1. Preliminary Statements,	177
§ 2. Apologetics of Anselm, Aquinas, and Bernard,	179
§ 3. Apologetics of Abelard,	186

CHAPTER IV.

Modern Defences of Christianity: A. D. 1517–1850.

§ 1. Preliminary Statements,	190
§ 2. Intellectual Deism of Herbert of Cherbury,	192
§ 3. Materialistic and sensual Deism,	196
§ 4. Replies to English Deism,	203
§ 5. French Encyclopædaism and German Rationalism,	216

BOOK THIRD.

HISTORY OF THEOLOGY (TRINITARIANISM) AND CHRISTOLOGY.

CHAPTER I.

General Doctrine of the Divine Existence.

§ 1. Name of the deity,	223
§ 2. Pantheism and dualism in the Church,	225
§ 3. Evidences of the Divine Existence,	229
§ 4. Divine Attributes,	240
§ 5. The Pagan Trinity,	243

CHAPTER II.

Ante-Nicene Trinitarianism.

§ 1. Preliminary Statements,	246
§ 2. Classes of Anti-Trinitarians,	253
§ 3. Trinitarianism of the Apostolic and Primitive Fathers,	261
§ 4. Origen's Trinitarianism,	288

CHAPTER III.

Nicene Trinitarianism.

	PAGE
§ 1. Preliminary Statements,	306
§ 2. Problem before the Nicene Council,	308
§ 3. Nicene doctrine of Eternal Generation,	315
§ 4. Nicene doctrine of the Holy Ghost,	355
§ 5. Terminology of Nicene Trinitarianism,	362
§ 6. Critical estimate of the Nicene controversy,	372

CHAPTER IV.

Post-Nicene Trinitarianism.

§ 1. Mediaeval Trinitarianism,	376
§ 2. Trinitarianism of the Continental and English Reformers,	378
§ 3. Unitarianism,	383
§ 4. Latitudinarian Trinitarianism in the English and German Churches,	385

CHAPTER V.

Doctrine of the Person of Christ.

§ 1. Principal Heresies in Christology,	392
§ 2. The Chalcedon Christology,	399

INTRODUCTION.

§ 1. *Methodology.*

DES CARTES: Dissertatio de Methodo (English translation published by Sutherland, Edinburgh, 1850). COLERIDGE: Essays on Method, Works II. 408–472, Harper's Ed. WHEWELL: History of Inductive Sciences (Introduction). AGASSIZ: Natural History (Essay on Classification).

BEFORE proceeding to investigate the several subjects that belong to a History of Christian Doctrine, it is necessary to make preliminary statements, respecting the general scheme and method, upon which the investigation will proceed. Methodology, or the science of Method, is never more important, and never yields greater fruit, than when applied to historical studies. At the same time, it possesses an independent value, apart from its uses when applied to any particular subject. Treating, as it does, of the scientific mode of approaching and opening any department of knowledge, it is a species of *philosophia prima*, or philosophy of philosophy, such as Plato and Aristotle were in search of. This, in their view, was the very highest kind of science; for the reason that it is not confined to some one portion of truth, as a specific science is, but is an instrument by which truth universally may be reached. It was what they denominated an *organon*,—an implement whereby the truth of any subject might be discovered. It, thus, resembled the science of logic. Logic does not, like philosophy or theology, enunciate any particular truths, but teaches those principles of universal reasoning, by which particular truths, in these departments or any other, may be discovered, and defended. If, now, we conceive of a science of investigation, that should stand in the same relation to all particular investigations, that logic does to reasoning generally, we shall have the conception of the science of Methodology; and it is one form of that primary philosophy which Plato and Aristotle were seeking for.

In the judgment of these thinkers, the *philosophia prima* was the most difficult problem that could be presented to the human mind; because, it was the problem for solving all problems. It was like those general formulas which the mathematician seeks, by means of which he may resolve a great number of particular questions. They did not claim to have constructed such a *prima philosophia*, yet they none the less regarded it as the goal, which should be continually kept in view, by the philosopher. And they would measure the progress of philosophic thought, from age to age, by the approximation that was made towards it. Even if the goal should never be reached, still the department of philosophy would be a gainer, by such a high aim. Lord Bacon himself regrets, that the eye had been taken off from it, and that thinkers had confined themselves to mere parts of truth. "Another error,"—he remarks, in enumerating the "peccant humors" of learning,—"is, that after the distribution of particular arts and sciences, men have abandoned universality, or 'philosophia prima'; which cannot but cease and stop all progression. For no perfect discovery can be made upon a flat or level, neither is it possible to discover the more remote and deeper parts of any science, if you stand but upon the level of the same science, and ascend not to a higher science."[1]

The science of Method seeks from this higher level to survey all the sciences, and from an elevated point of view, to discover, in each given instance, the true mode of investigation. It is the science of the sciences, because it furnishes the philosophic clue to all of them, and stands in the same relation to the whole encyclopædia of human inquiry, that a master-key does to all the locks which it opens. Its uses are evident; for if the method, or plan of investigation, is the avenue by which the human mind makes its entrance into a subject, then, upon its intrinsic adaptation to the case in hand, depends

[1] BACON: Advancement of Learning, Works I. 173, 193, Pa. Ed.

the whole success of the inquiry. If the method be a truly philosophic one, the examination of the topic proceeds with ease, accuracy, and thoroughness. But if it be arbitrary and capricious, the inquirer commences with an error, which, like a mistake in the beginning of an arithmetical calculation, only repeats, and multiplies itself, every step of the way.

Methodology seeks, in each instance, to discover *the method of nature*, as that specific mode of investigation which is best fitted to elucidate a subject. By the method of nature is meant, that plan which corresponds with the internal structure. Each department of human inquiry contains an interior order, and arrangement, which the investigator must detect, and along which he must move, in order to a thorough and symmetrical apprehension of it. The world of mind is as regular, and architectural, as the world of matter; and hence all branches of intellectual and moral science require for their successful prosecution, the same natural and *structural* modes of investigation, which a Cuvier applies to the animal kingdom, and a De Candolle to the vegetable. The method of the anatomist is a beautiful example of the method of nature. As in anatomy, the dissection follows the veins, or muscles, or nerves, or limbs, in their branchings off, so the natural method, everywhere, never cuts across, but along the inward structure, following it out into its organic divisions. The science of Method aids in discovering such a mode of investigation, and tends to produce in the investigator, that fine mental tact, by which he instinctively approaches a subject from the right point, and like the slate quarryman lays it open, along the line of its structure, and its fracture. The power of method is closely allied to the power of genius. A mind inspired by it attacks a subject with great impetuosity, and yet does not mar, or mutilate it, while it penetrates into all its parts. "I have seen Michael Angelo,"—says a cotemporary of that great artist— "at work after he had passed his sixtieth year, and although he was not very robust, he cut away as many scales from a block of very hard marble, in a quarter of an hour, as three young sculptors would have effected in three or four hours,—a thing almost incredible, to one who had not actually witnessed it. Such was the impetuosity, and fire, with which he pursued his labor, that I almost thought the whole work must have gone to pieces; with a single stroke, he brought down fragments three or four fingers thick, and so close upon his mark, that had he passed it, even in the slightest degree, there would have been a danger of ruining the whole; since any such injury, unlike the case of works in plaster or stucco, would have been irreparable."[1] Such is the bold, yet safe power, of a mind that works by an idea, and methodically.

The importance of a philosophic method is

[1] HARFORD: Life of Angelo.

nowhere more apparent than in the department of History. The materials are so abundant and various, that unless they are distributed in a natural order, they accumulate upon each other, and produce inextricable confusion. And yet, in no province is it more difficult to attain to a method at once comprehensive, and exhaustive. For History includes so much, that it is not easy to enclose it all at once; and it is so full of minute details, that many of them escape. And even when we separate some one division of the subject, such as Dogmatic History for example, and treat it by itself, the same difficulty remains. Such questions as the following immediately arise. Shall the whole system of Christian doctrine be described together, in its origin and gradual formation; or shall a single dogma be selected and followed out by itself? If the first mode be adopted, we secure comprehensiveness at the expense of exhaustiveness. If the latter be chosen, we cannot exhibit the reciprocal influence of doctrine upon doctrine, and lose the advantages of a comparative view of the whole, in securing those of minuteness and thoroughness in a part. A multitude of such questions immediately arises, when the dogmatic historian begins to lay out his plan of procedure, and he finds that almost every advantage is counterbalanced by some disadvantage. It only remains that he should exercise his best judgment, and produce the best method that is possible to him. The grade of its excellence can be known only by trial. Just so far as it proves itself to be a logical instrument of investigation, and actually divides and distributes the historical materials in a natural order, does it prove its author to be possessed of genuine philosophic talent.

Addressing ourselves, then, to the task of indicating a scientific method in Dogmatic History, it is evident, that the first step to be taken is, *to enunciate the generic idea of History itself.* What is History in its own nature? What is the fundamental conception involved in it? And inasmuch as Dogmatic History is a branch of Sacred, in distinction from Secular, or Profane History, it will become necessary to discriminate these two latter species from each other, so that the special subject of our investigations may be narrowed down to its real and distinctive elements. The definition, therefore, of History in its abstract nature, together with its subdivision into Sacred and Secular, must precede, and prepare the way for, the distribution of the dogmatic materials which we are to analyze, and combine.

§ 2. *Idea, and definition of History.*

History, in its abstract and distinctive nature, we define to be a *development.*[1] It is a gradual ex-

[1] The reader will find the author's views exhibited more at length, in his Lectures upon the Philosophy of History, Andover, 1856, and also in his Discourses and Essays, pp. 113–180, Andover, 1856.

pansion over a wider surface, of that which at the instant of its creation existed in a more invisible and metaphysical form. The development of a tree from a rudimental germ, for example, constitutes its historic process. Here the evolution, or expansion, is continuous from the seed, or rather from that invisible principle which contains the whole fabric potentially. For Cowper's lines upon the Yardley Oak are literally true:

> "Thou wast a bauble once, a cup and ball
> Which babes might play with; and the thievish jay,
> Seeking her food, with ease might have purloined
> The auburn nut that held thee, swallowing down
> Thy yet close-folded latitude of boughs,
> And all thy embryo vastness, at a gulp."

The idea of an evolution from a potential basis, is identical with that of a history. In thinking of one, we unavoidably think of the other, and this evinces an inward coincidence between the two conceptions. Unceasing motion, from a given point, through several stadia, to a final terminus, is a characteristic belonging as inseparably to the history of Man, or the history of Doctrine, as to that of any physical evolution whatever. In bringing before our minds, for example, the passage of an intellectual or a moral idea, from one degree of energy and efficiency to another, in the career of a nation, or of mankind, we unavoidably construe it as a continuous expanding process. The same law of organic sequence prevails in the sphere of mind, and of freedom, that works in the kingdom of matter and necessity. There is a *growth* of the mind, as truly and strictly as a growth of the body. The *basis* from which the one proceeds is, indeed, very different from that which lies at the foundation of the other. The evolution, in the first instance, is that of a spiritual essence, while that in the second is the unfolding of a material germ; but the process in each instance, alike, is an organically connected one. The history of matter, and the history of mind, though totally different from each other in respect to the substance from which the movement proceeds, and the laws that regulate it, are alike in respect to the *continuity* of the movement.

The essential substance of History, be it that of Nature or of Man, is continually passing through a motive process. The germ is slowly unfolding, as it is the nature of all germs to do. A corn of Egyptian wheat may sleep in the swathes and foldings of a mummy, through three thousand springs, but the purpose of its creation cannot be thwarted, except by the grinding destruction of its germinal substance. It was created to grow, and notwithstanding this long interval of slumbering life, the development begins the instant it is taken from the mummy, and cast into the moist earth. In like manner, an idea which inherently belongs to the mind of man may be hindered in its progress, and for ages may seem to be extinct; yet it is none the less in existence, and a reality. It is all the while a factor in the earthly career of mankind, and the historian who should throw it out of the account would misconceive, and misrepresent, the entire historic process. An idea of human reason, like popular liberty, for example, may make no external appearance for whole periods, but its reappearance, with an energy of operation heightened by its long suppression in the consciousness of nations, is the most impressive of all proofs, that it has a necessary existence in human nature, and is destined to be developed. A doctrine of Divine reason, like that of justification by Christ's atonement, is a positive truth which has been lodged in the Christian mind by Divine revelation, and is destined to an universal influence, a historical development, in and through the church; notwithstanding that some branches and ages of the church have lost it out of their religious experience. In brief, whatever has been constitutionally *inlaid* either in matter or in mind, by the Creator of both, is destined by Him, and under His own superintendence, to be evolved; and of all such germinal substance, be it in the sphere of Nature or of Man, we may say, that not a particle of it will be annihilated; it will pass through the predetermined stages of an expanding process, and obtain a full development. And this its development is its *history*.

§ 3. *Creation discriminated from Development.*

The doctrine of Development has been greatly misconceived, especially in modern speculation, and hence it becomes necessary to discriminate it still more carefully. Theorists have handled it in such a manner as to invalidate the principles of both natural and revealed religion. In the first place, substituting the idea of development for that of *creation*, they have constructed a pantheistic theory of the origin of the universe; and in the second place, confounding a development with an *improvement*, they have precluded the necessity of any supernatural and remedial methods for human welfare.

There are no two conceptions more diverse from each other, than those of Creation and Development. The one excludes the other. Development supposes existing materials; creation supposes none at all. Creation is from nothing;[1] development is

---

[1] See Cudworth's statement of the senses in which the dictum, "ex nihilo nihil fit," may be understood, Works III. 90 (Tegg's Ed.); also Anselm's Monologium, Caput VIII. (Ed. Migne); also Mosheim's Dissertation on creation out of nothing, in Cudworth's Intellectual System, III. 140 sq. (Tegg's Ed.). The clause "de nihilo" is vital in defining a creative act. For the human mind, involved in the unbroken chain of antecedents and consequents, is almost irresistibly prone to ask *from what stuff* is the created product made. The old objection, "de nihilo nihil fit," springs out of this proneness. Nothing comes from nothing, by the method of *development*, it is true; but not by the method of creation. The early fathers, owing to the prevalence of the Gnostic theory of world-making, were very careful to mark the differ-

from something. Creation indeed implies a preexisting Creator, but not as the substance or stuff out of which the creature is made. This would be emanation, or generation. The Creator, when he issues a creative fiat, does not send out a beam or efflux from his own substance, but by a miracle of omnipotence wills an absolutely new entity into being. This creative act is, of necessity, inexplicable, because explanation would imply the possibility of pointing out preëxisting materials of which the created product is composed. But by the very definition of creation, there are none. Development, on the contrary, implies the existence of rudimental and germinal matter. It supposes that a creative fiat has been uttered, and cannot be ac-

---

ence between creation, and composition or formation. THEOPHILUS (Ad Autolycum, II. 4) remarks: "Εἰ ὁ θεὸς ἀγένητος καὶ ὕλη ἀγένητος, οὐκ ἔτι ὁ θεὸς ποιητὴς τῶν ὅλων ἐστί." IRENAEUS (Adversus Haereses, II. x. 4) says: "Homines quidem de nihilo non possunt aliquid facere, sed de materia subjacenti ; Deus autem materiam fabricationis ipse adinvenit." AUGUSTINE (Confessiones, XII. vii), in the same strain remarks: "Fecisti coelum et terram non de te, nam esset aequale unigenito tuo; et aliud praeter te non erat, unde faceres ea, et ideo de nihilo fecisti coelum et terram." AMBROSE (Hexaëmeron, II. 2) teaches the same truth in a terse and lively manner. "Audi verba Dei, *Fiat* dicit. Jubentis est, non aestimantis. Imperat naturae, non possibilitati obtemperat, non mensuras colligit, non pondus exanimat. Voluntas ejus mensura rerum est. Sermo ejus finis est operis." AQUINAS's definition (Summa I. Quaest. lxv. 3) exhibits his usual exhaustiveness. "Creatio est productio alicujus rei secundum suam totam substantiam, nullo praesupposito, quod sit vel increatum, vel ab aliquo creatum."—" Creation," remarks FUSELI (Lecture III), "is an idea of pure astonishment, and admissible only when we mention Omnipotence."

counted for, except upon such a supposition. It requires a potential base from which to start, and this requires an act of absolute origination *de nihilo*. For there is nothing more absurd, than the pantheistic notion of an eternal potentiality, or, which is the same thing, that the Infinite is subject to the same limitations with the Finite, and must pass, by the method of development, from less perfect, to more perfect (yet ever imperfect) stages of existence, and in this manner originate the worlds. The idea of an absolute perfection implies, that the Being to whom it belongs, is immutable,—the same yesterday, to-day, and forever. The whole fabric of ancient and modern Pantheism rests upon the *petitio principii*, that the doctrine of evolution has the same legitimate application within the sphere of the Infinite and Eternal, that it has within that of the Finite and Temporal,—a postulate that annihilates the distinction between the two. The idea of undeveloped being has no rational meaning, except in reference to the Created and the Conditioned. Progressive evolution within the Divine Nature would imply a career for the deity, like that of his creatures, in which he was passing from less to more perfect stages of existence, and would thus bring him within the realm of the relative and imperfect. All latency is necessarily excluded from the Eternal One, by virtue of that absolute perfection, and metaphysical self-completeness, whereby his being is " without variableness or shadow of turning." His uncreated essence is incapable of self-expanding processes, and hence the created universe cannot be an effluent portion of his essence, but must be a secondary substance which is the pure make of his sheer fiat. To the question which still and ever returns: How does the potential basis which lies at the bottom of every finite development, itself come into existence? to what, or to whom, do these germs of future and ceaseless processes owe their origin? the theist gives but one answer. He applies the doctrine of creation out of nothing, to all germinal substance whatsoever. For the doctrine of evolution explains nothing at this point. A development is simply the unfolding of that which has been previously folded up, and not the origination of entity from nonentity. The *growth* of a germ is not the creation of it, but is merely the expansion of a substance already existing. All attempts to explain the *origin* of the universe, by the theory of development, or expansion, like the Indian cosmogony, drive the mind back from point to point in a series of secondary evolutions, still leaving the inquiry after the primary origin, and actual beginning of things, unanswered. Mere development cannot account for the origin of a strictly *new* thing. A germ can only protrude its own latency, and cannot inlay a foreign one. The significant fact in Natural History, not yet invalidated by the most torturing experiments of baffled theorists, that one species never expands into another, proves that though a process of development can be accounted for out of the latent potentiality at the base, the latter can be accounted for, only by recurring to the creative power of God. The expansion of a vegetable seed, even if carried on through all the cycles upon cycles of the geological system, never transmutes it into the egg of animal life; and this only verifies the self-evident proposition, that nothing can come forth, that has never been put in.

§ 4. *Development discriminated from Improvement.*

Of equal importance is it, to discriminate the idea of a Development from that of an *Improvement*. The abstract definition of history merely describes it as an evolution, or movement from some germinal point, but does not determine whether the movement be upward, or downward; from good to better, or from bad to worse. This depends upon the nature of the potential base from which the expanding process issues. Within the sphere of material nature, the germ, being a pure creation of God, can exhibit only a healthy and normal development. But within the sphere of *free-will*, the original foundation, laid in creation, for a legitimate growth and progress, may be displaced, and a secondary one laid by the abuse of freedom. This has occurred in the apostacy of a part of the angelic host, and of the entire human race. By this revolutionary act, the first potential basis of human history, which provided for a purer progress, and a grander evolution than man can now conceive of, was displaced by a second basis, which likewise provided for a false development, and an awful history, if not supernaturally hindered, all along through the same endless duration. It must, however, be carefully observed, that the secondary foundation did not issue out of the primary one, *by the method of development.* Original righteousness was not unfolded into original sin. Sin was a *new* thing, originated de nihilo, by the finite will. It had no evil antecedents, and was in the strictest sense a *creation* of the creature. As it is impossible that the creature should originate any good thing de nihilo, since this is solely the Creator's prerogative, so it is impossible that the Creator should originate evil de nihilo, since this implies a mutable excellence, and a possibility of self-ruin. Under and within the permissive decree of God, *sin is man's creation;* he makes it out of nothing. For the origin of moral evil cannot be accounted for, by the expansion of something already in existence, any more than the origin of matter itself can be. Original righteousness unfolded never so long, and intensely, will never be developed into original sin. The passage from one to the other must be by an absolutely *originant* act of self-will; which act, subject only to the limitation and condition above-mentioned, of the permission of the Supreme Being, is strictly creative from nothing. The origin of sin is, thus, the origination of a new historic germ, and not the unfolding or modification of an old one; and hence the necessity of postulating a creating, in distinction from a merely developing energy,—such as is denoted by the *possibilitas peccandi* attributed by the theologian to the will of the unfallen Adam.

The origination of a corrupt nature by the self-will of the first man, and the subsequent development of it in the secular life and history of the human generations, bring to view another aspect of the idea of development, and a different application of the doctrine of continuous evolution. This stubborn fact of apostacy compels the theorist to acknowledge what he is prone to lose sight of, viz.; that so far as the abstract definition is concerned, development may be synonymous with corruption and decline, as well as with improvement; that the organic sequences of history may be those of decay and death, as well as those of bloom and life. For there is no more reason for regarding evolution as synonymous with improvement alone, than with degeneracy alone. Scientific terms are wide and impartial. No particular truth is told, when it is asserted that there is a process of development going on in the world. This is granted upon all sides. On coming into the sphere of free agency, it is necessary, in order to any definite and valuable statement, to determine by actual observation, *what it is that is being expanded*; whether it is a primitive potentiality originated by the Creator, or a secondary one originated by the creature, *to either of which, the abstract conception of development is equally applicable.*

§ 5. *Distinction between Sacred and Secular History.*

This discrimination of the idea of development, from that of improvement, prepares the way for the *distinction between Sacred and Secular History.* Had the course of human history proceeded from the original basis, laid by the Creator, in the holiness and happiness of an unfallen humanity, human development would have been identical with human improvement. The evolution of the primitive historic germ would have exhibited a normal and perfect career, like that of the unfallen angels, and like that of the beautiful and perfect growths in the natural world. But we know, as matter of fact, that the unfolding of humanity does not now proceed from this first and proper point of departure. The creative idea, by the Creator's permission, is not realized by the free agent. The law of man's being is not obeyed, and his true end and destination is not attained. The original historic germ was crowded out by a second false one, from which the actual career of man now proceeds. But this illegitimate career, or development of a secondary and corrupted nature, exhibits all the characteristics of a continuous evolution. The depravation of humanity has been as organic a sequence from a common centre, as is to be found either in the realm of matter or of mind. The history of apostate man is as truly a development of moral evil, as the history of the angelic world is a development of moral good. And this species of history, by one of those spontaneous epithets which oftentimes contain a wonderful depth of truth, for the very reason that they are the invention of the common and universal mind, and not of a particular philo-sophical school, is well denominated *profane*. The secular career of man is a violation of sacred obligations, and of a divinely-established order. In reference to the Divine idea and intent, in the creation of man, it is a sacrilege. It displays downward tendencies, connected with each other, and acting and reacting upon each other, by the same law that governs any and every evolution. The acknowledged deterioration of languages, literatures, religions, arts, sciences, and civilizations; the slow and certain decay of national vigor, and return to barbarism; the unvarying decline from public virtue to public voluptuousness: in short, the entire history of man, so far as he is outside of the recuperating influences of Christianity, and unaffected by the supernatural intervention of his Creator, though it is a self-willed and guilty process, is, yet, in every part and particle of it, as organically connected, and as strict an evolution from a potential base, as is that other upward tendency, started in the Christian Church, and ended in the eternal state, by which humanity is being restored to the heights whence it fell.

For Sacred History is a process that results from the replacement of the original righteousness, and the original germ. It can no more be an evolution from the corrupted human nature, than this corruption itself can be a development of the pure and holy humanity. As we have seen, that the origin of the second, and false foundation for man's career upon the globe, can be accounted for, only by postulating an absolutely *originating* activity upon the part of the creature; so the origin of that new foundation which is laid for the upward and recuperative career of man, in the Christian Church, can be accounted for, only by postulating a *creative* energy and influence upon the part of God. This energy is found in Revelation, considered in its twofold direction, as a manifestation of truth, and a dispensation of spiritual influence. This supernatural energy, seizing upon the corrupt and helpless man, reinstates him in his original relations, and in the new birth of a principle of holiness, lays again the foundation for an upward career, which ends finally in the perfection with which he was originally created and endowed. Sacred History is thus differentiated from Secular, or Profane, by its underlying supernaturalism. In passing from Secular to Sacred History, we pass from the domain of merely human and sinful, to that of divine and holy agencies. For we do not find in the history of the world, as the opposite and antagonist of the church—of the natural, as distinguished from the renewed man,—any evidence of a special and direct intercommunication, between man and God. We find only the ordinary workings of the human mind, and such products as are confessedly within its competence to originate, evil included, and tinging all the elements with its dark stain. We can, indeed, perceive the hand of an overruling Providence throughout this realm, employed chiefly in restraining the wrath of man, but through the whole long course of false development, we see no signs, or products, of a supernatural and special interference in the affairs of men. Empires rise and fall; arts and sciences bloom and decay; the poet dreams his dream of the ideal, and the philosopher elicits and tasks the utmost possibility of the finite reason; and still, so far as its highest interests and destiny are concerned, the condition and history of the race remains substantially the same. It is not until a *communication* is established between the mind of man, and the mind of God; it is not until the Creator comes down to earth, by miracle and by revelation, by incarnation and by the Holy Ghost, that a new order of ages, and a new species of history begins.

This new and higher history, this new and higher evolution of a *regenerated* humanity, is the theme of the Church Historian. The subject matter becomes extraordinary. The basis of fact, in the career of the Church, is supernatural, in both senses of the term. In the first place, from the expulsion from Eden down to the close of the apostolic age, a positively *miraculous* intervention of Divine power lies under the series of events, momentarily withdrawn, and momentarily reappearing, throughout the long line of Patriarchal, Jewish, and Apostolic history,—the very intermittency of the action indicating, like an Icelandic geyser, the reality and proximity of the power. And if, in the second place, we pass from external events, to that inward change that was constantly being wrought in human character, by which the Church was called out from the mass of men, and made to live and grow in the midst of an ignorant, or a cultivated heathenism; if we pass from the miraculous to the simply *spiritual* manifestation of the divine agency, as it is seen in the renewal of the individual heart, and in the inward life of the Church, we find that we are in a totally different sphere from that of Secular History, and in a far higher one. There is now a positive intercommunication, between the human and the Divine, and the development that results constitutes a history far profounder, far purer, far more hopeful and beautiful, than that of the natural man, and the secular world.

§ 6. *Uses of these definitions and distinctions.*

In these definitions and discriminations, we find a proper introduction to Dogmatic History. For this portion of the general subject of Ecclesiastical History presents a very transparent and beautiful specimen of a historic evolution. The germ, or base of the process, is the dogmatic material given in the scriptures of the Old and New Testaments. In the gift of revelation, the entire sum, and rudimental substance, of Christian theology was given. But this body of dogma was by no means fully apprehended, by the ecclesiastical mind, in the outset. Its scientific and systematic comprehension is a gradual process; the fuller creed bursts out of the narrower; the expanded treatise swells forth growth-like from the more slender; the work of each generation of the Church joins on upon that of the preceding; so that the history of Christian Doctrine is the account of the expansion which revealed truth has obtained, through the endeavor of the Church universal to understand its meaning, and to evince its self-consistence, in opposition to the attacks and objections of scepticism.

The idea and definition of History, which we have thus enunciated, gives to this branch of inquiry all the advantages that flow from the dynamic theory, or the theory of organic connections, and at the same time protects it from the naturalism and pantheism which have too often invaded the province of history, in connection with the doctrine of development. The distinction between a creation and an evolution, carefully observed by the historian, preserves in his investigations, both the Supernatural and the Natural,—both the supernatural fiat or creative energy, from which everything takes its beginning of existence, and the natural process of development, that commences, and advances gradually from that point. And the distinction between Secular and Sacred History, if firmly grasped, likewise yields to the historical investigator all the advantages of the theory of connected and gradual processes, while, at the same time, it protects him from the error of those who overlook the fact of human apostasy, and who, consequently, see but one species of historical development in the world,—that, namely, of improvement and steady approximation to the ideal and the perfect. The distinction, in question, discriminates between normal and abnormal developments, and directs attention to the fact, that the total history of man upon the globe is not now a single current; that the stream of human history, originally one, was parted in the garden of Eden, and became two fountainheads, which have flowed on, each in its own channel and direction, and will continue to do so forevermore; and that there are now two kingdoms, two courses of development, two histories, in the universal history of man on the globe,—viz.:

the Sacred and the Secular, the Church and the World.[1]

§ 7. *Relation of doctrinal to external history.*

This enunciation of the idea of History brings us to the subject matter itself,—to the materials and elements of Dogmatic History. Our methodizing must now mark off the divisions of the doctrinal history of the Christian Church, in accordance with the actual structure of the subject, and arrange them in their natural order. These divisions will yield the topics that are to be investigated.

But, before proceeding to our analysis, it is worthy of notice, that although the external and doctrinal history of the Church can be distinguished from each other, they cannot be divided or separated from each other. The religious experience, the dogmatic thinking, and all the work-

---

[1] The assertion, "that God is in History," is sometimes made in such a manner and connection, as to obliterate the distinction between sacred and secular history, the church and the world. God is in secular history by his providence only; but he is in sacred history by an *inward* efficiency, the supernatural agency of his Spirit. In the first instance, he is the controller of the movement; in the latter, he is its inspiring life, and actuating energy. As the indwelling author of upright purposes and righteous designs, God is not in the history of Babylon, or of Rome, or of any portion of unregenerate humanity. Only where he works "to will and to do of his good pleasure," can it be said that God is *in* the process; and no one, surely, can find such an inward agency as this, in the sensual civilization of Babylon, or the ambitious civilization of Rome.

ings of the Christian mind and heart, exert a direct influence upon the outward aspects of Christianity, and show themselves in them. Improvement in one sphere leads to improvement in the other; and deterioration in the one leads to deterioration in the other. The construction of a creed oftentimes shapes the whole external history of a people. The scientific expansion of a single doctrine results in the formation of a particular type of Christian morality, or piety; which, again, shows itself in active missionary enterprises, and the spread of Christianity through great masses of heathen population. In these instances, the symbol and the dogma become the most practical and effective of agencies, and tend immediately to modify the whole structure of a Church, or a people,—nay of entire Christendom. In this way, the doctrinal history is organically connected with the external, and in the last result, with the whole secular history of man. Still, it is plain that we must distinguish parts of a subject, in order to discuss it with success. He who should attempt to grasp such a great theme as Ecclesiastical History, all at once, and to treat it in the entire comprehensiveness and universality with which it is acted out, and going on, would attempt a task too great for human powers. History occurs simultaneously, in all its parts and elements. Like Wordsworth's cloud, " it moveth all together, if it move at all." But although the history of an age is going on all at once, it cannot be written all at once. Missionaries are proceeding on their errands of love, theologians are constructing their doctrinal systems, persecutors are slaying the believer, prelates are seeking for supremacy, kings are checking the advance of the churchman,—all this, and an infinitude of detail, is going on in one and the very same period of time; but what historian can represent this whole simultaneous movement, with perfect success? He who would sketch an outline of such vast proportions, as to include all that has been thought, felt, and done, by the Christian Church, would make a sketch which no single human mind can fill up.[1]

The great whole, therefore, will be most completely exhibited, if the work is divided among many laborers, and each portion is made a special, and perhaps life-long object of attention, by a single mind. And it is for this reason, that the student must not rest satisfied with perusing a general history of the Christian religion and Church, however excellently composed. He must also study special histories,—the history of Doctrine, both general and special; the history of Creeds; the history of Polities; the history of Heresies; the history of Christian Philosophy, and of Christian Art; the

[1] NIEDNER has attempted to do this, in his manual. We can see the embarrassing effect of a universal outline, in NEANDER. The last part of his great work is not equal, in thoroughness, to the first, particularly in the dogmatico-historical section.

history of Missions; Monographs, or sketches of historic individuals. By thus examining one portion of the great subject, at a time and by itself, the mind obtains a more complete and symmetrical understanding of it, than is possible, in case only manuals and general treatises are read. Year after year, such a careful and discriminating study of special parts of the subject builds up the mind, in very much the same gradual mode and style, in which it has pleased the Head of the Church to spread his religion, and establish his kingdom upon the earth. The individual repeats in his own culture, the great historic process, and the result is a deep and clear apprehension of, Christianity, as a kingdom and a power among men.

§ 8. *Specification of the Method adopted.*

The Doctrinal History of the Church, in the method which we shall adopt, divides into the following topics:

I. The first division discusses the *Influence of Philosophical Systems, upon the construction of Christian Doctrine.*

We naturally begin the account of the internal history of Christianity, with the exhibition of philosophical opinions, because they have always exerted a powerful influence upon the modes and systems of theological speculation. We are obliged to take this influence into account, because we find it at work in the history itself. We have no concern with the question, whether philosophy ought to exert any influence upon the theological mind, in unfolding revealed truth. The settlement of this question belongs to the theologian, and not to the historian. But however the question be answered, it is a fact, that human speculation has exerted a very marked influence upon the interpretation of Scripture, and particularly, upon the construction of doctrines and symbols; and actual fact is the legitimate material, the true stuff and staple of history.

Moreover, we begin with considering the influence of Philosophy upon Christianity, because this influence shows itself at the very beginning. The human mind is already in a certain philosophical condition, before it receives Christianity, and even before Christianity is offered to it by the Divine Mind. In the history of man, that which is human precedes, chronologically, that which is divine. "That was not first which is spiritual: but that which is natural, and afterward that which is spiritual" (1 Cor. xv. 46). Men are sinners before they are made saints; and they are philosophers before they become theologians. When Christianity was revealed, in its last and fullest form, by the incarnation of the Eternal Word, it found the human mind already occupied with a human philosophy. Educated men were Platonists, or Stoics, or Epicureans. And if we go back to the time of the Patriarchal and Jewish revelations of the Old Testament, we find that there was in the minds of men, an existing system of natural religion and ethics, which was for that elder secular world what those Grecian philosophies were for the cultivated heathen intellect at the advent of Christ. A natural method in Dogmatic History must therefore commence with the influence of human philosophy, because this influence is actually existing and apparent at the beginning of the process. Christianity comes down from heaven by a supernatural revelation, but it finds an existing state of human culture, into which it enters, and begins to exert its transforming power. Usually it overmasters that culture, but in some instances it is temporarily overmastered by it. But the existing culture of a people is more the product of philosophy than of any other department of human knowledge; and hence the necessity of commencing the account of the doctrinal development of Christianity, with the exhibition of the influence of Philosophical Systems.

II. The second division, in the method we have adopted, comprises the *History of Apologies, or Defences of Christianity.*

We are naturally led to consider the manner in which the Christian religion has been maintained against attacks by the speculative understanding of man, after having first discussed the general influence of philosophy upon its interpretation and statement. For this second division is supplementary to the first. The defence of Christianity upon rational grounds, completes the philosophical enunciation of it. As matter of fact, we find that, so soon as the theologian has done his utmost to make a logical and systematic representation of revealed religion, he is immediately called upon by the skeptic to defend his representation. And having done this, his work is at an end.

But this is not the whole truth. For the relation between these two divisions is also that of action and reaction. The endeavor to defend Christianity very often elicits a more profoundly philosophic statement of it. The defence of the doctrine of the Trinity against Sabellian and Arian objections, resulted in a deeper view of the subject than had heretofore prevailed. The subtle objections, and dangerous half-truths of the Tridentine divines, were the occasion of a more accurate statement of the doctrine of justification by faith without works, than is to be found in the Ancient Church. Indeed, a clear, coherent, and fundamental presentation is one of the strongest arguments. Power of statement is power of argument. It precludes misrepresentations. It corrects misstatements. Hence, we find that the Defences of Christianity embody a great amount of philosophical expansion of Scripture doctrine; so that the history of Apologies is oftentimes, to a great extent, the history of the influence of Philosophy upon Christianity. In this, as we shall frequently have occasion to observe, we have an incidental, and therefore strong proof of the position, that history is organic in the connection and interaction of its divisions and elements.

Again, we see the propriety of discussing the History of Defences immediately after that of Philosophical Influences, from the fact, that both divisions alike involve the relation of reason to revelation. In the first division, reason receives and states the revealed truth; in the second, it maintains and defends it. But neither of these two functions can be discharged, without either expressly, or by implication, determining what is the true relation of the finite to the infinite reason, and coming to some conclusion respecting the distinctive offices of each.

III. The third division, in our general method of investigation, comprises the *History of individual Doctrines.*

Comparing the parts of the plan with each other, this is the most interesting and important of all. It is the account of the interpretation and systematic construction of Scripture truth, by the œcumenical Christian Mind. It is the Bible itself, as intellectually explored and apprehended by the Church universal.[1] It is the result of the scientific

---

[1] By the church universal is meant, all in every age who agree, in finding in the Scriptures the doctrines of grace and redemption. For the test of ecclesiastical catholicity is an agreement in doctrine; not in polity, or in any merely secondary matter. This was the ground taken by the Reformers. They denied that the Papal Church was a true church, and a part, consequently, of the

reflection of representative and leading theologians, of every age, upon the meaning and contents of revelation. Such is the general nature of this branch of the internal history of the church; but it is necessary to analyze it more particularly.

The History of Doctrines contains two subdivisions: 1. *General Dogmatic History;* 2. *Special Dogmatic History.*

The first treats of the general tenor and direction of dogmatic investigation; and is, in reality, an introduction to the second part of the subject. It serves to characterize the several stadia in the historic march and movement, and to periodize the time in which they occur. It is found for illustration, that one age, or one church, had a particular work to perform, in constructing the Christian system out of the contents of revelation, and that this imparted a particular tendency to the theological mind of that age or church. The Greek Church, during the first four centuries, was principally engaged with the doctrine of the Trinity, and, con-

---

universal catholic church, because Rome had falsified the truth, and doctrine of God. Thus, CALVIN remarks (Instit. IV. ii. 12), "While we refuse therefore to allow the Papists the title of the church, without any qualification or restriction, we do not deny that there are churches among them. We only contend for the true and legitimate constitution of the church, which requires not only a communion in the sacraments, which are the signs of a Christian profession, but above all, an *agreement in doctrine.* Daniel and Paul had predicted, that Antichrist would sit in the temple of God. The head of that accursed and abominable kingdom, in the Western Church, we affirm to be the Pope."

sequently, the general drift of its speculation was trinitarian, or *theological*, in the narrower sense of the term. The Latin Church, in the fifth and sixth centuries, was occupied with the subject of sin, in the Pelagian and Semi-Pelagian controversies, and its main tendency was *anthropological*. The doctrine of justification by faith was the absorbing theme for the Reformers, and the general tenor of Protestant speculation was *soteriological*. The specification, and exhibition of this particular function and work, in each instance, makes up the matter of General Dogmatic History.

Special Dogmatic History takes the doctrines one by one, and shows how they were formed, and fixed, by the controversies in the church and out of it, or by the private study of theologians without reference to any particular controversy. The doctrines of Christianity, as we now find them stated in scientific and technical terms, were constructed out of the Scripture phraseology very gradually. Sixteen hundred years must roll by, before the doctrine of the atonement could be analytically stated, and worded, as we now have it. Other doctrines received an expansion, and a systematic construction, sooner than this; but each and all of them were a slow and gradual formation. The account of this formative process, in each particular instance, constitutes Special Dogmatic History.

We cannot better exhibit the nature and characteristics of these two branches of Dogmatic History, which we have thus briefly discriminated, than by presenting examples of some of the methods that have been employed by dogmatic historians.

HAGENBACH finds five tendencies in doctrinal history; and, consequently, five periods, in the scientific development of revealed truth. They are as follows:

1. *The Age of Apologies;* when it was the main endeavor of the theological mind, to defend Christianity against infidelity from without the church. It extends from the end of the Apostolic Age, to the death of Origen: A. D. 70—A. D. 254.

2. *The Age of Polemics or Controversies;* when it was the main endeavor of the theological mind, to maintain Christianity against heresy from within the church. It extends from the death of Origen, to John of Damascus: A. D. 254—A. D. 730.

3. *The Age of Systematizing* past results, or of *Scholasticism,* in the widest signification of the word. It extends from John Damascene, to the Reformation: A. D. 730—A. D. 1517.

4. *The Age of Creed Controversy in Germany.* It extends from the Reformation, to the time of the Leibnitz-Wolfian Philosophy: A. D. 1517—A. D. 1720.

5. *The Age of Philosophizing upon Christianity.* This period is characterized by criticism, spec-

ulation, the reconciliation of faith with science, philosophy with Christianity, reason with revelation. It extends from A. D. 1720, to the present time.[1]

BAUMGARTEN-CRUSIUS finds three general tendencies in doctrinal history; but each one involves two special tendencies, so that the entire course of development presents six periods. The first general tendency is that of *construction;* the second is that of *establishment;* the third is that of *purification*. These three conceptions of constructing, establishing as authoritative, and purifying, the system of Christian doctrine, determine and rule the three principal stages which Baumgarten-Crusius finds in dogmatic history.

Subdividing each tendency, we have the following six periods:

1. *First Period:* Construction of the system of Christian doctrine, by pure thinking, and the influence of individual opinions. It extends to the Nicene council: A. D. 325.

2. *Second Period:* Construction of the system of Christian doctrine, through the influence of the church represented in general councils. It extends,

---

[1] The fourth and fifth of these tendencies are not sufficiently general to constitute historic periods. They are limited very much to the German Church, and do not comprehend the spirit of universal Christendom since the Reformation. Hagenbach, like his countrymen generally, yields to his national feeling, in constructing modern history, both secular and sacred, too exclusively in its relations to the Teutonic race. His periodizing, however, for the Ancient and Mediæval Church is excellent, and we have adopted it to some extent.

SPECIFICATION OF THE METHOD. 37

from the council of Nice, to the council of Chalcedon: A. D. 325—A. D. 451.

3. *Third Period:* Establishment of the system of Christian doctrine, as authoritative, through the hierarchy. It extends, from the council of Chalcedon, to Gregory VII: A. D. 451—A. D. 1073.

4. *Fourth Period:* Establishment of the system of Christian doctrine, through the church philosophy and scholasticism. It extends, from Gregory VII to the Reformation: A. D. 1073—A. D. 1517.

5. *Fifth Period:* Purification of the system of Christian doctrine, through the influence of ecclesiastical parties and controversies. It extends, from A. D. 1517—A. D. 1700.

6. *Sixth Period:* Purification of the system of Christian doctrine, through the influence of science and speculation. It extends, from A. D. 1700 to the present.

The method of ROSENKRANZ makes three periods, divided with reference to philosophical categories. The first period is that of *analysis*, and is represented by the Greek Church. The second period is that of *synthesis*, and is represented by the Latin Church. The third period is that of *systematizing*, and is represented by the Protestant Church.

ENGELHARDT's method finds the first period, to be that of *analytic* talent, engaged in the construction of individual doctrines, and extending from the Apostles to Scotus Erigena: A. D. 50—A. D. 850;

the second period, that of *synthetic* talent, employed in constructing Christianity as a universal system, marked by two tendencies, the scholastic and mystic, and extending from Scotus Erigena to the Reformation: A. D. 850—A. D. 1517; and the third period occupied with completing the three doctrinal systems of the Western Church,—the Lutheran, Papal, and Reformed,—and returning to the Biblical ideas, and elements, which had been neglected in the second period.

The method of KLIEFOTH is a combination of several. His *first period* is characterized by the construction of individual doctrines, by the Greek mind, in the analytic method, and with a prevailing theological (trinitarian) tendency. His *second period* is characterized by the construction of symbols by the Roman mind, in the synthetic method, and with a prevailing anthropological tendency. His *third period* is marked by the perfecting of doctrines and symbols, by the Protestant mind, in the systematizing method, and with a prevailing soteriological tendency. His *fourth period* is characterized by the dissolution of doctrines and symbols, confined to no particular church, and in no special method, but with a prevailing ecclesiastical tendency. The following table presents his scheme, at a glance.

1. Construction of single doctrines : Greek : Analytic : Theology.
2. Construction of symbols : Roman : Synthetic : Anthropology.
3. Perfecting of doctrines and symbols : Protestant : Systematic : Soteriology.
4. Dissolution of doctrines and symbols : ? : ? : Church.

It will readily be seen, that in following these main tendencies, which appear in the principal aeras and periods, General Dogmatic History finds a very rich amount of material. It exhibits the genius and spirit of particular ages, or leading churches; so that that monotony, which is complained of in some histories of the Christian Church, is entirely banished, and the inquirer finds himself in a region of great varied currents, and streams of tendency. One age is analytic; another is synthetic; another combines analysis and synthesis. Or, one age defends; another defines and authorizes; another eliminates and purifies; another is destructive and critical. In this way, the history presents a variety upon a grand scale; and the student who follows these courses and movements of the Ecclesiastical Mind feels an influence from the great whole, like that experienced by the voyager over the whole globe,—at one time, floating down the Amazon; at another opposing the mystic currents of the Nile; at another, "borne by equinoctial winds, stemming nightly toward the pole."

In respect to Special Dogmatic History, there is less variety in the methods employed. During each of these periods in General Dogmatic History, —viz.: the Apologetic, the Polemic, the Systematizing, etc.,—the theological mind also traverses the circle of individual doctrines; commonly, however, giving most attention to some one of them, or to some one kindred group of them. Take, for illustration, the Polemic period, in Hagenbach's method, extending from the death of Origen, to the time of John of Damascus,—the principal theologian of the Greek Church, after the division between the Eastern and Western Churches. The general tendency of this period was polemic; yet most of the fundamental doctrines of Christianity were more or less didactically investigated, and systematically constructed, during this controversial age, which included nearly five centuries (A. D. 254—A. D. 730). The various topics in *Theology* and *Christology:* viz., the evidences of the Divine existence, the unity and trinity of God, the two natures in the one person of Christ; in *Anthropology:* viz., the doctrines of sin, freedom, grace, and predestination; in *Soteriology:* viz., atonement, and justification; and in *Eschatology*, together with the doctrines of the Church and the Sacraments,—all these various, and varied, single topics were subjects of reflection and positive construction, during this controversial period. Yet not all to an equal degree, and extent. The two divisions of Theology and Anthropology were by far the most prominent; that of Soteriology being least considered. Thus we find special tendencies, in the midst of the great general one; single smaller but strong currents, in the one great polemic stream that was pouring onward. In the Greek Church, the polemic mind was most engaged with Theology. The doctrine of the trinity, together with the person of Christ, owes its systematic form to the subtle profundity of the Greek theologians. In the Latin Church, Anthropology excited most attention. The doctrines of sin, free will, and grace, awakened in the Occidental mind a preëminent interest, so that this anthropological cast characterizes its thinking.

These examples will suffice, to indicate the contents of the third, and most important division, in the internal history of the church.

IV. The fourth division in the method adopted comprises the *History of Symbols*.

The ultimate result of all this construction, authorization, and purification of doctrines, is their combination into a Creed, to constitute the doctrinal basis of a particular church. It is not enough to eliminate these doctrines, one by one, out of scripture, defend them against infidelity, define and establish them against heresy, and expand them into their widest form, and then leave them to stand, each for, and by itself. This whole process of doctrinal development, though it has its origin partly in a scientific temper, and satisfies an intellectual want, is nevertheless intended to subserve practical purposes, in the end. The church is not scientific, merely for the sake of science. It is not speculative merely for the sake of speculation. It runs through these stadia of Apologetics and Polemics, in order that it may reach the goal of universal influence, and triumph, over human error and sin This controversy, and toilsome investigation of revealed truth, is undergone, in order that the church may obtain a *system* of belief, a creed, or confession of faith, that shall withstand the attacks of infidelity, preclude the errors of heresy, and above all furnish a form of sound doctrine which shall be employed in moulding the religious experience of the individual believer. Personal Christian character is the object ultimately in view, in the formation of doctrinal statements, and the construction of symbols of faith.

The account of these Confessions, therefore, properly follows that of the single doctrines of which they are composed. *Symbolics*, as it is termed, is coördinate with the history of individual dogmas, and constitutes a general summary of the total results of theological speculation. It describes the origin and formation of those principal creeds which have been constructed, at different periods, by the universal church represented in a general council, or by the church of a particular country, to serve as the expression of its faith, and the theoretic foundation of its life and practice. It exhibits the history of such symbols, as the (so-called) Apostles' Creed, the Augsburg Confession, the Helvetic Confession, the Thirty-Nine Articles, the creeds of Dort and Westminster, the Boston Confession of 1680, the Cambridge and Saybrook Platforms.

If now we take in, at one glance, the whole field of investigation, opened before us in the third and fourth divisions of the general method we have adopted, we see that they are of themselves worthy of the undivided study of a lifetime. To trace the rise and growth of each of the great tendencies in dogmatic history; the elaborate formation of each and every one of the particular Christian doctrines, under the influence and pressure of the ruling spirit of the period; and then, the organization of all these general and special results, into creeds and confessions of faith, in order to strengthen and consolidate the individual and the general religious character: to do all this with profundity, and comprehensiveness, is a work worthy of the best scholarship, the deepest reflection, and the most living enthusiasm of the human mind.

V. The fifth and last division, in the method adopted, includes *Biographic History as related to the History of Doctrines.*

This presents sketches of those historic individuals, who, like Athanasius, Anselm, and Calvin, have contributed greatly by their intellectual influence, to shape either the single doctrines, or the symbols of the church, and who are, consequently, representatives of its philosophical and theological tendencies. A historic personage is one in whom the spirit of an age, or a church, is more concentrated and powerful than in the average of individuals. He is therefore history in the concrete; history in a single mighty and passionate personality.

This division, it is easy to perceive, contains a

greater variety of features, and more of popular and immediately impressive qualities, than either of the others. Indeed, if one were to choose a single portion of the wide field of Ecclesiastical History, as that in which he could labour with most ease, and exert the greatest popular influence, it would be that of biography. The lights and shadows play more strikingly and variedly, and there is far more opportunity for vivid sketching, brilliant description, and rapid narration, than in those more central parts of the subject which we have been describing. Biographic history, also, permits the writer to pay more regard to those secular characteristics, which throw a grace, and impart a charm. The influence of poetry, of art, and of science, in moulding and colouring religious character, can be exhibited far more easily while sketching the life of an individual, than when mining in the depths of doctrinal development. Biography invites and induces more flexibility and gracefulness in the style, than is possible in the slow but mighty movement of Christian science.

There is also an inexpressible charm in the biographic Monograph, especially when passing to it from the severer and graver portions of dogmatic history. We have been following the impersonal spirit of the age, the great tendency of the period, and now we come to a single living man, and a single beating heart. The forces of the period play through him, and that which had begun to appear somewhat rigid, though ever impressive and weighty, is now felt to have an intensely human interest, and a vivid vitality. Pass, for illustration, from the contemplation of the deep central movement of Scholasticism, to the study of the life and character of its noblest and best representative Anselm, and observe the agreeable relief, the grateful change. All this science, this dialectic subtlety and exhaustive analysis, which, contemplated, in the abstract, had begun to oppress the mind, while it astonished it, is now found in alliance with a piety as rapt and contemplative as that of a seraph, a simplicity as meek as that of a child, an individuality as marked and natural as that of a character in Shakspeare.

The biographic Monograph as related to the history of Opinions, constitutes, therefore, a very appropriate conclusion to the doctrinal history of the Christian Church.[1] It serves to connect the whole department with those active and practical aspects of Christianity, which are the immediate object of attention for the preacher and pastor. Beginning with the more speculative foundations of historical theology, and going along with its scientific development, the investigator concludes with its concrete and practical workings in the

---

[1] Such thoroughly wrought monographs, for example, as REDEPENNING's Origen, MÖHLER's Athanasius, HASSE's Anselm, and HENRY's Calvin, contain rich veins of information for the student in dogmatic history.

mind and heart of those great men who have been raised up by Providence, each in his own time and place, to do a needed work in the church. And while he is not to set up any one of them as the model without imperfection, and beyond which no man can go, he will find in each and all of those who are worthy to be called historic men, something to be revered, and to be imitated; something that serves to remind him of that only perfect model, the great Head of the Church, who made them what they were, and who reflects something of His own eternal wisdom and infinite excellence, in their finite, but renovated natures.

Such men were Athanasius and Augustine of the Ancient Church; Anselm and Aquinas of the Mediaeval Church; Luther and Calvin of the Modern Church. Each pair is a dual man. The six are three representatives of the three great general tendencies in ecclesiastical history,—those of construction, authorization, and purification. But we have seen that there are tendencies within tendencies, subordinate movements in the great general movement, the river Rhone in Lake Geneva. These, also, have their representatives, whose career and influence belong to biographic history. Such are Tertullian and Origen of the Apologetic period; Basil, the two Gregories, and Chrysostom, of the Polemic period; Scotus Erigena the lonely theologian of one of the darkest ages in church history, Abelard, Bernard, and the two interesting mystics

Richard and Hugh St. Victor, of the Scholastic period; Melanchthon and Zuingle of the Reformatory period.

Such, it is conceived, is a natural Method for the investigation of the internal or dogmatic history of the Christian Church. And in closing this statement of the Methodology of the subject, it may be remarked, that this plan for a written volume is also a plan for a life-long course of private study and investigation. Upon examination, it will be perceived, that it allows of indefinite expansion as a whole, and in each of its parts. The entire history in its general aspects may be investigated wider and wider, and deeper and deeper, or a single section may be made the subject of study for years. The history of an individual doctrine may be selected, and the student find matter enough in it to occupy him a lifetime. What an interest would be thrown around the clerical life of one, who in the providence of God is separated from educated men and large libraries, by collecting about him the principal works upon the doctrine of the atonement, e. g., from the patristic, scholastic, reformed, and present periods, and making them his study for a few hours every week. What a varied, yet substantially identical soteriology would pass slowly, but impressively, before his continually expanding and strengthening mind. Carrying him back continually, as such investigation naturally and spontaneously would, to an examination of the scripture matter, out of which this body of dogmatic literature has been expanded, what a determined strength, and broad comprehensiveness of theological character would be gradually and solidly built up, like a coral isle, in that man's mind.

In closing this statement of the general method, therefore, may it not be recommended as the basis of one important part of that life-long course of study, which every clergyman is solemnly bound to begin and carry along? No man, in any department of literature, or in any profession or calling, ever regrets subjecting himself to the history of his department. It is a safe and generous influence that comes off upon the mind from History; and there is no way so certain to secure an impression ever deeper and purer from this great intellectual domain, as to lay down in the outset a method that is natural, organically connected, and self-expanding. Then, the inquirer may begin in any section; work backwards, or forwards; contemplate the whole, or only a part. He will find connections all along the line, and be in communication with the great whole, at each and every point of his investigation.

BOOK FIRST.

HISTORY

OF THE

INFLUENCE OF PHILOSOPHICAL SYSTEMS,

UPON THE

CONSTRUCTION OF CHRISTIAN DOCTRINE.

LITERATURE.

AUGUSTINUS: De Civitate Dei, Lib. VIII, Cap. iii—xii.
CUDWORTH: Intellectual System of the Universe.
GALE: Court of the Gentiles.
STILLINGFLEET: Origines Sacrae.
RITTER: History of Ancient Philosophy; translated by Morrison.
RITTER: Geschichte der Christlichen Philosophie.
ACKERMANN: The Christian element in Plato; translated by Asbury.
BAUR: Das Christliche des Platonismus.
LEWIS: The Platonic Philosophy.
BUTLER: Lectures on Ancient Philosophy.
ULLMANN: Reformers before the Reformation.
HAMPDEN: Lectures upon the Scholastic Philosophy.
HAUREAU: De la Philosophie Scolastique.
WHEWELL: History of the Inductive Sciences (Mediaeval Philosophy).
CHALYBÄUS: Historical Survey of Speculative Philosophy from Kant to Hegel; translated by Tulk.

CHAPTER I.

PHILOSOPHICAL INFLUENCES IN THE ANCIENT CHURCH:
A. D. 1—A. D. 730.

§ 1. *General features of Platonism and Aristotelianism.*

IN investigating the influence which secular Philosophy has exerted upon the construction of Christian Doctrine, the limits to which we are shut up by the character of this work will not permit an examination of the great multitude of schemes of human speculation, that have made themselves felt in the intellectual history of the church. We shall, therefore, confine our attention to those two systems, by which the theoretical apprehension of revealed truth has been the most decidedly modified, and for the geatest length of time. These two systems are *Platonism*, and *Aristotelianism.*

Before proceeding to the discussion of the subject, it is worthy of notice, that there are some advantages in being limited to the examination of only these two philosophies.

1. In the first place, they have exerted more influence upon the intellectual methods of men, taking in the whole time since their appearance, than all other systems combined. They certainly influenced the Greek mind, and Grecian culture, more than all the other philosophical systems. They reappear in the Roman philosophy,—so far as Rome had any philosophy. We shall see that Plato, Aristotle, and Cicero, exerted more influence than all other philosophical minds united, upon the greatest of the Christian Fathers; upon the greatest of the Schoolmen; and upon the theologians of the Reformation, Calvin and Melancthon. And if we look at European philosophy, as it has been unfolded in England, Germany, and France, we shall perceive that all the modern theistic schools have discussed the standing problems of human reason, in very much the same manner in which the reason of Plato and Aristotle discussed them twenty-two centuries ago. Bacon, Des Cartes, Leibnitz, and Kant, so far as the first principles of intellectual and moral philosophy are concerned, agree with their Grecian predecessors. A student who has mastered the two systems of the Academy and Lycaeum will find in Modern philosophy (with the exception of the department of Natural Science) very little that is true, that may not be found for substance, and germinally, in the Greek theism.

In being shut up to these systems we are, therefore, subjected to no great disadvantage.

2. Secondly, these two philosophies contain more of truth than all other systems that do not draw from them, or are opposed to them. They contain a representation of the powers and functions, the laws, operations, and relations, of the human mind, that is nearer to the actual matter of fact, than can be found in other alien and differing systems. They are therefore the best instrument to be employed in evoking the powers of the human mind; in forming and fixing its methods of intellectual inquiry; and in guiding it in the investigation of the legitimate subjects that are presented to it. We are speaking only comparatively, it will be noticed. We are comparing things human with things human; systems of finite reason with systems of finite reason. Neither Platonism nor Aristotelianism is free from grave errors. Plato, in some places, certainly, teaches a defective theory of moral evil, in deriving it from the ὕλη, and regarding it as the involuntary imperfection which necessarily belongs to the finite.[1] Aristotle indi-

---

[1] "The relation of man to sin," remarks ACKERMANN (Christian element in Plato, p. 265), "his subjection to its power and dominion, is with Plato not so much (as according to the Christian view) one made by himself and proceeding from the free act of his will, as rather one founded in the constitution of nature and the world, and into which man has fallen merely from ignorance." The following extracts illustrate this. "Almost all intemperance in pleasure and disgraceful conduct (ἀκρατία καὶ ὄνειδος) is not properly blameworthy like voluntary evil. For no one is vol-

rectly fosters pantheism, in speculating so much more upon τὸ ὄν than upon ὁ ὤν, and in denying the immortality of the *individual* soul, though con-

untarily evil (κακὸς μὲν γὰρ ἑκὼν οὐδείς); for the evil man becomes evil through a kind of bad habit of body (πονηρὰν ἕξιν τινὰ τοῦ σώματος), and an ill-regulated training." *Timaeus*, 86. d. "He who commends justice speaks the truth, but he who disparages it says nothing sound and salutary; nor does he disparage intelligently what he disparages. ..... Let us then mildly persuade him, for he does not willingly err (οὐ γὰρ ἑκὼν ἁμαρτάνει)." *De Republica*, IX. 589. d. "For Simonides was not so ill-informed as to say that he praised those who did no evil willingly; as if there were those who did evil willingly (ὡς ὄντων τινῶν οἱ ἑκόντες κακὰ ποιοῦσιν). For I am about of the opinion that no wise mar supposes that any one errs willingly (ἑκόντα ἐξαμαρτάνειν), or willingly commits base and wicked acts; but that all men well know. that those who commit base and wicked acts do so involuntarily (ἄκοντες ποιοῦσι)." *Protagoras*, 345. d. At the same time, it is needless to remind the reader, that Plato's doctrine of law and justice, and particularly of the divine vengeance upon evil, is in utter contradiction with such representations as these.—— Aristotle alludes to this view of the involuntariness of sinful habits, and combats it, in the *Nicoma-* *chean Ethics*, (Book III. Chap. v. Bohn's Ed. p. 68). "But as to the saying, that 'no person is willingly wicked, nor unwillingly happy,' it seems partly true and partly false; for no one is unwillingly happy, but vice is voluntary. .... Legislators punish people even for ignorance itself, if they appear to be the *cause* of their own ignorance; just as the punishment is double for drunken people; for the principle is in themselves, since it was in their own power not to get drunk, and this drunkenness is the cause of their ignorance. And they punish those who are ignorant of anything in the laws which they ought to know; and likewise in all other cases in which men appear to be ignorant through negligence; upon the ground that it was in their own power not to be ignorant; for they had it in their own power to pay attention to it. ..... But if any one by an uncompelled ignorance does unjust acts, he is unjust voluntarily; nevertheless he will not be able to leave off being unjust, and to become just whenever he pleases. For the sick man cannot become well [by his own volition], even though it so happen that he is voluntarily ill, owing to a debauched life, and from disobedience to physicians. At the time, therefore, it

ceding it to mind in its generic nature.[1] Yet both of these systems, taken together as a whole, were antagonistic to the atheism, the materialism, and even the polytheism of the pagan world. The Greek theism, as represented in these two systems, notwithstanding its defects, affirmed the existence of god, and of one supreme god,[2] and taught a spiritual

---

was in his own power not to be ill, but when he has allowed himself to become ill, it is no longer in his own power; just as it is no longer in the power of a man who has thrown a stone, to recover it; and yet the throwing and casting it was in his own power; and thus *in the beginning* it was in the power of the unjust and the intemperate man not to become such; and therefore they are so voluntarily; but when they have become so, it is no longer in their own power to avoid being so." The ethics of Aristotle here agree with the Augustinian position in the Pelagian controversy, that power having been given by creation, if lost by apostasy (which is an act of unforced self-will), the creature is still under obligation.

[1] It is the opinion of RITTER (Ancient Philosophy, III. 648) that Aristotle differed from Plato, in holding that the soul is special or individual only so far as it exists in a determinate body, and that, therefore, as individual it is perishable. The early Christian Fathers supposed that Aristotle denied the immortality of the soul, and MOSHEIM coincides with them. But CUDWORTH is inclined to explain the skeptical phraseology of Aristotle upon this point, by referring it to the animal soul, and not to the rational. Yet, he thinks that Aristotle is not as explicit as Plato, in affirming the soul's immortality. (Intellectual System, Book I. Ch. xlv., and Mosheim's Note.)

[2] The early Fathers, in their defences of Christianity against the pagan opponent, contend that the better pagan writers themselves agree with the new religion in teaching that there is one Supreme Being. LACTANTIUS (Institutiones, I. 5), after quoting the Orphic Poets, Hesiod, Virgil, and Ovid, in proof that the heathen poets taught the unity of the supreme deity, affirms that the better pagan philosophers agree with them in this. "Aristotle," he says, "although he disagrees with himself, and says many things that are self-contradictory, yet testifies that one supreme mind rules over the world. Plato, who is regarded as the wisest philosopher of them all, plainly and

theory of man and human life. Hence we are justified in saying that these two systems are, comparatively, the best which the unaided reason of man

openly defends the doctrine of a divine monarchy, and denominates the supreme being, not ether, nor reason, nor nature, but as he is, *god;* and asserts that by him this perfect and admirable world was made. And Cicero follows Plato, frequently confessing the deity, and calls him the supreme being, in his treatise on the Laws. Furthermore, when he discusses the nature of the gods, he argues that the world is governed by this supreme deity in the following manner: 'Nothing is more excellent than god; therefore it must be that the world is governed by him. Hence god is not obedient or subject to any other existence of any kind; consequently, he governs all other existences.' What god is, he thus defines in his tract On Consolation: 'The deity whom we are speaking of cannot be defined otherwise than as a free and unrestrained intelligence (mens soluta quaedam, et libera), distinct from all mortal concretion or mixture, perceiving and moving all things.' Seneca also, who was the most zealous of even the Roman stoics,—how often does he praise the supreme deity. For when he is speaking of premature death he says: 'Dost thou not perceive the authority and majesty of thy judge, the ruler of the world, the god of heaven and of all gods, upon whom these several single divinities whom we adore and worship are dependent?'" AUGUSTINE takes the same ground (De Civitate Dei, IV. 24, 25, 31; VII. 6.). PLATO (Euthyphron, 6. b. c) represents Socrates as asking Euthyphron: "Do you then think that there is in reality war among the gods one with another, and fierce enmities and battles, and many other things of the kind, such as are related by the poets, and with representations of which by good painters the temples have been decorated? Must we say that these things are true, Euthyphron?" The charge of atheism brought against Socrates was probably founded upon his denial of the philosophic and real truthfulness of the popular polytheism. PLUTARCH (De sera numinis vindicta) employs the expressions τὸ δαιμόνιον, πρόνοια, θεός indifferently in the singular or plural. He also speaks of the mythological gods, Jupiter, Apollo, etc., as subordinate to a higher power, and not as sharing a divided empire over the world. For a full account of the difference between the monotheistic and the polytheistic paganism, compare: CUDWORTH's Intellectual System, I. iv. 24, et passim; HOWE's Living Temple, Part L

has constructed, and that there are some advantages in being forced to pass by all secondary and opposing systems, when discussing the influence of philosophical systems upon Christianity.

3. A third advantage in confining our attention to these two systems, is found in their essential agreement with each other. Platonism and Aristotelianism differ only in form, not in substance. This is evident upon testing each by the great standing problems of philosophy. In reference to the principal questions and topics, both give the same answers, and both are found upon the same side of the line that divides all philosophies into the material and the spiritual, the pantheistic and the theistic. There is a substantial agreement between Plato and his pupil Aristotle, respecting the rationality and immortality of the mind as mind, in distinction from matter; respecting the nature and origin of ideas; respecting the relative position and importance of the senses, and of knowledge by the senses. But these are subjects which immediately reveal the general spirit of a philosophic system.

Ch. ii; STILLINGFLEET's Origines Sacrae; GROTII De veritate Christianae religionis; EPISCOPII Institutiones; HORSLEY's Prophecies of the Messiah dispersed among the heathen; HARVEY's Preliminary Essay to Irenaeus; GLADSTONE's Homer, II. 1 sq.; MORGAN's Trinity of Plato and Philo, p. 93 sq.; NAGELSBACH's Homerische Theologie.——There is nothing of a saving or *redemptive* nature in the mere doctrine of the divine unity. The devils are monotheists (James, ii. 19.) But there is great condemning power in the doctrine, if, as was the case with the pagan world, "when they knew God, they glorified him not as God " (Rom. i. 21).

Let any one read the ethical treatises of Plato and Aristotle, and he will see that both held the same general idea of the deity as a moral governor; of moral law; and of the immutable reality of right and wrong. The political writings of both, teach that man possesses an innate political nature, and both breathe the same political spirit. Noticing these resemblances, the student who passes from the one to the other author perceives that he has not passed into a different philosophical division, but is all the while upon the high ground of theism and spiritualism.[1]

[1] RITTER, in his History of Ancient Philosophy (Vol. III), states the coincidences between Plato and Aristotle as follows: (1) Aristotle adopts Plato's divisions in philosophy, viz.: Logic (Aristotle, Metaphysics), Physics, Ethics (Aristotle, Politics); and the Platonic terminology generally. pp. 15, 63. (2) Aristotle like Plato teaches that the knowledge of the ultimate ground of all things, alone, is science, and that this universal principle upon which all sciences depend, as their initiative and leading clue, [corresponding to Bacon's "form of induction"] is necessary, and not hypothetical. pp. 35, 39. (3) Plato sought this necessary first ground or principle, in the idea of God; Aristotle sought it in the idea of [necessary] Being, τὸ ὄν, as distinguished from [contingent] matter,—[i. e. in Spirit as distinguished from Nature]. p. 53. (4) Plato's "dialectic" is the same as Aristotle's "first philosophy." p. 53. (5) Aristotle uses Plato's arguments against the Eleatic School, which asserted that one thing is as true as another, hence that there is no absolute truth at all. p. 75. (6) Aristotle *generally*, like Plato, carefully distinguishes the sensuous representation, and whatever belongs to the province of the senses, from rational thought, or the ideas of reason,—which latter faculty is indifferently denominated νοῦς or διάνοια by both writers. Aristotle, however, does not make so wide a separation between sense and reason as Plato does. p. 89.—" The disagreement," says Ritter (p. 343), "between Plato and Aristotle is only apparent, or at least it is only upon matters of subordinate interest. Upon all

The method of each is indeed different, though the matter remains the same. And inasmuch as the method sometimes exerts even more influence than the matter upon the mind of the student, it is not surprising, if, upon looking too exclusively at the divergence of men and schools at the end of the line, and after this difference between the two methods has been aggravated and exaggerated by time and mental temperaments, he is strongly inclined to believe, that there must be an essential diversity between the two systems themselves. The synthesis and poetry of Plato, for illustration, at one extreme, become Gnosticism, while the analysis and logic of Aristotle, at the other extreme, become extravagant subtilty, and minute Scholasticism. And inasmuch as but little resemblance can be traced between Gnosticism and Scholasticism, it is hastily concluded that there can be no sameness of essential matter, and oneness of fundamental principle, between the original systems from which they sprang, and by the abuse of which they came into existence. For we shall find that the evil which Christianity has suffered from these philosophical systems, has originated from an exaggera-

---

essential points there is unanimity." With this, CUDWORTH coincides. "Though the genius of these two persons was very different, and Aristotle often contradicteth Plato, and really dissents from him in several particulars; yet so much, I think, may be granted to those reconcilers (Porphyry, Simplicius, and others) that the main essentials of their philosophies are the same." (Intellectual System, I. 94. Tegg's Ed.)

tion of one particular element in each, and its sole employment in philosophizing upon Christianity, to the neglect of the remaining elements of the system. Letting go of the sober and truthful ideas of the system itself, which served to fill out and substantiate the method, the speculator held on upon the mere hollow method alone. In this way, Platonism, under the treatment of the New-Platonics, degenerated into an imaginative theosophy; and Aristotelianism, in the handling of the later Schoolmen, became mere hair-splitting,—both systems, in this way, each in its turn, contributing to the corruption of Christianity.

With this preliminary account of the relations of Platonism and Aristotelianism to each other, we pass to consider the extent to which these philosophies have prevailed in the church, and the estimate in which they have been held.

§ 2. *Philosophy at the time of the Advent.*

At the time of the advent of Christ, and in the age immediately preceding, the philosophical world was in a state of deep decline, and of growing corruption. Philosophy, like all other departments of human inquiry, as well as the general intellectual condition of mankind, was at the lowest point. The system most extensively prevalent was the *Epicurean*, because this is most congenial to corrupt human nature, and possessing little or nothing of a scientific character is more easily understood and received by the masses. Epicureanism is the most natural and spontaneous philosophical scheme for earthly minds, and hence prevails in those periods when the fallen humanity runs its career with greatest swiftness, and with least resistance, from religion, or from the better philosophical systems.

Yet, at the time when the Eternal Word became flesh, and dwelt among men, the system that exerted most influence upon the nobler class of minds was Platonism. The Jewish Philo, and the Pagan Plutarch and Pliny, are representatives of a class of men of earnest minds, in this period, who could not be satisfied with the prevailing Epicureanism and Sensualism in speculation. We cannot call them Platonists in the strictest use of the term; for Philo and Plutarch were New-Platonists,[1] and Pliny was of the Stoic school. Still, employing the term in a wide signification, to denote a great *philosophical tendency* opposed to Epicureanism and Sensualism, these men belonged to one and the same general division in philosophy,—that of the *Grecian Theism*. For New-Platonism, though a degenerate type, was yet tinctured strongly with the characteristics of the system from which it had degenerated; and Stoicism upon the side of ethics has much in common with the system of Aristotle.

---

[1] CUDWORTH (Intellectual System, I. 332) shows that Plutarch adopted dualism, to account for the origin of evil; Mosheim combats him, but ineffectually.

We find then the fact to be, that in the century preceding and succeeding the advent of our Lord, Platonism, in the wide acceptation of the term, was the philosophy that was moulding the minds of the most thoughtful and earnest men, and that these men, although a very small minority, yet like such minorities generally, were destined to exert a greater influence upon the history of Opinions than the opposite majority of Epicureans.

§ 3. *Philosophy in the Apologetic Period:* A. D. 70—A. D. 254.

Passing into the Apologetic period, we find the facts in respect to the philosophical influences operating within the Christian church to be as follows:

Philosophy is now within the church itself. In the preceding period, it was outside of it. The Plutarchs, Plinys, and Philos, were not Christians; and the Apostolic Church, being under the direct guidance of the Apostles, had little or nothing to do with systems of human speculation. In this period, however, we find that philosophy has been adopted by the Christian as distinguished from the Pagan mind, and that within the sphere of the church it is now more successfully cultivated, and more legitimately employed, than in the sphere of the world. The secular mind now employs philosophy, and even this more lofty and ethical philosophy of which we are speaking, in attacking Christianity; while the ecclesiastical mind employs it to repel their attacks. Lucian was indeed an avowed Epicurean; but Celsus pretends at least to Platonism,[1] and Porphyry was a New-Platonist; and the substance of the attack upon Christianity, in this period, was the work of these two latter minds. The consequence is, that the Christian apologist is compelled to study, and employ this same general system of speculation, for his own higher purposes. He perceives that a system of philosophy like the Platonic is favourable to the principles of ethics and natural religion; that it does not, like the Epicurean, undermine all morality and religion; and therefore insists, and with right, that so far as it can properly go, it is not unfriendly to the system of revealed truth.[2] Indeed, the controversy between the Platonic infidels Porphyry and Celsus, and the

[1] NEANDER (I. 160) regards Origen as mistaken, in attributing the work against Christianity to Celsus the Epicurean, the friend and contemporary of Lucian. CUDWORTH (II. 340) remarks that "though Celsus were suspected by Origen to have been indeed an Epicurean, yet did he at least *personate* a Platonist too. The reason whereof might be, not only because the Platonic and Pythagoric sect was the divinest of all the Pagans, and that which approached nearest to Christianity and the truth (however, it might by accident therefore prove the worst, as the corruption of the best thing), and by that means could with greatest confidence hold up the bucklers against Christianity and encounter it; but also because the Platonic principles, as they *might* be understood, would, of all others, serve most plausibly to defend the pagan polytheism and idolatry."

[2] Justin Martyr and Clement of Alexandria frequently cite the monotheistic views of Plato, respecting the popular divinities, in proof of the nothingness of the heathen deities, and the folly of idolatry.

Platonic apologists Justin Martyr and Origen, did not relate so much to the question whether Platonism was substantially correct, but whether it was all that man needed; not whether the first principles of ethics and natural religion are true and valid, but whether natural religion is able to secure the eternal interests of mankind,—a question which is constantly recurring, and which constitutes the gist of the controversy between skepticism and Christianity at this very moment, as much as it did in the first ages of the church.

The consequence was, that this system of human philosophy, the Greek theism, upon being brought into the church and employed in defending Christianity, received a more exact definition, and a more legitimate application, than it obtained while employed by the secular and skeptical mind. It thereby came nearer to the original form in which it was first promulgated by Plato and Aristotle. Let any one examine the philosophical positions of Justin, Origen, and even that earnest hater of philosophy Tertullian, and he will see that there is a much closer agreement between these Christian Apologists and Plato and Aristotle, than there is between these latter and the New-Platonic skeptics. For the New-Platonic skeptics did not confine Platonism within its true limits. It was their desire to establish human philosophy upon the ruins of Christianity, as a universal religion,—sufficient to meet the wants of humanity, and therefore rendering the revealed system superfluous. Hence the human system itself was enlarged by deductions that were illegitimate, and by additions that were alien to its true meaning and substance; so that the imaginative New-Platonism that resulted is quite different from the more sober and circumscribed philosophising of Socrates, Plato, and Aristotle.[1]

[1] The difference between Platonism and New-Platonism has been often overlooked, notwithstanding that writers of high authority have directed attention to it. BRUCKER (Historia Philosophiae II. 364, De Secta Eclectica) remarks, "Totum quoque systema Platonicum adulterandum, et mutandum, adjiciendum et ex aliis systematibus inserendum erat, quo factum est, ut tota fere facie a Platonis imagine deficisset." NIEBUHR (Later Roman History, Lectures LXX. and LXXVIII.) agrees with this in saying, that "the [hostile] relation in which New-Platonism placed itself towards Christianity introduced something downright untrue into the Platonic philosophy, which was now made to prop up paganism." Besides this motive which the New-Platonic skeptic found in his opposition to Christianity, to adulterate the Socratic Platonism, there was the natural tendency to corruption in a philosophical system as taught by the disciple, who is always an inferior mind compared with the originator of the system. BACON (Advancement of Learning, Book I.) remarks the tendency in the disciple to falsify and injure the system of the master, in the following terms. "Hence it hath come that in arts mechanical the first deviser comes shortest, and time addeth and perfecteth; but in sciences the first author goeth farthest, and time leaseth and corrupteth. So, we see, artillery, sailing, printing, and the like were grossly managed at the first, but by time accommodated and refined: but contrariwise, the philosophies and sciences of Aristotle, Plato, Democritus, Euclides, Archimedes, of most vigor at the first, and by time degenerate and embased; whereof the reason is no other, but that in the former, many wits and industries have contributed in one; and in the latter, many wits and industries have been spent about the wit of some one, whom many times they have rather depraved than illustrated."—The opposition of New-Platonism to Christianity, in its endeavor to establish itself

The fact then, in relation to the Apologetic period is, that Platonism, in the widest acceptation, was the dominant philosophy, so far as the theologian made any use of human speculation. To use the summary conclusion of Baumgarten-Crusius, "the church adhered to Platonism, notwithstanding all the varied and injurious influences that were experienced from the exaggerations or misapplications of this system, as that philosophical doctrine or school which was not only the most extensively prevalent, but appeared to be most akin, in its general spirit and tendency, to Christianity."[1]

It ought, however, to be added, that at the close of this Apologetic period, Aristotelianism began to appear in a more distinct and independent manner than before, so that the dim beginnings of that dialectic spirit which did not attain any very considerable influence till the great outburst of Scholas-

---

as a system sufficient to meet the wants of mankind, showed itself in three forms: (1) Open attack, by Porphyry, Julian, Proclus, and Plotinus. (2) By exaggerated sketches of distinguished pagan philosophers to take the place of the gospel narratives,—such as Jamblichus's life of Pythagoras, Philostratus's life of Apollonius of Tyana. (3) By forged writings containing some Biblical ideas mixed with errors, which were to be disseminated as of equal authority with the canonical books. It is with reference to this latter class of writings that COLERIDGE (Works V., 267) remarks that, "from the confounding of Plotinism with Platonism, the English Latitudinarian divines fell into the mistake of finding in the Greek philosophy many anticipations of the Christian faith, which in fact were but its echoes. The inference is as perilous as inevitable, namely, that even the mysteries of Christianity needed no revelation, having been previously discovered and set forth by unaided reason."

[1] Dogmengeschichte, I. § 13.

ticism, may be traced here and there. It was, however, the method, rather than the matter of this system that exerted an influence, and attracted attention at this time. So far as the substance of Aristotelianism is concerned, it was, as we have shown, one with Platonism, and therefore really at work in the general mind of this period; but so far as its logical forms are concerned, it now began for the first time to exert a slight influence, which was not regarded with favour by the leading ecclesiastical minds. The school of Alexandria, where the Platonic spirit was more intense and extreme than elsewhere, were particularly opposed to Aristotelianism, as it had then appeared, and as they understood it. But the writings themselves of Aristotle were not much known, and as a consequence both adherents and opponents proceeded from an imperfect apprehension of his system. Baumgarten-Crusius remarks, that in the church of the first centuries Aristotelianism was almost synonymous with sophistry, and hair-splitting. Irenaeus says that "minuteness and subtilty about curious questions is characteristic of Aristotelianism."[1] Tertullian, speaking of the heretics he was opposing, alludes to the "wretched Aristotle, who invented their logic for them."[2] The fact seems

---

[1] Adversus Haereses, II. 14. "Minutiloquium, et subtilitas circa quaestiones, Aristotelicum est."

[2] De praescriptionibus haereticorum, vii. "Miserum Aristotelem! qui illis dialecticam instituit, artificem struendi et destruendi versipellem, ... omnia retractantem, ne quid omnino tractaverit."

to have been that Aristotelianism, during the 2d and 3d centuries, was employed chiefly by the heretical mind,[1] merely as an acute logical method, and almost wholly in discussions respecting the origin of the world, and the nature of the deity. Among the erroneous doctrines advanced at this time in connection with this system, was that of the eternity of the world.

§ 4. *Philosophy in the Polemic Period.* A. D. 254 —A. D. 730.

Passing into the Polemic period, we find the same Grecian theism to be the dominant philosophical system. As the ecclesiastical mind now became more scientific than in the Apologetic age, it was natural that the Platonic philosophy should be still better understood, so that we find the vagueness and fancifulness of New-Platonism gradually disappearing, and giving place to a more correct apprehension of the genuine Socratic Platonism united with more of the Aristotelian element. The attention of Augustine, the greatest theologian of this important period, had been directed to

---

[1] "The Artemonites busied themselves a good deal with mathematics, dialectics, and criticism; with the philosophy of Aristotle, and with Theophrastus. ...... We perceive here the different kinds of influence exerted by the systems of philosophy; the Platonic being employed to defend the doctrine of Christ's divinity, while the opposite direction of mind, tending to combat that doctrine, leaned to the side of Artemonism." NEANDER I. 581.

Christianity by the aspirations awakened during his Platonic studies,[1] which, he discovered, as Plato himself did, could not be realized by anything human. "In Cicero and Plato and other such writers," he says, "I meet with many things acutely said, and things that awaken some fervor and desire, but in none of them do I find the words, 'Come unto me all ye that labor and are heavy laden, and I will give you rest.'"[2] In his Confessions, he speaks of the broad prospect opened before him by the Platonic writings, but of their utter insufficiency to empower the mind to reach the region thus displayed,—of the immortal longing united with the eternal hopelessness. "For it is one thing,"—he says, in that deep-toned eloquence of his, which so often stirs the depths of our being like a choral anthem,—"for it is one thing, from the mountain's shaggy top to see the land of peace and find no way thither; and in vain to strive towards it, in ways beset by fugitives and deserters, and opposed by their captain, the lion and the dragon; and another thing, to keep on the way thither, guarded by the hosts of the heavenly general. These things did wonderfully sink into my soul, while I read the least of thy apostles, and

---

[1] He read Plato in a Latin translation. Confessions VII. ix.

[2] Augustine (Confessions, VII. ix) discriminates very clearly between the teachings of Plato and those of revelation. He finds the doctrine of the Logos in the Greek philosopher, but not that of the *incarnate* Logos; the doctrine that God is the light of the mind, enlightening every man that cometh into the world (John i. 9), but not that God in the flesh died for the ungodly.

meditated upon thy word, and trembled exceedingly."[1]

The influence of Platonism is also very apparent in the scientific, as well as practical theology of the Polemic period. The anthropological views called out in the controversy between Augustine and Pelagius exhibit unmistakable signs of the prevalence of this system. The Augustinian view of the origin and nature of sin is closely connected with the Platonic view of the nature and endowments of the human soul. The doctrine of innate ideas harmonizes with that of innate depravity. In the other great controversy of this period,—that respecting the Trinity,—those theologians who exerted most influence in forming, and establishing the final creed-statement, had been disciplined by the Greek intellectual methods. Athanasius, Basil, and the two Gregories, were themselves of Greek extraction, and their highly metaphysical intellects had been trained in Grecian schools. Athanasius was a reverent student of Origen, though by no means a servile recipient of all of Origen's opinions;

---

[1] Confessions, VII. xxi. "To Simplicianus then I went, the spiritual father of Ambrose (a bishop now), and whom Ambrose truly loved as a father. To him I related the mazes of my wanderings. But when I mentioned that I had read certain books of the Platonists, which Victorinus, sometime rhetoric professor at Rome (who had died a Christian, as I had heard), had translated into Latin, he testified his joy that I had not fallen upon the writings of other philosophers, full of fallacies and deceits after the rudiments of this world, whereas the Platonists many ways lead to the belief in God, and His Word." Confessions, VIII. ii.

and Basil, Gregory Nyssa, and Gregory Nazianzen, were thoroughly versed in classical antiquity. Such a discipline as this would naturally introduce these leading minds of the 4th century, to the philosophy of Plato, whose influence was felt through the whole Hellenic culture of the period.

But as we pass along in this Polemic age, we find that, although the same general estimate is put upon Platonism, as during the Apologetic period, yet the theological mind is forced to employ, and does imperceptibly employ, more and more of the logic and dialectics of Aristotle's system.[1] In constructing the doctrine of the Trinity and the Person of Christ, the mind of an Athanasius is compelled to an analysis, distinction, limitation, and definition, which has perhaps even more affinity with the dialectic spirit and method of Aristotle, than with that of Plato. Let us look a moment, for illustration, at a statement of the doctrine of the trinity ascribed to Athanasius, but which probably proceeded from the school of Augustine,—commonly called the *Symbolum Quicumque*. A few positions

---

[1] Dans la primitive Eglise, les plus habiles Auteurs Chrétiens s'accommodoient des pensées des Platoniciens, qui leur revenoient le plus, et qui étoient le plus en vogue alors. Peu à peu Aristote prit la place de Platon, lorsque le goût des Systémes commença à régner, et lorsque la Théologie même devint plus *systématique* par les decisions des Conciles Généraux, qui fournissoient des Formulaires précis et positifs. LEIBNITZ: Théodicée, Ed. Erdmann, p. 481.——The heretical mind, in this period, also made use of the Aristotelian logic. Aëtius, the Arian, employed the categories of Aristotle in defending his views. SOCRATES: Eccl. Hist. II. xxxv.

taken from it will suffice to show that the theological mind, in drawing up a form of doctrine that should contain all the Scripture elements, was forced to employ that niceness of discrimination, and sharpness of distinction, which is so characteristic of the Aristotelian system. "This is the catholic faith: that we worship one God in a trinity, and a trinity in a unity. Neither *confounding* the persons, nor *dividing* the substance." Here the logical conceptions of "confusion" and "division" are carefully distinguished. "The *person* of the Father is one; the *person* of the Son is one; the *person* of the Holy Spirit is one." Here, the conception of "person" is discriminated from that of "nature," or "essence," by the affirmation that there are three persons. "But of the Father, and of the Son, and of the Holy Spirit, the divinity is one, the glory equal, the majesty equal. Such as is the Father, is the Son, and the Holy Spirit. The Father is uncreated, the Son is uncreated, the Spirit is uncreated. The Father is infinite, the Son is infinite, the Spirit is infinite. The Father is eternal, the Son is eternal, the Holy Spirit is eternal." Here the notion of "equality" in the persons is enunciated. "And yet there are not three eternal *beings*, but one eternal *being;* there are not three uncreated, nor three infinite *beings*, but one uncreated and one infinite *being.*" Here, the conception of "being" or "essence" is discriminated again from that of "person," by the affirmation that there is but one *being*.

No one can look, for a moment, at these statements involving such logical conceptions as "confusion," "division," "essence," "person," etc., or can follow the course of the controversy with Sabellianism on the one side, and Arianism on the other, without perceiving that although the theological mind had not derived this subtlety from the study of Aristotle in any very formal manner, it had nevertheless felt the influence of that close and powerful method which is to be seen in the more dialectic dialogues of Plato, and which was carried to a still greater energy of abstraction, and power of analysis, in the writings of his successor.[1]

In this manner, we think, the combined system of *Platonico-Aristotelianism* may be said to have been the dominant one in this Polemic period, when the scientific statements of Scripture truth were forming. We do not, indeed, find that the entire works of Aristotle were translated, commented upon, and taught by distinguished men in the church, during this period, as we shall in the next. So far as a text book was concerned, Plato was still the great philosophical authority. Nevertheless, the writings of Aristotle were beginning to attract the attention of students,[2] and the dim be-

---

[1] We do not hesitate to affirm, that the four Orations of Athanasius against the Arians contain a dialectics as sharp and penetrating, and a metaphysics as transcendental as anything in Aristotle or Hegel.

[2] BOËTHIUS, in the 5th century, translated a part of the Organon. CASSIODORUS, in the 6th century, made a sketch of the Aristotelian logic. AUGUSTINE, passing in review his early studies, and contrasting the meagreness and in-

ginnings of that formal Aristotelianism which reaches its height of influence in the Scholastic age, may be traced in all the more acute and subtle workings of the theological mind in this controversial period.

sufficiency of human knowledge with the fulness and sufficiency of revelation, remarks (Confessions, IV. xvi): "What did it profit me, that scarce twenty years old, a book of Aristotle called the ten Predicaments, falling into my hands (on whose very name I hung, as on something great and divine, so my rhetoric master at Carthage, and others accounted learned, often mouthed it with cheeks bursting with pride), I read and understood it unaided?" The knowledge of Aristotle's writings, however, was confined to his logical treatises. His Morals, his Metaphysics, his Physics and his Natural History, were not read in the church until the Scholastic age.

CHAPTER II.

PHILOSOPHICAL INFLUENCES IN THE MEDIAEVAL CHURCH:
A. D. 730—A. D. 1517.

§ 1. *Platonism of the Mystic Theologians.*

PASSING, now, into the Systematizing Period, extending from John Damascene to the Reformation, we enter into a sphere of more intense philosophical activity than any in the history of the church. Even the speculative movement of the German mind for the last half-century, confined though it has been to a single nationality, and not shared by the church at large, and therefore more likely to become intense, is inferior in energy, subtlety, and depth, to mediaeval Scholasticism. Probably the church will never again see a period in which Scripture and theology will be contemplated so exclusively from a philosophical point of view; in which the desire to rationalize Christianity (in the technical sense of the term), to evince its absolute reasonableness, will be so strong and overmastering. We are, therefore, passing into the most speculative period in Church-History; and hence it is well denominated the period of Systematizing.

In the outset it may be remarked, as it was in relation to the two preceding periods, that the Greek philosophy, as formed and fixed by Plato and Aristotle, was the prevalent system. We shall indeed find here and there tendencies to a pantheistic philosophy in individual minds; but the weight and authority of both intellectual and moral character is almost entirely upon the side of the Grecian theism. But instead of the collocation employed in speaking of the two previous periods, we must now change the position of the two philosophies, and say that the general philosophical system of this Scholastic period was *Aristotelo-Platonism*, instead of Platonico-Aristotelianism. The basis of speculation was now the Aristotelian analysis, with more or less of the Platonic synthesis superinduced and interfused; while in the Apologetic and Polemic periods, the ground form was the Platonic idea, more or less analyzed and cleared up by the Aristotelian conception. But in both cases, it was the one general system of theism and spiritualism, as opposed to the general system of pantheism, naturalism, and sensualism.

We have less difficulty in detecting the presence of the Platonic element during this Scholastic age, than we had in detecting the Aristotelian element in the preceding periods. For we find it formally and distinctly existing. In the first half of the Systematizing period,—viz.: from John of Damascus to Anselm (A. D. 730—A. D. 1109)—the philosophical character of the Polemic time is still very apparent, though beginning to wane before the growing scholastic tendency. Platonism, says Hagenbach, constituted the red morning dawn of the mediaeval philosophy, and was not entirely eclipsed by formal and established Aristotelianism in the schools, until the 13th century. It is, remarks Ritter, the notion of ignorance which affirms that in the Middle Ages men were given up solely to the Aristotelian philosophy. The foundation of Anselm's mode of thinking, says Baumgarten-Crusius, was a free Platonism in the spirit of Augustine.[1]

Platonism in the Systematizing period displays itself very plainly and powerfully in the Mystic Theology. All along through this age of acute analysis and subtile dialectics, there runs a vein of devout and spiritual contemplation, which stands out in striking contrast with the general scholastic character of the time. It appears in its best form in the *Mystic Scholastics*. This was a class of men of naturally meditative temper, and of deep religious devotion, who found more satisfaction in contemplating the objects of faith and religion, than in

---

[1] HAGENBACH: Dogmengeschichte, § 150; RITTER: Geschichte der Christlichen Philosophie, VII. 70; BAUMGARTEN-CRUSIUS: Dogmengeschichte, I. § 97. 1.

philosophizing upon them,—especially in that extremely analytic manner in which the mind of the period delighted. Such men discovered in the writings of Plato,—and more particularly in the more ethical and practical portion of his writings, —a philosophy that harmonized with their cast of mind, and favoured their contemplative disposition. But although they were predominantly contemplative, they must carefully be distinguished from that small circle of Mystics who appeared in the century immediately preceding the Reformation, and who possessed far less of that systematic and scientific spirit which must ever be united with the contemplative, in order to a symmetrical theological character. These *Mystic Scholastics* of whom we are speaking, and whom we have so denominated because they were Schoolmen with an infusion of mysticism, felt the influences of the time in which they lived, and especially of the Aristotelianism that was dominant in the schools; so that while by their writings and teachings they helped to check the excessive subtilty and speculation of the period, by keeping in view the more practical and contemplative aspects of Christianity, they were themselves preserved from that degenerate mysticism which ends in a vague and feeble pantheism and naturalism, because it neglects the scientific aspects of religion, and decries all creed-statements.[1]

---

[1] "It is an error to suppose Mysticism as the perpetual antagonist of Scholasticism; the Mystics were often severe logicians;

For it is important to discriminate between the two species of Mysticism which appeared not only in the Middle Ages, but appear more or less in every age. In itself, and abstractly considered, Mysticism was a healthful reaction against the extremely speculative character of Scholasticism. It served to direct attention to the fact that religion is a life, as well as a truth. But, on the other hand, Mysticism was sometimes an unhealthy reaction against a moderate Scholasticism. It forgot that Christian dogma is the support and nutriment of all genuine Christian life; and that there is no trustworthy religious experience that is not grounded in the perception of religious doctrine. The mystic of this species disparaged discriminating and accurate statements of biblical doctrine, and was often the violent enemy of scientific theology and churchsymbols. In this instance, Mysticism soon run itself out into positive and dangerous errors.

The first class of Mystics, the *Mystic Scholastics*, were those who held the hereditary orthodoxy of the church, and sought to reach the meaning of the old symbols and doctrines by a contemplative and practical method; yet not to the entire exclusion of the speculative and scientific. Such men were Bernard († 1153), Hugh St. Victor († 1141), Richard St. Victor († 1173), William of Champeaux († 1121), Bonaventura († 1274).

the Scholastics had all the passion of the Mystics." MILMAN: Latin Christianity, Book XIV. Chap. iii.

A second class of Mystics, whom we denominate the *Heretical Mystics*, were those who rejected, in greater or less degree, the historical theology, and sought to solve the mysteries of religion either by an intensely speculative, or a vague and musing method. Hence, there were two subdivisions in this class, both of which were characterized by a common undervaluation of the church orthodoxy. The representative of the first subdivision is Scotus Erigena († 880),—a theologian who diverged from the catholic faith into pantheism, by the use of a very refined and subtile dialectics, and who, in his treatise De Divisione Naturae, anticipates some of the positions of Spinoza. Representatives of the second subdivision are Eckart († 1329), and Ruysbröck († 1384), who likewise lapsed into pantheistic views from the other side,[1] by the rejection of all logical methods, and the substitution of mere feelings and intuitions, for clear discriminations and conceptions.

Between the Mystic Scholastics and the Heretical Mystics, there stood a third interesting class, the *Latitudinarian Mystics*, who partook of the

[1] Some of the most extreme positions of this class were the following: Quam cito deus fuit, tam cito mundum creavit. Deus est formaliter omne quod est. Nos transformamur totaliter in deum et convertimur in eum, simili modo sicut in sacramento panis convertitur in corpus Christi.— Quidquid proprium est divinae naturae, hoc totum proprium est homini justo et divino. Propter hoc iste homo operatur, quidquid deus operatur, et creavit una cum deo coelum et terram, et est generator Verbi aeterni; et deus sine tali homine nesciret quicquam facere. NIEDNER: Kirchengeschichte, 505.

characteristics of both. They agreed with the Mystic Scholastics in holding the church orthodoxy in honor, but from the neglect of scientific investigation lost sight of some parts of the catholic system. The piacular work of Christ and the doctrine of justification, in particular, were misconceived and sometimes overlooked. The best representatives of this class are Von Cölln († 1329), Tauler († 1361), Suso († 1365), Gerson († 1429), Thomas à Kempis († 1471), and the author of the work which goes under the title of "Theologia Germanica." These writers, though the harbingers of the Reformation, and in general sympathy with the evangelical system, are not complete representatives of the historical orthodoxy.[1]

§ 2. *Aristotelianism of the Scholastic Theologians.*

But while there was this very considerable amount of Platonism in the Systematic period, Aristotle's method was by far the most influential. The Crusades had opened a communication with the East, and had made the Western Church acquainted with the Arabic translations of Aristotle, and commentaries upon him. The study of Aristotle commenced with great vigor, and notwithstanding the prohibition of the church, the system of the Stagirite

---

[1] See ULLMANN's Reformers before the Reformation; VAUGHN's Hours with the Mystics; HELFFERICH's Christliche Mystik; LIEBNER's Hugo St. Victor.

took possession of all the principal schools, and of all the leading minds. The 13th century exhibits Scholasticism in its finest form. Minds like Alexander Hales († 1245), Albertus Magnus († 1280), and Thomas Aquinas († 1274), employ the Aristotelian analysis in the defence of the traditional orthodoxy of the church. Their reverence for the faith of the church kept them from deviating into those errors into which philosophy is liable to fall, when it is not restrained and guided by revelation; so that although we find in their writings a very acute and intense speculation, we discern in them nothing of pantheism or naturalism. The fundamental principles of ethics, and Christian theism, have found no more powerful defenders than the great Schoolmen of the thirteenth century.

But this moderation in the use of Aristotle's method did not long continue. In the 14th century and onward, we find a class of Schoolmen who are characterized by more or less of departure from the doctrines of revelation, and an extreme subtilizing and refinement in ratiocination. It is from this class that Scholasticism has too often obtained its bad reputation in modern times. Minds like Duns Scotus († 1308), Occam († 1347), and Gabriel Biel († 1495),[1] not content with analysing truth down to its ultimate elements, attempted to analyse

[1] Compare the brief and lively sketching of their characteristics, by MILMAN: Latin Christianity, Book XIV. Ch. iii.

these ultimates themselves; so that there were for them no strictly first principles, but everything must undergo division and subdivision indefinitely.[1] Distinctions without differences, innumerable distinctions that had no existence in the real nature of things, were drawn, and Christian philosophy as well as theology was unsettled. An influx of barbarous terms was one consequence; and these terms had not even the merit which often atones for uncouthness of phrase—that of exactly defining a real philosophic idea, or discriminating a really scientific distinction. Dialectic ingenuity was expended in the attempt to answer all possible questions. Such queries as the following were raised: "Is it a possible supposition that God the Father can hate God the Son? Is it possible for God to substitute himself (suppositare se) for the devil, for an ass, for a gourd, for a flint? In case he can, then in what manner would the gourd preach, work miracles, or be affixed to the cross?" Then, again, "there were," says Erasmus, "innumerable quibblings about notions, and relations, and formalitations, and quiddities, and haecceities, which no eye could

---

[1] "The main principles of reason," remarks HOOKER (Eccl. Pol. Book I. Chap. viii), "are in themselves apparent; for to make nothing evident of itself unto man's understanding were to take away all possibility of knowing anything. And herein that remark of Theophrastus is true: 'They that seek a reason of *all* things do utterly overthrow reason.' In every kind of knowledge some such grounds there are, as that being proposed, the mind doth presently embrace them as free from all possibility of error, clear and manifest without proof."

follow out but that of a lynx, which is said to be able, in the thickest darkness, to see things that have no existence."[1]

The 14th century exhibits Scholasticism in its most extreme forms. The Aristotelian logic and analysis is now applied, in the most ingenious and persistent manner, to the dogmas of the Papal Church. Most of these not only afforded opportunity for the display of acuteness and ingenuity, but absolutely required it. Such doctrines as absolution or the forgiveness of sins by the Church, the meritoriousness of works, works of supererogation, refusal of the cup to the laity, purgatory, and particularly transubstantiation, elicited all the intellectual force of the Schoolman. In his reasoning, he made much more use of the form, than of the substance of Aristotelianism. The logic of Aristotle was disconnected from both his metaphysics and politics, so that the ideas of the Stagirite upon all the higher problems were lost sight of, and only the Aristotelian categories were employed to make distinctions which the discriminating intellect of the Greek never would have made, and to defend tenets which, had he lived in the days of Duns Scotus, his sagacious understanding never would have defended. Thus we find, in the 14th century, the system of Aristotle employed in the same one-sided and merely formal manner in which we have

[1] ERASMI Stultitiae Laus. Bas. 1676. p. 141 sq.

seen that of Plato employed in the 2d and 3d centuries,—Scholasticism, in the narrow sense, being the result in the former instance, and Gnosticism in the latter.

§ 3. *Reaction against extreme Aristotelianism, from the Later Mystics and the revival of Greek Literature.*

But this extreme tension of the human intellect, and this microscopic division and subdivision, could not last, and the reaction came on apace. Even in the 14th century, while the highly speculative dispute between the Thomists and Scotists was going on, that middle division of the mediæval Mystics of which we have spoken,—the Latitudinarian Mystics,—began to appear, and by its warm devoutness and musing contemplativeness, contributed to soften the theoretic hardness, and render flexible the logical rigidity of the period. Such men as Von Cölln († 1329), Tauler († 1361), and Henry Suso († 1365), with much less of that scientific spirit which we have seen to have coexisted with the contemplative tendency in the Bernards and St. Victors, and hence not so interesting to the theologian, or so influential upon the development of doctrine, nevertheless exerted considerable practical influence through their preaching, and works of devotional theology. Sermons like those of Tauler, and tracts like that entitled "Theologia Germanica," which

Luther praised so highly, and like the "Imitation of Christ" by à Kempis, were composed and spread abroad, during the close of the 14th and beginning of the 15th centuries. We begin to see the dawn of the Reformation, in this inclination toward a more contemplative method, and a more devout and practical apprehension and use of Christian doctrine.

This tendency, moreover, was strengthened by the revival of Greek literature, in the 14th and 15th centuries. A very interesting school of Platonists sprang up in Italy, in the latter part of the 15th century; at the head of which stood Marsilius Ficinus (†1499), who translated the writings of Plato into Latin, and Picus Mirandola (†1494), who awakened a wonderful enthusiasm by his lectures and commentaries upon the philosophy of the Academy. Though the influence of this school contributed nothing toward the revival of evangelical Christianity, but on the whole tended to deism, its intellectual effects were favorable to a spirit of inquiry, and assisted in undermining the superstitions of the Papal system.[1] The Italian literature of the 14th century is also pervaded with Hellen-

[1] "The Platonic Academy established at Florence by Cosmo de Medici, who placed Ficinus at the head of it, was much involved in New-Platonism. Its apprehension of Christianity was very inadequate, and its leaders, had they not feared the charge of heresy, would have substituted the natural religion of the best Pagan theists for the doctrine of Redemption." See HARFORD's Life of Angelo, Vol. I.

ism. Boccaccio († 1375), and Petrarch († 1374) his friend and teacher, show everywhere in their writings the influence of Greek culture, and also, what is more noticeable still, a veiled but deeply seated opposition to the Papacy. It is from the Italian writers of the 14th and 15th centuries that that large infusion of Platonism flowed, which came into the English literature of the Elizabethan age. Spenser, Surrey, Wyatt, Sidney, Herbert, Vaughn, Shakspeare, and Milton, all, either directly or indirectly, felt the influences of the Italian poets and novelists, and borrowed more or less from them. In the preceding 13th century, Dante († 1321) composed a poem which from beginning to end is luminous and distinct with the metaphysics of Aquinas, and the abstraction of Aristotle. This poem also, like the writings of Boccaccio and Petrarch, breathes a spirit of opposition to the Papacy; but the utterance is much more unambiguous and fearless.

These influences began to be felt also within the Papal church itself, long before the Reformation of the 16th century. The English Wickliffe († 1384), the "morning star" of Protestantism, had been trained up in the most rigorous scholasticism. He was an admirer of Occam, one of the most intense dialecticians of the 14th century. But he had read Aristotle diligently in the translations of the day, and had become somewhat acquainted with the Platonic philosophy through the writings of Augustine,—the writings of Plato himself not being current in his time. The influence of these studies is apparent. He rejected the nominalism of Occam and the century, and adopted the theory of realism in philosophy. From the first awakening of his intellectual and religious life, he had been a diligent student of the Scriptures, the whole of which he translated into English. He contended for the rights of the laity, in opposition to the claims of the hierarchy ; and labored for the promotion of the political and educational interests of England, in opposition to the aims of the Papacy.[1] Contemporaneously with Wickliffe, Chaucer († 1400) exerted that wonderfully creative and vivifying influence upon the English mind, language, and literature which they have not yet lost, although this most original writer has become obsolete to the majority of his countrymen. And like the Italian Dante, the whole spirit of his writings favored the downfall of the Papal superstition, and prepared the way for Luther and the Reformation.

[1] BAUMGARTEN-CRUSIUS: Dogmengeschichte, I. § 115.

CHAPTER III.

PHILOSOPHICAL INFLUENCES IN THE MODERN CHURCH:
A. D. 1517—A. D. 1860.

§ 1. *Philosophy of the Reformers.*

WE have arrived now, in our rapid survey, at the age of the Reformation, and shall throw into one period the whole time since 1517 down to the present, in continuing this account of the influence of the two cognate philosophical systems of Plato and Aristotle, upon Christian theology.

The Reformers were *Platonico-Aristotelian*, so far as they employed any system of human speculation. In this age we find the basis reversed from what it was during the Systematic period, and perceive the same general order and proportion of the two elements, that we saw in the Polemic period. The theological mind once more proceeds from the contemplative and practical side of the Grecian theism, as its point of departure, but in its controversies, especially, employs its logic and analysis. Luther's mission and function was a practical rather than a scientific one, and we do not find his mind strongly interested in any portion of human science. The abuse of philosophy, and particularly of the Aristotelian, by the Scotuses, the Occams, and the Biels, and still more the employment of it in the defence of the formalism and ungodliness of the Papacy, excited in his mind such a strong aversion to Aristotle, that he is said, with exaggeration probably, to have trembled with rage at the sound of his name, and to have affirmed that if the Greek had not been a man, he should have taken him to be the devil himself. But the deep and real sentiment of Luther, in regard to philosophy, as well as in regard to revelation itself, must be derived from a comparison of all his views and statements, and not from some particular sentiments expressed in certain connections, and drawn out by the polemic temper of the moment. If certain isolated expressions are to be taken as the exponent of his ulterior opinions respecting the authority of Scripture, the modern rationalist, who insists upon subjecting the inspired Canon to the tests of an individual opinion, really is, as he claims to be, a lineal descendant of that bold spirit who threw the Epistle of James out of the Canon, and spake violently against the Apocalypse.

But this is not a correct view. As Luther did undoubtedly, in his inmost soul, completely submit his reason to that divine revelation, whose normal authority over the Church and tradition, he was such a mighty instrument of restoring; so in his sober judgment he did recognize the importance of a true and proper science of theology, and of a true and proper science of the human mind, to be employed in building it up out of the matter of revelation. Even in reference to Scholasticism itself, he remarks in a letter to Staupitz, "I read the Scholastics with judgment, not with closed eyes. I do not reject everything they have advanced, neither do I approve of everything."[1]

Calvin and Melanchthon were the theologians for the two branches of the Protestant Church, and in these minds the influence of Platonism is very visible and marked. Melanchthon was one of the ripest Grecians of his time, and his whole intellectual method is the spontaneous product of a pure and genial sympathy with the philosophy of the Academy. Calvin, though less intensely and distinctively Platonic, because his mind was naturally more logical and dialectic, and this tendency had been strengthened by his early legal studies, exhibits a symmetrical union of the two systems whose influence we are describing. No one can read the first five chapters of the first book of the Institutes, without perceiving plainly, that this mind, which

[1] Ego Scholasticos cum judicio, non clausis oculis lego, ... Non rejicio omnia eorum, sed nec omnia probo. LUTHER's Works, I. 402 (De Wette's Ed.).

has done so much to shape and mould modern systematic theology, had itself been formed and moulded, so far as philosophical opinions and methods are concerned, by the Grecian Theism.[1]

§ 2. *Philosophy of the English and Anglo-American Churches.*

Respecting the prevalence of Platonism and Aristotelianism since the time of the Reformation, our limits will permit only a very concise statement. These two systems exerted upon the English theology of the 17th century, both of the Established Church and of the Nonconforming divines, a very powerful influence. Selecting Hooker as the representative of the first, and Howe of the last, we see that the Platonic philosophy never in any age of the church moulded the theological mind more pervasively and thoroughly, than in this instance. In Baxter and Owen, both of whom were also very diligent students of the Schoolmen, we perceive more of the influence of the Aristotelian system.[2] This body of divinity, which without

---

[1] The authors most quoted are Plato, Cicero, Aristotle, Plutarch, and Xenophon of the Pagans; and Augustine, Lactantius, and Boëthius of the Ecclesiastical writers. Simon Grynaeus, the famous Platonist, was one of the most intimate friends and associates of Calvin.

[2] "Next to practical divinity, no books so suited with my disposition as Aquinas, Scotus, Durandus, Occam, and their disciples; because I thought they narrowly searched after truth, and brought things out of the darkness of confusion. For I could never from my first studies en-

question is the most profound that the English mind has originated, owes its systematic form and structure to the Grecian intellectual methods. Respecting the influence of philosophy upon the English and Anglo-American theologies of the 18th and 19th centuries, we briefly remark the following. The system of Locke, which held undisputed sway in both countries during the 18th century, is antagonistic in its first principle to the Platonico-Aristotelian system. Its primary position that all knowledge comes from sensation and reflection, if rigorously construed, renders it a sensuous system, and brings it into affinity with those ancient Epicurean and materializing schools which it was the endeavour of Socrates, Plato, and Aristotle to overthrow. The French philosophers of the 18th century put this strict construction upon Locke's affirmation respecting the source of all ideas, and built up a system from which all spiritual ideas and truths were banished. The Scotch philosophers,

---

dure confusion. Till equivocals were explained, and definition and distinction led the way, I had rather hold my tongue than speak; and I was never more weary of learned men's discourses, than when I heard them wrangling about unexpounded words or things, and eagerly disputing before they understood each other's minds, and vehemently asserting modes, and consequences, and adjuncts, before they considered of the *Quod sit*, the *Quid sit*, or the *Quotuplex*. I never thought I understood anything till I could anatomize it, and see the parts distinctly, and the conjunction of the parts, as they make up the whole. Distinction and method seemed to me of that necessity, that without them I could not be said to know; and the disputes that forsook them, or abused them, seemed but as incoherent dreams." BAXTER's Narrative of his Life and Times.

on the contrary, put a loose construction upon Locke's dictum, and regarded "reflection," in distinction from "sensation," as the source of that particular class of ideas which are the foundation of morals and religion, and which cannot, confessedly, be derived through sensation. The system of Locke, as interpreted by the French school, run itself out into sheer materialism and atheism. The system of Locke, as interpreted by the Scotch mind, was brought into affinity with the theism of the past,—though only by elevating the function of "reflection" into a coördinate rank with that of "sensation," and making it a *second* and *independent* inlet of knowledge.

The English and American theologies of the 18th and 19th centuries have felt the influence of the Locke philosophy, in the modified form of the Scotch school; while the earnest and practical religious spirit, which has characterized these churches, has tended to neutralize the materializing elements that still remained in it. During the last quarter of the present half-century, both countries have felt the influence of a revived interest in that elder system whose history we have been delineating,—an interest that is growing deeper and stronger, and from which, if not allowed to become extreme to the neglect of the theological and practical religious interests of the church and the world, the best results for Christian science may be expected.

§ 3. *Philosophy of the German Church.*

A very important and influential movement of the theological mind, since the Reformation, appears in the German theology of the last half of the 18th and the first half of the 19th centuries. We are too near this, in time, to be able to judge of it in the best manner, for we have yet to see its final issue. One thing, however, is certain, that so far as it is a truthful and really scientific method of theologizing, it is due greatly to the influence of the Grecian masters in philosophy, and their successors.

The Germanic mind has been influenced during the last hundred years, by two entirely antagonistic systems of human speculation,—that of Theism, and that of Pantheism. The former, as we have seen, has come down from Plato and Aristotle; the latter, though not unknown to the ancient world, yet received its first scientific construction in the mind of that original and powerful errorist, Baruch Spinoza. The revival of the interest in philosophy, which began as soon as the general European mind had become somewhat tranquillized, after the deep central excitement of the Reformation and of the theological controversies which followed it had partially abated, showed itself in the rise of the systems of Des Cartes, Leibnitz, Wolff, and Kant. All these systems are substantially theistic. They reject the doctrine of only one Substance, and strongly mark the distinction between finite and infinite Being. They are all of them, in greater or less degree, influenced by the systems of Plato and Aristotle, and are in the same general line of philosophical speculation. But the deep and solid foundation for pantheism that had been laid by Spinoza, and the imposing architectural superstructure which he himself had reared upon it, gave origin to another, and totally different philosophical tendency and system of speculation. For although Des Cartes, Leibnitz, and Kant differ from each other, and upon important points, yet their systems are all theistic, and therefore favorable to the principles of ethics and natural religion. The systems of Spinoza and his successors Schelling and Hegel, have, on the other hand, had a more uniform agreement with each other. They are fundamentally and scientifically pantheistic; and therefore are destructive of the first principles of morals and religion. By their doctrine of only one Substance, only one Intelligence, only one Being, they annihilate all the fixed lines and distinctions of theism, —distinctions like those which imply the *metaphysical* reality of an uncreated and a created essence or being, and lines like those which distinguish right and wrong, free-will and fate, from each other, as *absolute* contraries, and *irreconcilable* opposites.

So far therefore as the theological mind of Germany has been influenced by the earlier Germanic philosophy, and more especially so far as it has felt the influence of the Platonic and Aristotelian systems themselves, it has adopted the historical theism, and its philosophical thinking has harmonized with that of the church from the beginning.

It is true, that in the eighteenth century, the German Church was largely infected with rationalism and deism; but this should be traced primarily to a decline of the religious life itself,—to the absence of a profound consciousness of sin and redemption. The existence of a living, and practical experience of New Testament Christianity in the heart, does not depend ultimately upon a system of philosophy, good or bad, though it is undoubtedly favored or hindered by it, but upon far deeper and more practical causes. At the same time it should be noticed, that if the church must make its choice between two such evils, as an arid and frigid deism, or an imaginative and poetic pantheism, it chooses the least evil, in electing that system which does not annihilate the first principles of ethics and practical morality, and which, if it does not accept a revealed religion, does at least leave the human soul the truths of natural religion. An unevangelical, though serious-minded Lord Herbert of Cherbury, or Immanuel Kant, who insists upon the absolute validity of the ideas of God, freedom, and immortality, together with the immutable reality of right and wrong, is a less dangerous enemy to the gospel, than an unevangelic pantheist, who denies the metaphysical reality of each and all of these ideas, as apprehended and accepted by the common human mind, and destroys the foundations not merely of revealed religion, but of all religion, by affirming that God is the only Substance, and the only Being, and that all that has been, is, and ever shall be, is his self-evolution and manifestation.[1]

On looking at the scientific theology of Germany, during the present century, we find it modified by both of these two great philosopical tendencies. The two systems of theism and pantheism have been conflicting in this highly speculative country, with an energy and intensity unequalled in the history of philosophy; so that the theological mind of Germany exhibits a remarkable diversity of opinions and tendencies. Even in the anti-

---

[1] In the annual report of the American Board of Foreign Missions for 1857, a missionary to India represents the passage from the Hindoo pantheism to Christianity, as sometimes mediated and facilitated by the temporary reception of deistical views in the place of pantheistic ones. "Mr. Ballantine," says the Report, "calls attention to certain facts which are instructive, and, for the most part, encouraging. (1.) The progress of deistical principles among the Hindoos. This is great. It is an effect of education, and the multiform influence of European ideas engrafted into the native mind. It professes to be the religion of nature, admitting the existence of one God, and denying a revelation from him. The number who hold these sentiments is so large, as to produce a perceptible weakening effect on the power of caste, and the bondage to Hindooism [pantheism]. It is not, in general, of the malignant type of infidelity in Christian lands, and to a certain extent is auxiliary to the gospel; with many, it is a stepping-stone from Hindooism to Christianity."

rationalistic or spiritual school, this same opposition between the historical Theism and Spinozism is to be seen. The theology of Schleiermacher, which has exerted a great influence upon classes that disagree with it—upon the Rationalist on the one hand, and the Supernaturalist on the other, and upon all the intermediates between these—is characterized by a singular heterogeneity of elements. Its founder was a diligent student of Plato, and an equally diligent student of Spinoza. Hence, while we find in this system, a glowing and devout temper that is favorable to a living theism, and a vital Christianity, we also find *principles* that are subversive not merely of revealed but of natural religion.[1] In fact, this system presents, in one respect, the most remarkable phenomenon in the whole

---

[1] Schleiermacher's definition of religion, as "the feeling of dependence upon the Infinite," does not involve theism, unless the Infinite is defined to be a *person*. But in a correspondence with the elder Sack, published posthumously in the Studien and Kritiken, 1850 (Heft I. 158-9), Schleiermacher expressly asserts, in answer to the inquiry of his correspondent, that the existence of this feeling of dependence does not of necessity require that the Infinite should be personal. NEUDECKER (Münscher—Von Cölln, Dogmengeschichte, III. § 28) quotes the following from Schleiermacher (Glaubenslehre, I. § 42), in proof that he held the theory of an eternal creation of the world. Speaking of the Mosaic account of creation, he remarks: "Jene ganze Frage setzt einen zeitlichen Anfang der Welt schon als entschieden voraus, allein unser unmittelbares Abhängigkeitsgefühl findet in dieser Annahme keine bestimmtere Befriedigung als in einen ewigen Schöpfung der Welt." This quotation is not to be found in the Berlin edition of 1852; but on page 200 (Vol. I.) it is remarked, that it is indifferent to the Abhängigkeitsgefühl, whether the doctrine of a temporal or an eternal creation be adopted.

history of theology and philosophy,—the phenomenon of a system mainly pantheistic, instrumental at a particular crisis in the history of a national mind, in turning its attention to the more distinctively spiritual and evangelical doctrines of Christianity. Having served this purpose, however, its work is done, and it cannot, as the course of thinking now going on in Germany itself plainly indicates, continue to satisfy the wants of the theological mind, but must either be adopted in all its logical consequences, and thereby become the destruction of evangelical religion, or else be rejected and left behind, in that further progress towards, and arrival at New Testament Christianity, which it was instrumental, by a logical inconsistency however, in initiating.

The final judgment, consequently, in respect to the real worth and influence of the philosophic movement of the German mind, must be held in reserve, until the final issue appears. The estimate which the future historian will form of it, will be determined according as the German Church of the future shall draw nearer to the symbols of the Reformation, or shall recede further from them. But the same may be said of German theologizing, that has been remarked of theological science in the former periods, and in other countries,—viz : that so far as it has been influenced by the Platonic and Aristotelian systems, it has been theistic in its principles and methods, and has been favorably formed and moulded.

BOOK SECOND.

HISTORY
OF
APOLOGIES.

LITERATURE.

FABRICIUS: Delectus argumentorum, et syllabus scriptorum, qui veritatem religionis Christianae adversus Atheos, Naturalistas, etc. asseruerunt.

TZSCHIRNER: Geschichte der Apologetik (unfinished).

RÖSZLER: Bibliothek der Kirchen-Väter.

RITTER: Geschichte der Christlichen Philosophie, I. 289–564.

ERSCH und GRUBER: Encyklopädie (Artikel Apologetik).

THOLUCK: Ueber Apologetik (Vermischte Schriften, I. 149–373).

KAYE: Justin Martyr, Clement of Alexandria, Tertullian.

BOLTON: Evidences of Christianity as exhibited in the writings of its Apologists down to Augustine.

LECHLER: Geschichte des Englischen Deismus.

HAGENBACH: Kirchengeschichte des 18 und 19 Jahrhunderts.

LELAND: View of the principal Deistical Writers.

SCHLOSSER: History of the Eighteenth Century; translated by Davison.

CHAPTER I.

DEFENCES OF CHRISTIANITY IN THE APOLOGETIC PERIOD.
A. D. 70—A. D. 254.

§ 1. *Preliminary Statements.*

THE History of Apologies is the next subject to be investigated, in our course through the internal history of the Christian Church. As we proceed, we shall find that we are examining the workings of the Christian Mind, in its endeavour to harmonize revelation and reason. The history of the Defences of Christianity is, therefore, one of the best sources whence to derive a true philosophy of Christianity. As we pass along through this branch of Dogmatic History, we shall observe that substantially the same objections are urged by the skeptical mind, from age to age, and that substantially the same replies are made. Perhaps in no part of Church History, do we observe so striking verification of the proverb that man is the same being in every age, as in the history of Apologies.

Infidelity is the same over and over again; reappearing in new forms, it is true, so that it looks to the time and the church in which it appears, like a new thing under the sun, yet ever remaining identical with itself, it makes very much the same statements, and elicits very much the same replies.

At the same time, the investigation of the process discloses the fact of a diversity in the unity. The skepticism of one period is not a mere fac simile of a preceding. It springs up out of the peculiar culture of the age, and takes on a hue by which it can be distinguished. At one time it is deistic infidelity; at another pantheistic. At one time an epicurean naturalism is the warm and steaming soil, in which it strikes its roots; at another a frigid and intellectual rationalism. And the same variety is seen in the Apologies. Like meets like. Each form of errour is counteracted by a correspondent form of truth, and thus the great stream of debate and conflict rolls onward.

Commencing with the Apologetic period, we find that this first age of the church is very properly denominated the Age of Apologies. The great work to be performed by the Christian Mind was to repel attacks. Christianity, during the whole of this period of two centuries, was upon the defensive. Less opportunity, consequently, was afforded for constructing the positive system of scripture truth, so that the theological interests of the church in this age were subordinated to its apologetic effort, and Christian science received only that indirect, though important investigation, which is involved in the discussion of the relations of reason to revelation.

The attacks upon Christianity during this period, proceeded from two general sources: *Judaism* and *Paganism*. Judaism held the doctrine of a special revelation, in common with Christianity, and consequently the objections which it raised were of a different character from those urged by a Pagan philosophy which did not acknowledge any special and supernatural communication from God. The attacks upon Christianity that proceeded from the Judaistic opposer had a constant and immediate reference to the Old Testament, as he understood it. He did not, like the pagan skeptic, attack Christianity because it claimed to be a divine revelation; but because it claimed to be a form of revelation more final and conclusive than that first and ancient form whose authority he believed to be valid, and which he supposed was to be entirely annihilated by the new religion. Hence the question between the Judaistic skeptic and the Christian apologist involved the whole subject of the relation of the New to the Old Dispensation. The Pagan opponent of Christianity, on the other hand, received neither the Old nor the New Testament as a divine revelation, and the objections which he urged related to the possibility, and reality of any special communication from the infinite to the finite mind.

It is to these two general forms of skepticism, and the replies that were made by the Christian apologist, that we now turn our attention.

§ 2. *Ebionite Skepticism, and Christian replies.*

The first species of opposition to Christianity, from the direction of Judaism, and having reference to the meaning and authority of the Old Testament, was *Ebionitism.*

The Ebionite, judging from the somewhat conflicting statements of the early fathers, was the apostate Jewish-Christian of the 2d century. The Jewish-Christian, originally evangelical, had by this time lapsed down to a humanitarian position respecting the person and work of Christ, and the nature of Christianity. He rejected the doctrine of Christ's deity, and of his miraculous birth, and held him to be the son of Joseph and Mary.[1] At the

---

[1] Ἐβιωναῖοι δὲ ὁμολογοῦσι τὸν κόσμον ὑπὸ τοῦ ὄντως Θεοῦ γεγονέναι, τὰ δὲ περὶ τὸν Χριστὸν ὁμοίως τῷ Κηρίνθῳ καὶ Καρποκράτει μυθευοῦσι. IRENAEUS: Adv. Haer. I. xxii. Ed. Harvey. There seems to have been some variety in the views of the Ebionites respecting the grade of Christ's being; some regarding him as a much more exalted creature than others did. But all of them agreed in denying his deity, and his place in the trinity. EUSEBIUS (Eccl. Hist. III. 27) describes the Ebionites as holding Christ to be a common man, born of the virgin Mary by ordinary generation. EPIPHANIUS (Haer. XXX. 3) represents them as regarding him to be an exalted spirit, created before all other creatures. ORIGEN (Cont. Celsum, V. 61) distinguishes two classes of Ebionites, one of which admitted the supernatural birth of Christ, and the other denied it; but neither class admitted his deity.—One portion, and that probably a small one, of the Ebionites were mystical rather than literal in their

same time, however, he regarded Jesus as the Messiah promised in the Old Testament; believing that he was set apart for his work by the inspiration of the Holy Spirit, at the time of his baptism by John. He made use of a Hebrew gospel, now lost, which was probably that of Matthew, with the omission of such portions of it as teach his miraculous birth, and his divine nature. The remainder of the New Testament canon he rejected, particularly the epistles of Paul, whom he regarded as the corrupter of genuine Christianity.

The Ebionite was thus pseudo-Jewish in all essential particulars. With the exception that he believed the Messiah to have made his appearance, and that Christ was he, he stood upon the same position with the Pharisee who opposed Christ in the days of his flesh, and with the Jew whom Paul found his bitterest enemy. The Messiah of the Old Testament was not a divine being in his view; circumcision and the observance of the Mosaic ritual were requisite to salvation; and salvation was by the works of the law.

Having this conception of the Messiah, and of

spirit. Their Judaism was mingled with theosophic tendencies, and they herald the approaching Gnosticism. The Elcesaites were probably a branch of these. Those Jewish Christians who accepted the evangelical system, and at the same time adhered to their national ceremonial (as they were permitted to do, by the Apostolic convention, Acts xv), were not called Ebionites but *Nazarenes*, and existed down to the close of the 4th century.—Compare NEANDER: I. 341–366; GUERICKE: § 43; OLSHAUSEN: Commentary on Acts xv. 1.

the Old Testament dispensation generally, the Ebionite could see no affinity between the Christianity of the catholic Church, and Judaism. On the contrary, he saw only an irreconcilable opposition between them; so that one was the entire extinction of the other, to its inmost substance and fibre. He could not, to use the fine phrase of Augustine, see the New Testament in the Old, and of course he could not see the Old Testament in the New.

This preparatory statement will now enable us to understand the nature of the objections urged by the Ebionite against the faith of the Church, which were the following:

(1.) The Christ of the New Testament, as the Church received and interpreted the New Testament,[1] was contrary to the representations of the Messiah contained in the Old. The portraitures did not agree. The person depictured in the four canonical Gospels was not the person described in the Jewish Scriptures. The Old Testament Messiah, the Ebionite contended, was not an incarnation of a divine Person, but only a supernaturally born and inspired man.

(2.) The Christ of the catholic Church, the Ebionite asserted, was contradictory to the Old Testament conception of God. The divinity of Christ, it was contended, was incompatible with the mono-

[1] It will be remembered that the Ebionite professed to believe in Christ as an authorized messenger from God, and the Messiah who was to come; and also that he accepted a part of the New Testament.

same time, however, he regarded Jesus as the Messiah promised in the Old Testament; believing that he was set apart for his work by the inspiration of the Holy Spirit, at the time of his baptism by John. He made use of a Hebrew gospel, now lost, which was probably that of Matthew, with the omission of such portions of it as teach his miraculous birth, and his divine nature. The remainder of the New Testament canon he rejected, particularly the epistles of Paul, whom he regarded as the corrupter of genuine Christianity.

The Ebionite was thus pseudo-Jewish in all essential particulars. With the exception that he believed the Messiah to have made his appearance, and that Christ was he, he stood upon the same position with the Pharisee who opposed Christ in the days of his flesh, and with the Jew whom Paul found his bitterest enemy. The Messiah of the Old Testament was not a divine being in his view; circumcision and the observance of the Mosaic ritual were requisite to salvation; and salvation was by the works of the law.

Having this conception of the Messiah, and of

spirit. Their Judaism was mingled with theosophic tendencies, and they herald the approaching Gnosticism. The Elcesaites were probably a branch of these. Those Jewish Christians who accepted the evangelical system, and at the same time adhered to their national ceremonial (as they were permitted to do, by the Apostolic convention, Acts xv), were not called Ebionites but *Nazarenes*, and existed down to the close of the 4th century.—Compare NEANDER: I. 341–366; GUERICKE: § 43; OLSHAUSEN: Commentary on Acts xv. 1.

the Old Testament dispensation generally, the Ebionite could see no affinity between the Christianity of the catholic Church, and Judaism. On the contrary, he saw only an irreconcilable opposition between them; so that one was the entire extinction of the other, to its inmost substance and fibre. He could not, to use the fine phrase of Augustine, see the New Testament in the Old, and of course he could not see the Old Testament in the New.

This preparatory statement will now enable us to understand the nature of the objections urged by the Ebionite against the faith of the Church, which were the following:

(1.) The Christ of the New Testament, as the Church received and interpreted the New Testament,[1] was contrary to the representations of the Messiah contained in the Old. The portraitures did not agree. The person depictured in the four canonical Gospels was not the person described in the Jewish Scriptures. The Old Testament Messiah, the Ebionite contended, was not an incarnation of a divine Person, but only a supernaturally born and inspired man.

(2.) The Christ of the catholic Church, the Ebionite asserted, was contradictory to the Old Testament conception of God. The divinity of Christ, it was contended, was incompatible with the mono-

---

[1] It will be remembered that the Ebionite professed to believe in Christ as an authorized messenger from God, and the Messiah who was to come; and also that he accepted a part of the New Testament.

theism of the Jewish Scriptures, and was a species of idolatry and polytheism.

(3.) The Ebionite affirmed that the superseding, or, as he preferred to term it, the annulling of the Old Testament law by the catholic Christianity, was in conflict with the doctrine of the divine origin of the law, and the immutable necessity of its observance.

As these objections proceeded from a defective and erroneous apprehension of the Jewish religion, the chief labour of the Christian apologist consisted in imparting more correct views of the inward and real nature of the Old Testament Dispensation, and thereby justifying his own denial of these positions of the Ebionite. The moment the spiritual character of Judaism, as portrayed in Moses, and especially in the Psalms and the Prophets, could be seen, its essential harmony with catholic Christianity would appear, and the assertion of an irreconcilable hostility between the two systems would fall to the ground of itself. Hence the Christian apologist replied as follows to the Ebionite skeptic.

(1.) All that pertains to the person of Christ, as described in the canonical gospels, is essentially to be found in the Old Testament prophecies and types concerning the Messiah. The apologist was guided to this counter-assertion, and upheld in it, by such sayings of Our Lord as: "Search the [Old Testament] Scriptures, for they are they which testify of *me*. Had ye believed Moses, ye would have believed me; for he wrote of *me*. But if ye believe not his writings, how shall ye believe my words" (John v. 39, 46, 47). He was also emboldened to make the counter-assertion, and to defend it, by that remarkable example set by Christ, when in his last conversation upon earth with his disciples, " beginning at Moses and all the Prophets, he expounded unto them, in all the [Hebrew] Scriptures, the things concerning *himself*" (Luke xxiv. 27).

The consequence was, that the Christian Apologist first of all took issue with the Ebionite opponent, in respect to the alleged fact itself, of a contradiction between the Messiah of the Old Testament and the Christ of the Gospels. The appeal was made directly to the Jewish Scriptures, and particularly to the prophecies in Isaiah respecting the supernatural birth, and exalted character, of the promised Messiah. The divinity of the Messiah being proved from this source, the Apologist harmonized it with monotheism by means of the doctrine of the trinity, though he made little attempt to construct this difficult doctrine.

(2.) The second and further reply to the Ebionite was, that the Old Testament itself teaches and expects the future superseding of Judaism by Christianity,—not however by annihilating that which was permanent and spiritual in Judaism, but by unfolding all this still more fully, and abrogating only that which was national, ceremonial, and local in it. The promise that *all* the nations of the earth should be blessed in the seed of Abraham; the glowing and beautiful description in Isaiah of the calling of the Gentiles; the prayer for the conversion of the whole world, as in Psalm lxvii; the emphasis laid upon a tender and contrite heart in comparison with a formal and hypocritical offering of sacrifice; and the repeated assertion of Christ that he came not to destroy, but to fulfill the Law and the Prophets,—all this set the Apologist upon the track of discovering the true relation of the two dispensations to each other, and imparted earnestness and confidence to the tone with which he made the counter-assertion.

Furthermore, the terrible and unexpected destruction of Jerusalem, so fresh in the experience of the Jewish nation, was cited by the Christian Apologist to prove that all that was national and external in Judaism, was destined to pass away. This was an *argumentum ad hominem* that had, as such arguments generally have, even more weight than those which were drawn from a deeper source, and are of more value for all time. The actual demolition of the Jewish temple and overthrow of the Jewish cultus, the destruction of a central point where the nation could gather itself together and maintain its religious nationality, and its dispersion to the four winds of heaven, were triumphantly cited by the early Christian apologete, as convincing arguments for the divinity of Christianity as the true crown and completion of Judaism.[1]

[1] There was so much similarity between the Ebionite and the Jew, that in the absence of documents relating to Ebionitism, the nature of the Ebionite objections to Christianity, and of the Apologists' reply to them, may be seen to some extent from the course of thought in a portion of Justin Martyr's *Dialogue with the Jew Trypho.* The following particulars are in point: (1) Trypho urges that the ceremonial law is the ordinance of God, and therefore ought still to be observed. Justin replies, that the ceremonial law was given to the Jews on account of the hardness of their hearts. All its ordinances, its sacrifices, its Sabbath, the prohibition of certain kinds of food, were designed to counteract the inveterate tendency of the Jews to fall into idolatry. They who lived before Abraham were not circumcised, and they who lived before Moses neither observed the Sabbath, nor offered sacrifices, although God bore testimony to them that they were righteous. (2) Trypho quotes Daniel vii. 9 to prove that the Messiah was to be a great and glorious personage; whereas the Messiah of the Christians was unhonoured and inglorious, and fell under the extreme curse of the law. Justin's answer is, that the Scriptures of the Old Testament speak of two advents of the Messiah; one in humiliation, and the other in glory, and the Jews, blinded by prejudice, looked only at those passages which foretold the latter. (3) Trypho objects that the Christian doctrine of the pre-existence and divinity of Christ, and his subsequent assumption of humanity, contradicted the Jewish idea of the Messiah; and also that Elias was to be the precursor of the Messiah, but that Elias had not yet appeared. To this Justin replies by referring to the prophecy of Isaiah (Chapter vii), in which the birth of the Messiah from a Virgin is foretold; and asserts that the prophecies respecting Elias had, with respect to Christ's first coming, been accomplished in John the Baptist; and that before Christ's second advent, Elias would himself appear. Furthermore, Justin contends that the Messiah must have already come, because, after John the Baptist, no prophet had arisen among the Jews; and they had lost their national independence agreeably to the prediction of Jacob. (4) Trypho calls upon Justin to show, that in the Old Testament mention is ever made of another God, strictly so called, besides the Creator of the universe. Justin answers, that whenever in Scripture God is said to appear to man, we must under-

§ 3. *Gnostic Skepticism, and Christian replies.*

The second form of opposition to Christianity, during the Apologetic period, which also like Ebionitism involved the relation of the New to the

stand the appearance to be of the Son, not of the Father; as when God appeared to Abraham at the oak of Mamre, to Lot, to Jacob, to Moses out of the burning bush, and to Joshua. Justin also appeals to Ps. cx and Ps. xlv, to show that David speaks of another Lord and God, besides the Creator of the universe; and quotes Proverbs viii, and Gen. i. 26, iii. 22, to prove the pre-existence of Christ. (5) Trypho asserts, that although Jesus might be recognized as the Lord, and the Messiah, and God, by the Gentiles, yet the Jews, who were the worshippers of the absolute God who made him (Christ) as well as them (the Gentiles), were not bound to recognize or worship him. Justin, in answer, quotes Ps. xcix and Ps. lxxii, to show that even among the Jews they who obtained salvation, obtained it only through Christ. (6) Trypho asserts, that the New Testament accounts respecting the birth of Christ could only be compared to the fables respecting the birth of Perseus from Danae, and the descent of Jupiter under the appearance of a shower of gold. It would be better at once to say, that the Messiah was a mere man, and elected to the office on account of his exact compliance with the Mosaic law, than to hazard the incredible assertion, that God himself submitted to be born, and to become a man. Justin, in answer, again quotes Isaiah liii. 8, to prove that the Messiah was not to be born after the ordinary manner of men; and Isaiah xxv, to show that the Messiah was to effect miraculous cures; and Isaiah vii, which, he argues, could not apply to Hezekiah. He also charges the Jewish teachers with having expunged from the Septuagint version, several passages clearly prophetic of the Messiah. (7) Trypho at length says: "The whole Jewish nation expects the Messiah. I also admit that the passages of Scripture which you have quoted apply to him; and the name of Jesus or Joshua, given to the son of Nun, inclines me somewhat to the opinion that your Jesus is the Messiah. The Scriptures moreover manifestly predict a suffering Messiah; but that he should suffer death upon the cross, the death of those who are pronounced accursed by the law fills me with perplexity."

8

Old Testament, was *Gnosticism*. The same fundamental questions were agitated in the controversy with this form of errour, as in the contest with Ebionitism; and in reality the reply to the Ebionite, which resulted as we have seen in the clear exhibition of the connection between Judaism and Christianity, was a reply to the Gnostic.

The limits of this work do not, of course, permit a detailed account of that amorphous system of speculation which sprang up in the second and

---

Justin answers that the curse applied only to those who were crucified on account of their personal transgressions; whereas Christ was sinless, and submitted to this ignominious death, in obedience to the will of his Father, in order that he might rescue the human race from the penalty due to their sins. Then, after quoting Ps. iii. 5, Is. lxv. 2, and Is. liii. 9, as prophetic of the Messiah's crucifixion, Justin shows at considerable length that Ps. xxii is descriptive of the perfect humanity, of the sufferings, death, and resurrection of the Messiah. (8) Trypho inquires of Justin whether he really believed that Jerusalem would be rebuilt, and that all the Gentiles as well as the Jews and Proselytes would be collected there under the government of the Messiah. Justin, in answer, admits that this belief was not universal among the orthodox Christians; but that he himself held that the dead would rise again in the body, and live for a thousand years in Jerusalem, which would be rebuilt, beautified, and enlarged. He appeals in support of his opinion to Isaiah, and to the Apocalypse, which he ascribes to John, one of Christ's apostles. (9) Justin finally comes to speak of the conversion of the Gentiles; and contends that the Christians are the true people of God, inasmuch as they fulfil the spiritual meaning of the law, and do not merely conform, like the Jews, to the letter. They have the true circumcision of the heart; they are the true race of priests, typified by Jesus the High Priest in the prophecy of Zechariah; they offer the true spiritual sacrifices agreeably to the prophecy of Malachi; they are the seed promised to Abraham, because they have the faith of Abraham; they are, in a word, the true Israel. See KAYE's Justin Martyr, p. 24 sq.

third centuries, with an ingenuity of speculation, and a perverse perseverance of mental power, never excelled in the history of human errours. Only the most general characteristics can be specified.

The Gnostics claimed to be in possession of the true philosophy of Christianity. They were of two classes: *Judaizing* and *Anti-Judaizing*. The former, like the Ebionite, acknowledged the authority of the Old Testament, but unlike him was not satisfied with a literal interpretation of its teachings. The Judaizing Gnostic recognized the distinction spoken of by Paul in his Epistle to the Romans, and employed by the Christian Apologist himself against the Ebionite,—that, viz., of a Jew outwardly and inwardly. But this distinction he entirely misapprehended. He regarded it to be the same as that found in all Oriental philosophies (by which his own intellectual methods had been chiefly formed) between the esoteric and exoteric, the initiated and uninitiated, the philosophic and the unphilosophic mind. The consequence was a hyperspiritualizing of the Old Testament, in such a manner as to evacuate it of all its practical and salutary truths, and the introduction of a system of emanation, which was not only directly contrary to the Mosaic doctrine of creation de nihilo and the spiritual monotheism of the Old Testament, but was in reality a system of polytheism, resulting in that "worshipping of angels and voluntary (or gratuitous) humility" against which St. Paul warns the Colossians as early, probably, as the beginning of the seventh decade from the birth of Christ. This class of Judaizing Gnostics were originally Jews, who attempted to apply the doctrines of the Oriental theosophies in connection with those of New Platonism, to the interpretation of the Hebrew Scriptures. Hence their disposition like the Ebionite to proceed from the Old Testament as a point of departure.

The *Anti-Judaizing* Gnostics, on the other hand, were originally Pagan philosophers or theosophers, who passed over to a nominal Christianity directly, and not through Judaism, and hence cherished a profound contempt for the whole Old Testament Dispensation. They tore Judaism out of all connection with Christianity, and regarded the true philosophic apprehension or $\gamma\nu\tilde{\omega}\sigma\iota\varsigma$ of Christianity, as consisting in the elimination from it of everything distinctively Jewish or Mosaic. The consequence was, that those two doctrines which are the life and life-blood of Christianity,—the doctrines of guilt and atonement,—were thrown out of the scheme of the Anti-Judaizing Gnostic. These came down from the Old Testament, and in reality are the substance of pure spiritual Judaism. In their place the Gnostic inserted absurd theories respecting the origin of the universe and of evil; theories by which creation was no longer the created, and sin was no longer sinful.

It is plain that Gnosticism in both of its forms,

like Ebionitism, was to be met most successfully, and overcome most triumphantly, by the plain and clear enunciation of the real relation of Christianity to Judaism. All three of these errours sprang out of a false conception, and were therefore to be overcome only by furnishing the true one. The thoroughness with which men like Irenaeus († 202), Tertullian († 220), Clement of Alexandria († 212–220), and Origen († 254),[1] investigated the Scriptures, in order to exhibit Judaism and Christianity in the true light, and in their mutual connection and harmony, is worthy of all admiration, and it may be added of imitation in any age. For every age of the Church is somewhat exposed to a revival of Anti-Judaistic Gnosticism, from the disposition among men of a speculative turn to reject, or at least to neglect the Old Testament; chiefly upon the ground of the vividness of its representations of the Divine personality, and the severe spirituality of its conception of sin and atonement.

§ 4. *Pagan Skepticism, and Christian replies.*

While the Christian apologist of this period was thus called to defend Christianity against objections that originated in a formal and unspiritual apprehension of Judaism on the one hand, and a

[1] IRENAEUS: Adversus Haereses. TERTULLIANUS: Adversus Marcionem; De prescriptionibus haereticorum; Adversus Valentinos; Contra Gnosticos scorpiacum. CLEMENS ALEXANDRINUS and ORIGEN, passim.

false spiritualism that rejected the Old Testament altogether on the other, he was at the same time compelled to meet that species of infidelity, common to every age, which rejecting revelation altogether, contends that the principles of natural reason and natural religion are adequate to meet the religious wants of mankind, and affirms that the Christian system is contradictory to them.

We have therefore to consider the attacks and defences of this period, so far as concerns the purely *Pagan Opposition to Christianity*. These attacks, unlike those of Ebionitism and Gnosticism, stood in no sort of connection with the religion of the Jewish nation, but were founded upon those views of human nature and of God, which belonged to the entire heathen or Gentile world.

The principal objections urged against Christianity by such pagan philosophers and speculatists as Celsus (150), Porphyry († 304), and Hierocles (300), were the following:

(1.) Christianity they asserted was irreligous and unethical; because it was founded upon an anthropopathic idea of God, particularly in the Old Testament, and contained absurd representations of the deity that were unfavourable to religion,— for example, the account of the creation and fall of man, the birth of Christ, his miracles, his death, and especially his resurrection. Porphyry and Celsus compared the account of the life and actions of Christ recorded in the gospels, with the popular narrations in the Greek and Roman mythologies, and placed him in the catalogue of the pagan heroes and demi-gods. They did not deny his historical existence, it should be noticed, but asserted that his disciples had craftily given currency to an exaggerated and false picture of the life of a sincere and good man.

(2.) Christianity claimed to be a supernaturally revealed religion; but revelation of this species is impossible and irrational. The pagan skeptic would concede the possibility of a general communication from the deity, such as appears in nature, and the human mind, but denied the reality of such a special and written revelation as the church claimed to possess in the canonical Scriptures.

The first of these objections was chiefly of a practical character, and hence was met in a practical manner by the apologist. The earliest defenders of Christianity against the heathen skepticism, Justin Martyr (†163), Tatian (†174), Athenagoras (†177),[1] laid much stress upon the transforming power of Christianity; upon the joyful deaths of Christians; and upon the greater safety

[1] The apologists who replied with most effect to the objections of the Pagan skeptic were: JUSTIN MARTYR: Apologia I and II; TATIAN: Λόγος πρὸς Ἕλληνας; ATHENAGORAS: Πρεσβεία περὶ Χριστιανῶν; CLEMENS ALEXANDRINUS: Cohortatio ad Gentes, a searching examination of the pagan mythologies; ORIGEN: Contra Celsum; TERTULLIAN: Apologeticus, De Idolatria; CYPRIAN: De idolorum vanitate; MINUCIUS FELIX: Octavius. See GUERICKE: Church History, §§ 29, 57–59.

in accepting Christianity, even if it should prove to be a delusion.

These were plain facts that could not be denied. The charge of immorality, which originated in unmixed malice and falsehood, and which Gibbon has re-stated with that minuteness of rhetorical amplification which accompanies a desire to convey an impression without daring to make an assertion, was easily refuted by a stern morality in the early church, that carried multitudes to the stake, or the amphitheatre, and a purity of life that was in dazzling contrast with the morals of heathenism. With respect to the theological representations of the Old and New Testaments, the early Christian Apologists had to perform a labour similar to that in the contest with the Ebionite and Gnostic,—the labour, viz. of bringing out to view the whole truth in the case. The objection that the Biblical representation of the deity is anthropopathic was met by directing attention to the fact, overlooked designedly or undesignedly by the Pagan skeptic, that the Jewish religion prohibited idolatry, and taught the unity and spirituality of the deity, at a time when the rest of the world was polytheistic and material in its theological conceptions, and employed these anthropopathic representations in a figurative manner only, as the inadequate but best means of communicating to a creature of time and sense the great spiritual idea with which it was labouring. Furthermore, living, as the first Christian Apologists did, so near to the age in which the events recorded in the Evangelists occurred, the historical argument for the authenticity and genuineness of the New Testament could be urged with even a greater confidence and success than it has been, or could be, since.[1]

The answer to the second objection of the Pagan opponent, viz. that revelation is contrary to reason, involved a much deeper examination of the whole subject upon grounds of reason and philosophy. This is the great standing objection of skepticism in all ages, and the history of Apologies, after the Apologetic period, is little more than the account of the endeavour of the Christian Mind to harmonize faith with science, religion with philosophy.

So far as concerns the defences of this earliest period in Apologetic History, it may be remarked, generally, that while the primitive fathers affirmed the intrinsic reasonableness of Christianity, and made some attempts to defend it upon philosophic grounds, it was not the favourite and predominant method with them. They feared philosophy as

---

[1] "For what motive," says JUSTIN MARTYR (Apologia I. Ch. 53), "could ever possibly have persuaded us to believe a crucified man to be the first begotten of the unbegotten God, and that he should hereafter come to be the judge of all the world, had we not met with those prophetic testimonies of him [in the Old Testament] proclaimed so long before his incarnation? Were we not eye-witnesses to the fulfilling of them? Did we not see the desolation of Judea, and men out of all nations proselyted to the faith by his apostles, and renouncing the ancient errors they were brought up in?"

taught in the different ancient schools; and regarded the various and conflicting systems as the sources of heresy.[1]

The abuse of philosophy by the Gnostics, especially, made them cautious in employing speculation in defending revealed religion, and even somewhat

---

[1] "Heresies themselves," says TERTULLIAN (De praescriptionibus haereticorum, Ch. 7.), "are tricked out by philosophy. Hence the 'aeons,' and I know not what infinite 'forms,' and 'the trinity of man' according to Valentinus: he was a Platonist. Hence the god of Marcion, more excellent by reason of his indolence: he belonged to the Stoics. And the doctrine that the soul dies is maintained by the Epicureans; and the denial of the resurrection of the body is taken from the united school of all the philosophers; and where matter is made equal with God, there is the doctrine of Zeno; and when aught is alleged concerning a god consisting of fire, there comes in Heraclitus. The same matter is turned and twisted by the heretics and by the philosophers; the same questions are involved: Whence comes evil? and wherefore? and whence man? and how? and (what Valentinus has lately propounded), whence God? to wit, from a mental evolution and an abortive birth (enthymesi et ectromate). Wretched Aristotle! who has taught them the dialectic art, cunning in building up and pulling down, using many shifts in sentences, making forced guesses at truth, stiff in arguments, busy in raising contentions, contrary even to itself, dealing backwards and forwards with every subject, so as, really, to deal with none...... What then has Athens to do with Jerusalem? What the Academy with the Church? What heretics with Christians? Our school is of the porch of Solomon, who himself also has delivered unto us, that we must in simplicity of heart (Wisdom i. 1) seek the Lord. Away with those who have brought forward a Stoic, and a Platonic, and a Dialectic Christianity." ACKERMANN (Christian Element in Plato, p. 24) remarks with much truth, that the early fathers favoured or feared philosophy according as it claimed to be a handmaid to Christianity, or a substitute for it; and that this explains the fact, that we so often find in the same church fathers contradictory expressions concerning Platonism and philosophy generally.

guarded in their assertion that it is defensible upon rational principles. They preferred, as we have seen, to employ the exegetical, historical, and practical arguments in opposition to the skeptic. This is true particularly of the defences that were composed in the second century by the Latin Apologists, Tertullian and Minucius Felix.[1] They defined and defended Christianity more with reference to its practical nature, and its influence upon private and public life. Still, even the vehement Tertullian, whose abhorrence of Gnosticism led him to inveigh with a bitterness not always discriminating against philosophy, appeals to the "testimonium animae naturaliter Christianae,"—to the witness of that real and true human nature which is in favour of the truth. This he would find, previous to its corruption and sophistication by philosophy falsely so called, in the spontaneous expressions of man in his most serious and honest moments. "Soul," he says, "stand thou forth in the midst,—whether thou art a thing divine and immortal according to most

---

[1] TERTULLIAN (De praescrip. Ch. 8) remarks that one part of the church were more inclined to philosophize upon Christianity than the other. "I come, therefore, to that point, which even our own brethren put forward as a reason for entering upon curious enquiry, and which heretics urge for bringing in curious doubt. It is written, they say, 'seek and ye shall find.' Let us remember when it was that our Lord uttered this saying: in the first beginning, I think, of his teaching, when it was yet doubted by all men whether He were the Christ; when as yet not even Peter had declared him to be the Son of God. ...... With good cause therefore was it *then* said: Seek and ye shall find, seeing that He was yet to be sought, who was not yet acknowledged."

philosophers, and therefore the less able to speak falsely, or as seems to Epicurus alone, whether thou art in no way divine, because material and mortal, ... whether thou hadst thy beginning with the body, or art sent into the body after it is formed,—from *whatever* source, and in whatever manner thou makest man a rational creature, more capable than any of understanding and of knowledge, stand thou forth and testify. But I summon thee not such as when formed in the schools, trained in the libraries, nurtured in the academies and porches of Athens, thou utterest thy crude wisdom. I address thee as simple, and rude, and unpolished, and unlearned; such as they have thee who have nothing but thee; *the very and entire thing that thou art in the crossroads, in the public squares, in the shops of the artisan.*[1] I have need of thy uncultivation (imperitia), since in thy cultivation however small no one puts faith. I demand of thee those truths which thou carriest with thyself into man, which thou hast learned to know either from thyself, or from the author of thy being, whoever he be. Thou art not, I know, a Christian soul; for thou art not born a Christian, but must be made one. Yet now the Christians themselves demand a testimony from

---

[1] "By philosophy I mean neither the Stoic, nor the Platonic, nor the Epicurean and Aristotelian. But whatever things have been properly said by each of those sects, inculcating righteousness and devout knowledge, this whole selection I call philosophy." CLEMENS ALEXANDRINUS: Stromata, Lib. I. p. 288. Ed. Paris, 1640.

thee, who art a stranger, against thy own friends, that they may blush even before thee, for hating and scoffing at us, on account of those very things which now detain thee as a party against them."[1]

This eloquent and vehement North African father appeals in the same way to the spontaneous convictions of man, in proof of the Divine Existence. "God," he says, "proves himself to be God, and the one only God, by the very fact that he is known to all nations; for the existence of any other deity than he would first have to be demonstrated. The consciousness of God is the original dowry of the soul; the same and differing in no respect in Egypt, in Syria, and in Pontus; for the God of the Jews is the one whom the *souls* of men call their god. We worship one God, the one whom ye all naturally know, at whose lightnings and thunders ye tremble, at whose benefits ye rejoice. Will ye that we prove the divine existence by the witness of the soul itself, which although confined by the prison of the body, although circumscribed by bad training, although enervated by lusts and passions, although made the servant of false gods, yet when it recovers itself as from a surfeit, as from a slumber, as from some infirmity, and is in its proper condition of soundness, calls God by *this* name only, because it is the proper name of the true God.[2]

[1] TERTULLIAN: De testimonio animae, Ch. 1.
[2] The deity is addressed by the pagan in this "sound" unsophisticated condition as "deus," and not as Jupiter, or Apollo, or by any other name.

'Great God,' 'good God,' and 'God grant' [deus not dii] are words in every mouth. The soul also witnesses that He is its judge, when it says 'God sees,' 'I commend to God,' 'God shall recompense me.' O testimony of a soul naturally Christian! [or monotheistic]. Finally, in pronouncing these words it looks not to the Roman capitol but to heaven; for it knows the dwelling place of the true God; from him, and from thence it descended."[1] These are the affirmations of one who in another place denominates philosophers the "patriarchs of

[1] TERTULLIAN: Adversus Marcionem, I. 10; Ad Scapulam, 2; Apologeticus, 17.—The following passages from pagan writers corroborate these affirmations of Tertullian: "There is a god (est deus) in heaven who hears and sees what we do." PLAUTUS: Captivi. "Be of good cheer, my child, there is a great god (Ζεύς) in heaven who beholds and rules all things." SOPHOCLES: Electra, 175. "*Alcibiades.* But what ought I to say? *Socrates.* If God will (ὅτι ἐὰν Θεὸς ἐθέλη)." PLATO: Alcibiades I. 135. MINUCIUS FELIX (Octavius, 18, 19) maintains that the wiser pagans taught the unity of God. See also AUGUSTINE (De Civitate. Lib. VIII) respecting the opinions of Plato. CALVIN (Institutes I. 10) sums up the whole of this view in the following manner: "In almost all ages, religion has been generally corrupted. It is true indeed, that the name of one supreme God has been universally known and celebrated. For those who used to worship a multitude of deities, whenever they spake according to the genuine sense of nature, used simply the name of God in the *singular* number, as though they were contented with one God. And this was wisely remarked by Justin Martyr, who for this purpose wrote a book 'On the Monarchy of God,' in which he demonstrates, from numerous testimonies, that the unity of God was a principle universally impressed on the hearts of men. Tertullian (De Idolatria) also proves the same point from the common phraseology. But since all men without exception have become vain in their understandings, all their natural perception of the Divine unity has only served to render them inexcusable." Compare ante, p. 55 (Note).

heretics," and Plato himself the author who "furnishes the sauce and seasoning of all the heretical speculations."[1]

In the same strain of reasoning, Minucius Felix argues. He speaks of the natural rationality of man in which Christianity finds a corroboration, and describes it as a power of apprehension "that is not produced by study, but is generated by the very make and structure of the human mind."[2] This writer, also, refers to the partial agreement of the heathen philosophy with Christianity, yet makes a violent attack upon Socrates, in which he speaks of him, after the phrase of Zeno probably, as that Attic jester (scurra Atticus).

Passing to the Greek Apologists of this period, Justin, Athenagoras, and Tatian, we find philosophy much more identified with Christianity, than in the Occidental defences. The distinction between natural and revealed religion is not very carefully made by them.[3] They were somewhat inclined to regard all religious truth as a revelation from God, and referred it partly to a supernatural communication from the Divine mind, and partly to the light of nature. Hence they did not always dis-

---

[1] " Philosophi patriarchae haereticorum " (De Anima, 3, and Adv. Hermogenem, 8). " Plato omnium haereticorum condimentarius " (De Anima, 23).

[2] " Ingenium quod non studio paratur, sed cum ipsa mentis formatione generatur" (Octavius, 16).

[3] This tendency is very strong in Lactantius, of the polemic period, who confounds ' religio ' with ' sapientia ' to such a degree, as to result in latitudinarian views of the gospel.

criminate with sufficient care between that which is the product of the human mind left to its spontaneous operations, and that which is communicated to it by a *special* revelation. Sometimes we find the same mind passing from one view to the other; at first blending natural and revealed religion together, and afterwards separating them. Justin Martyr is an example of this. In his earlier apologies, addressed to the Roman emperor, he recognizes the resemblance between the principles of natural religion and the ethics of Christianity, in order to render the philosophic and virtuous Marcus Aurelius, or Antoninus Pius, indulgent towards the new religion.[1] But in his later work, aimed

---

[1] "To lay before you [the emperor] in short, what we expect, and what we have learned from Christ, and what we teach the world, take it as follows: Plato and we are both alike agreed as to a future judgment, but differ about the judges; Rhadamanthus and Minos are his judges, Christ ours. And moreover we say that the souls of the wicked being reunited to the same bodies shall be consigned over to eternal torments, and not as Plato in the Timaeus will have it, to the period of a thousand years only. If then we hold some opinions near of kin to the poets and philosophers in greatest repute among you, and others of a diviner strain, and far above out of their sight, and have demonstrations on our side into the bargain, why are we to be thus unjustly hated, and to stand distinguished in misery above the rest of mankind? For in saying that all things were made in this beautiful order by God, what do we seem to say more than Plato? When we teach a general conflagration, what do we teach more than the Stoics? When we assert departed souls to be in a state of consciousness, and the wicked to be in torments, but the good free from pain and in a blissful condition, we assert no more than your poets and philosophers. When Plato (Repub. lib. x) said that 'the blame lies at his door who wills the sin, but God wills no evil,' he borrowed the saying from Moses." JUSTIN MARTYR: Apol. I. Ch. 8, 18, 57. The

against those who asserted that natural religion and ethics were adequate to meet the wants of man, and could therefore supersede Christianity, he takes the ground that the doctrines of a Plato and a Socrates had come to the Greeks by the way of the Jews through Egypt.[1]

The Apologist thought himself to be conducted to this view of the homogeneity of reason and revelation, by certain representations in Scripture, particularly by those portions of the writings of the Apostle John which speak of the Logos as enlightening every man that comes into the world. Some modern writers have supposed that the idea of the Logos, or the manifested Reason of God, which appears so frequently in the apologetic writings of the primitive fathers, was chiefly derived from the Platonic philosophy, and the writings of the Jewish

---

'Christian' in the Octavius of 'MINUCIUS FELIX says: "I have explained the opinions of almost all the philosophers, whose most illustrious glory it is that they have worshipped one God, though under various names; so that one might suppose either that the Christians of the present day are philosophers, or that the philosophers of old were already Christians."

[1] Cohortatio, 15, in NEANDER: I. 666. THEOPHILUS GALE's Court of the Gentiles, and CUDWORTH's Intellectual System, contain much to favour this view. AUGUSTINE expresses himself doubtfully: De Civitate Dei, VIII. 11, 12. CLEMENT OF ALEXANDRIA goes so far as to maintain "that the Greeks derived even their strategical skill from the Jews; and that Miltiades, in his night march against the Persians, imitated the tactics of Moses in conducting the children of Israel out of Egypt." He also "traces the first idolatrous columns of the ancients to their hearing of the fiery and cloudy pillar that went before the people of God." BOLTON: Evidences, pp. 82, 118, 123.

Philo. But it is the remark of Baumgarten-Crusius, who is not led to it by any merely theological interest or feeling, that the Logos-idea of the New Testament was more influential in forming the general philosophical notions of the church at this time, than was the department of secular philosophy itself. Clement of Alexandria, and the school of Origen generally, attribute the better religious knowledge of the heathen world, at one time to the Logos, and at another to the scriptures,[1] because they held that it was one and the same Supreme Reason that communicated the knowledge in both forms. They are however careful to observe that

[1] Respecting the source whence St. John derived the idea of the Logos, NEANDER (I. 575) remarks as follows: "The title 'Word of God,' employed to designate the idea of the Divine self-manifestation, the Apostle John could have arrived at within himself, independent of any outward tradition; and he would not have appropriated to his own purpose this title, which had been previously current in certain circles, had it not offered itself to him, as the befitting form of expression for that which filled his own soul. But this word itself is certainly not derived, any more than the idea originally expressed in it, from the Platonic philosophy, which could furnish no occasion whatever for the choice of this particular expression. The Platonic philosophy led rather to the employment of the term νοῦς, as a designation of the mediating principle in the deity. It is, rather, the translation of the Old Testament term דָּבָר; and it was this Old Testament conception, moreover, which led to the New Testament idea of the Logos. An intermediate step is formed by what is said in the epistle to the Hebrews concerning a Divine Word (See Bleeck's Commentary); and thus we find in the latest epistles of Paul from the first epistle to the Corinthians and onward, in the epistle to the Hebrews, and in the gospel of John, a well constituted series of links in the progressive development of the apostolic Logos-doctrine."

the unwritten revelation is imperfect, sporadic, and inadequate to meet all the religious wants of a sinful race, while the written word is perfect, full, and sufficient.[1]

§ 5. *Recapitulatory Survey.*

Having thus sketched the course of apologetic thinking during the second and first half of the third centuries, we bring the results into the following recapitulation.

The scientific mind of the Church, so far as it contended with Ebionitism and Gnosticism, was occupied chiefly with a clear and consistent exhibition of the real nature of Judaism, and of its essential agreement and oneness with Christianity. This correct apprehension of the first form of special revelation was of itself a refutation of those arguments which attempted to prove, either that Christianity was in hostility to all preceding special revelations from God, and that therefore it must be rejected, or else that there had been no preceding special revelations, and that therefore it must expel and annihilate every element of Judaism from itself.

And so far as the Church had to contend with Pagan philosophy, which derived its arguments wholly from the operations of the human mind, and rejected both of the special revelations, the sub-

---

[1] The unwritten word is termed μέρος τοῦ λόγου, σπερματικός λόγος.

stance of its counter-argument was, that even if the principles of natural religion should be regarded as the pure efflux of the unassisted human mind, they did not run counter to the doctrines of Christianity, but really required them, in order to their own spread and efficiency among men; that the human mind, when its real and deep convictions were revealed, was monotheistic, or naturally Christian, as Tertullian states it; but that, more than all, it was most probable that this natural religion itself was the remains of a primitive revelation, which had been made to the race in the earliest ages of its existence, and which had been waning and growing dimmer and dimmer, as the process of corrupt human development went on.

CHAPTER II.

DEFENCES OF CHRISTIANITY IN THE POLEMIC PERIOD:
A. D. 254—A. D. 730.

§ 1. *Preliminary Statements.*

WE pass now, in the history of the Defences of Christianity, into the Polemic Period. In this age we shall find Apologetics assuming a more profound and scientific character, than it has hitherto borne. We perceive the beginning of that great *methodical* conflict between religion and philosophy, faith and science, which is renewed in every age, and in some form or other will probably continue to the end of human history.

Even in the last part of the Apologetic period, the distinctions between natural and revealed religion, faith and science, the supernatural and the natural, began to be drawn with more clearness. The controversy between Origen and Celsus, the ablest upon both sides of the great question that occurred in these first centuries, brought out these distinctions somewhat, from the latent state in which for the most part they had existed in the earlier defences, and compelled both parties to see that nothing but a more precise and scientific discussion of the contradictions between Christianity and skepticism could settle the questions at issue. Religion in the first two centuries had existed mainly in the form of feeling. It was now to take on the form of scientific cognition; and the commencement of the change, not in the matter of Christianity, for this remains the same in all ages, but, in the form of apprehending it, is seen first of all in the altered manner of defending it against the skeptic. In the school of Alexandria, with Origen at its head, the apologetic science of the first period set with a splendour that was the herald of a yet more glorious dawn in the Polemic age that was to follow.[1]

As the dogmatic material now becomes more abundant and various, and the defences more systematic and elaborate, it will facilitate the investigation of the apologetic history of this period, to distribute it under the following principles of classification: (1.) The distinction between revelation and reason. (2.) The distinction between faith and

[1] The principal apologetic work of the first period is that of Origen against Celsus, "composed," says BAUMGARTEN-CRUSIUS (Dogmengeschichte, I. § 21), "with the confidence of victory, and with a most comprehensive knowledge of the nature and history of Christianity, as well as of the skepticism of its opponents."

science. (3.) The distinction between the natural and the supernatural. In exhibiting the mode in which the Apologetic Mind of this period apprehended these distinctions, and stated the relation of each idea to the other, we shall bring to view the whole course of doctrinal developement. For the ideas of revelation and reason, faith and science, the miraculous and the natural, were the leading ones in the controversy with the skeptic, and the whole dispute took form and character from them.[1]

§ 2. *Mutual relations of Revelation and Reason.*

1. In considering the manner in which the reciprocal relations of revelation and reason were conceived of in the Apologetic History of this period, the first characteristic that meets us is the fact, that the line between the two was now more strictly and firmly drawn, than it had been. The preceding age, as has been observed, referred everything to God, because its religious consciousness was of that warm and glowing character which is disinclined to distinguish, in a scientific manner, what proceeds from a supernatural and what from a natural source. All truth, provided it was truth, was conceived as coming from God, in some form or other. This view was sometimes expressed, even by the Christian apologist, in such a strong

[1] For this rubric, together with a portion of the materials, we are indebted to the very excellent manual of BAUMGARTEN-CRUSIUS.

and unguarded manner as to expose Christianity to the charge of being but little superior to natural religion, if not identical with it. Justin Martyr, in his Apology addressed to the Roman emperor, expresses himself as follows: "They who live according to reason are Christians, even though they are regarded as godless ($ἄθεοι$); such for example were Socrates and Heraclitus among the Greeks."[1] He probably ventured upon such an assertion from a partial understanding of corresponding ones in the scriptures. Paul (Rom. ii. 14) remarks that, "whenever ($ὅταν$ with subj. $ποιῇ$) the Gentiles, which have not the law, do by nature the things contained in the law, they are a law unto themselves." Peter (Acts x. 35) affirms that, "in every nation he that feareth God and worketh righteousness is accepted with him." Overlooking the fact that these are both of them hypothetical statements introduced for the sake of an argument, and that whenever there is any *categorical* affirmation made in the scriptures respecting the actual fact of sinless obedience, the pagan man is represented as being disobedient to the law written on the heart, and that therefore every mouth must be stopped, and the whole world become guilty before God (Rom. iii. 19, 20),—overlooking the concessive nature of the hypothesis, the apologist in this instance affirms what he could not know, that in the instances of Socrates and Heraclitus there had been

[1] Apologia I. 46.

a perfect obedience of the law of reason and righteousness.

Hence it became necessary to distinguish between those spontaneous workings of the human mind which are to be seen in the Pagan philosophy and theology, and those higher phenomena of the human soul which appear only after it has felt the influence of a higher manifestation of truth and spiritual influences. This naturally led to a technical distinction between natural and revealed religion, and to a demarcation of that which issues from man left to himself, from that which proceeds in a special and peculiar manner from the Divine Mind.[1] As the Christian apologist was compelled to a still more close and rigorous defence, by an increasingly close and rigorous attack, he found it necessary to draw some lines that had not been drawn before, and to score more deeply some lines that had been but faintly described. Revelation now began to be taken in its stricter and narrower signification, to denote that communication of truth, by *direct* inspiration, which had been recorded in the Jewish scriptures, and in the New Testament canon,— which latter had by the beginning of the Polemic period been determined and fixed by the authority of the Church. The application of the term in its widest signification begins now to disappear, so that the contest between the Christian and the skeptic,

---

[1] Upon the use of the term "revelation" in a general and a special sense, see TWESTEN: Dogmatik, I. 320 (Note).

became, what it has been ever since, the conflict between scripture on the one hand, and speculation on the other.

2. A second characteristic in the Apologetic History of this period is, that the question respecting the possibility of a revelation, in the *generic* meaning of communication between the human and the Divine, was not raised by the skeptic, and of course not by the apologist. This question, which enters so largely into the conflict between Christianity and infidelity in modern times, is wholly a modern one. The denial of the possibility of *any* revelation from God to man began with Spinoza, one of the most original and powerful of skeptics, and has been followed with more vigour and acuteness by Hume, than by any other succeeding mind.

But in this age of the Church, both parties acknowledged the possibility and reality of a revelation of some sort. The testimony of the Greek philosophers, particularly Plato, to the need of a divine communication in order that the darkness overhanging human life and prospects might be cleared away, was frequently cited by the Christian apologist, and admitted by the skeptical opponent. The confession of Plato in the Timaeus,[1] "to find the maker and father of all this universe

---

[1] Τὸν μὲν οὖν ποιητὴν καὶ πατέρα τοῦδε τοῦ παντὸς εὑρεῖν τε ἔργον, καὶ εὑρόντα, εἰς πάντας ἀδύνατον λέγειν. Timaeus, 28 c. Ed. Steph. "What we asserted at the beginning appears now to be really the fact, that it is not possible for any excepting a very few men to be perfectly happy and blessed." Epinomis, Ch. 13.

of existence, is a difficult work, and when he is found, it is impossible to describe him to the mass of mankind," was a classical passage, and often cited by the early fathers. Origen[1] quotes the Platonic passage in which it is said: " human nature is not competent to seek out God and find him in his pure reality, unless the being seeking is assisted by the being sought" (μὴ βοηθηθεῖσα ὑπὸ τοῦ ζητουμένου).

So far therefore as the acknowledgment of the *need* and *possibility* of a revelation is concerned, the apologist of this period was not required to elaborate a defence in this reference. His great labour was to convince the skeptic that those more general forms of revelation in nature, and in providence, were not sufficient to meet the wants of *sinful* man. A certain and reliable knowledge was craved by the human soul respecting some subjects about which the human mind of a Socrates or a Plato could give only conjectures and express strong hopes.[2] The apologist contended that the doctrines

---

[1] Contra Celsum, VII. xlii.

[2] Plato's belief in the immortality of the soul and the reality of a future life was accompanied with more or less of doubt at times, to which he gives frank utterance. "To affirm *positively*, indeed, that these things are exactly as I have described them, does not become a man of sense. But that, either this, or something of the kind, takes place with respect to our souls and their habitations,—seeing that the soul seems to be immortal (ἐπείπερ ἀθανατόν γε ἡ ψυχὴ φαίνεται οὖσα), —appears to me most fitting to be believed, and worthy the hazard for one who trusts in the reality. For the hazard is noble (καλὸς γὰρ ὁ κίνδυνος), and it is right to allure ourselves with such views as with enchantments (ἐπᾴδειν)." Phaedo, 114. c. Ed. Steph.

of the soul's immortality, and of a future state of rewards and punishments, though dimly appearing in the pagan philosophy, could be made an absolutely clear and certain knowledge, only by the testimony of one who like Christ came out from eternity, and went back into it; who came from God and went to God; who actually died, rose from the dead, re-appeared on earth for a season, and then ascended up where he was before. Hence the Christian apologist of this period made great use of the facts of Christ's incarnation and resurrection, to corroborate the truths of natural religion and make them absolutely certain,—a species of proof which the modern church does not emphasize with such energy as did the ancient, to the diminution of its faith, and lively realizing of invisible things.

But, more than this, the apologist contended that a knowledge was required by the human soul respecting still other subjects, about which natural religion was totally silent. Whether the deity could pardon sin; whether he would, and, if so, the method in which; whether the human race was to continue on from century to century in sin and sorrow and suffering, as it had for centuries and ages before, or whether any remedial system would be introduced, to interrupt this natural developement downward, and start a new order of ages, and begin a new species of history,—about such questions as these, which were far more vital and important than any others, the Christian apologist contended, and with truth, that human reason, and the general teachings of nature and providence were totally silent. Unless, therefore, a *special* communication should be made, man must be left without any answer to the most anxious and important of his questions. Such a special answer to such special questions had been made. It was contained in the scriptures of the Old and New Testaments, to which the term revelation in the high and strict sense was now applied and confined.

3. A third characteristic of the Apologetics of this period is the insisting upon revelation, in this strict sense, as an infallible authority for the human mind. The idea of an infallible norm or rule of faith, though not a new one, by any means, in the mind of the church, now begins to be more clearly enunciated. The conception of a special and peculiar revelation led to that of infallibility. Revelation, in the broad and loose signification in which, we have seen, it was sometimes employed by the earlier apologists, and acknowledged by their heathen opponents, leaves room and play for errour and misconception. That general communication of truth which God makes to the human mind, through its own constitution and through the works of creation and providence, though reliable to a certain extent, is not reliable beyond the possibility of errour; though true, is not infallibly true. For this species of revelation is mixed with human corruption, and darkened by human blindness. It is

not as pure and accurate as it was in the beginning, because, as St. Paul teaches (Rom. i. 18–25), that which may be known of God in a natural manner and by natural reason has not been retained in its original simplicity and genuineness. While therefore the Christian apologist was disposed to give human reason its due, and to make use of all the statements of the pagan philosophers respecting the general truthfulness of man's natural intuitions, he at the same time insisted that natural religion could not be construed into a divine *authority*, and an *infallible* norm or rule. Being but a form of human consciousness, it was liable to all the fluctuations of consciousness, and to all the deteriorations of consciousness,—at one time being considerably free from foreign and contradictory elements, as in the instance of a Plato or a Plutarch; at another mixed and mingled with the most crude and absurd notions and opinions, as in the vagaries of New-Platonism, and the fanciful dreams of the Gnostic philosophers. Hence the apologist maintained that a further and peculiar species of revelation was needed, that should not only answer questions and supply wants that were unanswered and unsupplied by natural religion, but should also be fixed in a *written* form. In this way, it would be exempt from liability to corruption and alteration from the fluctuations of human consciousness, and would go down from age to age unchangeable amidst the changeable, and infallible amidst the fallible.

The Western Church, particularly, under the guidance of Augustine, urged the necessity of an infallible authority in matters of doctrine and practice. This necessity was affirmed in connection with the doctrine of human apostacy and sinfulness. It was therefore a *relative* necessity. Had man continued in his primitive state, he would have remained in such a close and living union with his Creator that no special and written revelation would have been needed, but the spontaneous operations of his mind, and the holy communion of his heart with God, would have afforded all the religious knowledge necessary. But inasmuch as he had apostatized, and no longer enjoyed that original intercourse with his Creator, a special interposition was called for, to clear up and rectify his now only imperfectly correct natural conceptions, and still more to impart an additional knowledge, respecting the possibility and method of his restoration to the Divine likeness and favour.

This attribute of *authority*, which was now asserted of revelation, was emphasized all the more from the fact that the idea of the Church was now a more definite and influential one than it had been. The infallibility of the scriptures was urged in connection with the growing authority of the one only catholic Church, as opposed to schismatical and heretical sects.[1] This connection we shall find in

---

[1] TERTULLIAN (De praescript. Ch. 36.), in the preceding period, traces the doctrine of the one catholic church to revelation as

the next period to have become so close as to be converted into identity, and tradition together with ecclesiastical decrees takes the place of scripture. The beginnings of this may be seen in the last half of the Polemic period, but not in the first half. The theology of the 4th and 5th centuries was too much controlled by Augustine to allow of the co-equality of tradition with revelation.[1] Much as that powerful mind was inclined to quote the general opinion of the Church, respecting the meaning of scripture, in opposition to the heretical parties with which he was in continued conflict, he never attributed *infallibility* to any human opinion. A saying of his which occurs in his controversy with the Manichaeans has been frequently quoted by Roman Catholic writers, to prove his substantial agreement with the Papal theory of the relation of biblical to ecclesiastical authority. It is this. "I should not believe (have believed) the gospel, unless the authority of the catholic Church moved (had moved) me to."[2] Calvin, Bucer, and the elder Protestant writers generally, construe the imperfect

---

its source. "The church acknowledges one God, the Lord, the Creator of the universe, and Christ Jesus the Son of God the Creator, born of the virgin Mary, and the resurrection of the flesh. She joins the law and the prophets with the writings of the evangelists and apostles, and *thence* drinks in her faith."

[1] "Titubabit fides, si scripturarum sacrarum vacillet auctoritas." AUGUSTINE: De doctrina christiana, I. xxxvii.

[2] "Evangelio non crederem, nisi me ecclesiae catholicae commoveret auctoritas." AUGUSTINE: Contra Epistolam Fundamenti, Ch. v. (Ed. Migne, VIII. 176). Compare also, TERTULLIAN: De praescriptionibus, Ch. 28.

as the pluperfect in this passage, and interpret Augustine as affirming that when he was "an alien from the Christian faith, he could not be prevailed upon to embrace the gospel as the infallible truth of God, till he was convinced by the authority of the Church."[1] In other words, if when examining into the claims of Christianity to be the absolute religion, he had found the Christian Church disputing within itself respecting the canon of scripture upon which this religion professed to be founded, and also in respect to the cardinal doctrines of Christianity contained in this canon, he as a pagan should have stood in doubt of the whole matter, and would not have received a book, and a system, respecting which those who professed to adopt it were constantly wrangling. But the entire unanimity of the Church respecting the authenticity and authority of the canonical scriptures determined him in their favour. Had he found the same diversity of opinion in the Church, that he saw among the heretical parties, respecting the written revelation, he should not have found rest in it. The

---

[1] CALVIN: Institutes, I. vii. 3. LUTHER (Table Talk, "Of the Fathers") remarks in his characteristic manner that "the Pope to serve his own turn, took hold on St. Augustine's sentence, where he says, *evangelio non crederem*, &c. The asses could not see what occasioned Augustine to utter that sentence, whereas he spoke it against the Manichaeans; as much as to say: 'I believe not *you*, for ye are damned heretics, but I believe and hold with the Church, the spouse of Christ.'" See also, the explanation of this sentiment of Augustine by STILLINGFLEET: Grounds of the Protestant Religion, Pt. I. Ch. vii.

passage read in its connections in the argument, and interpreted in the light of that stricter view of revelation which, we have seen, Augustine did so much towards establishing, merely affirms, in the words of Hagenbach,[1] "a subjective dependence of the believer upon the authority of the Church universal, but not an objective subordination of the Bible itself to this authority." The individual, in the opinion of Augustine, is to respect the authority of the Church in seeking an answer to the questions: What books are canonical, and what apocryphal? and what is the doctrinal system contained in them? In answering these questions, he contended, that the Church universal had an authority higher than that of any one member; and higher, particularly, than a man like Manichaeus who claimed to be an inspired apostle.[2] When therefore, a single individual, or a particular party like the Manichaeans, insisted that they were right in rejecting certain portions of the canon that had been, and still were, deemed canonical by the Church at large,[3] and in deriving from the portions

---

[1] Dogmengeschichte, § 119.

[2] He began his treatise thus: "Manichaeus apostolus Jesu Christi, providentia Dei Patris. Haec sunt salutaria verba de perenni et vivo fonte." AUGUSTINE: Cont. Ep. Fundamenti, c. 5.

[3] Respecting the alterations of scripture by heretical parties, see EUSEBIUS, V. 28; NEANDER I. 582. TERTULLIAN (De praescriptionibus, c. 17, 38, 39) remarks that, "heresy does not receive certain of the scriptures, and whatever it does receive, it twists about according to its own plan and purpose, by adding to it and subtracting from it. And if to a certain extent it accepts the scriptures entire, nevertheless by devising different expositions it perverts them. An adulteration by

of it which they acknowledged to be of divine authority, a set of doctrines respecting the origin and nature of evil, such as the apostolic and catholic Church did not find in the scriptures,—when the individual, and the heretical party, in this way opposed their private judgment to the catholic judgment, Augustine denies the reasonableness of the procedure. He affirms the greater probability of the correctness of the Catholic Mind, in comparison with the Heretical or Schismatic Mind, and thereby the *authority* of the Church in relation to the individual, without dreaming however of affirming its absolute *infallibility*,—an attribute which he confines to the written revelation.

The position which the Church sustains to the individual is indicated, remarks Augustine, in the words of the Samaritans to the Samaritan woman: "Now we believe, not because of thy saying, for we have heard him ourselves, and know that this is indeed the Christ, the Saviour of the world" (John iv. 42). The individual first hears the concurrent testimony of the great body of believers in

---

imposing a false sense is as much opposed to the truth, as a corruption by the pen." CLEMENS ALEXANDRINUS (Stromata, VII. xvi) makes the same charge. "But if some of those who follow after heresies venture to employ the prophetical writings, in the first place, they do not employ all of them; and in the second place, they do not employ them as a consistent whole, according to the substance and context. But selecting what is spoken ambiguously, they conform this to their own theory, besprinkling here and there a few texts, not regarding their meaning, but employing the bare letter." Compare also, IRENAEUS: Adversus Haereses, II. x. 1.

every age, and then verifies it for himself. He finds a general unanimity in the Church catholic respecting the canonical and apocryphal books, and also respecting their meaning and doctrinal contents. He goes to the examination with the natural expectation of finding that the general judgment is a correct one, and in so far, he comes under the influence of traditional or catholic opinions. This is the "ecclesiastical authority" which has weight with him. At the same time he exercises the right of private judgment; the right namely to examine the general judgment and to perceive its correctness with his own eyes. The Samaritans put confidence in the testimony of the woman, but at the same time they went and saw, and heard for themselves. They came into agreement with her by an active, and not by a passive method. In employing this illustration, Augustine adopts the Protestant, and opposes the Papal theory of tradition and authority. The Papist's method of agreeing with the catholic judgment is passive. He denies that the individual may intelligently verify the position of the Church for himself, because the Church is *infallible*, and consequently there is no possibility of its being in error. The individual is therefore shut up to a mechanical and passive reception of the catholic decision. The Protestant, on the other hand, though affirming the high probability that the general judgment is correct, does not assert the infallible certainty that it is. It is conceivable and possible that the Church may err. Hence the duty of the individual, while cherishing an antecedent confidence in the decisions of the Church, to examine these decisions in the light of the written word, and convert this presumption into an intelligent perception, or else demonstrate their falsity beyond dispute. "Neither ought I to bring forward the authority of the Nicene Council," says Augustine (Contra Maximianum Arianum II. xiv. 3), "nor you that of Ariminum, in order to prejudge the case. I ought not to be bound (detentum) by the authority of the latter, nor you by that of the former. Under the authority of the Scriptures,[1] not those received by particular sects, but those received by all in common,[2] let the disputation be carried on, in respect to each and every particular."

[1] GIESELER (History, Vol. I. § 90) remarks, that down to the council of Chalcedon, in 451, "in answering opponents men did not endeavour to prove [merely] that the council was oecumenical, but [also] that its decision was true according to scripture and tradition."

[2] AUGUSTINE's mind, while he was inquiring and doubting, and before he attained to Christian faith, was much influenced by the fact that the scriptures and the Christian system were the faith of the *world*. He argued that God would not have permitted a system of *error* to have obtained such universal currency, and so wide-spread influence. "Since we are too weak to find out truth by abstract reasonings, and for this very cause need the authority of Holy Writ, I began to believe that Thou wouldest never have given such excellency of authority to Scripture in all lands, hadst Thou not willed thereby to be sought and believed in. . . . . . It is no vain and empty thing, that the excellent dignity of the authority of the Christian faith hath overspread the whole world." Confessions, VI. v. xi. TERTULLIAN: (De praescriptionibus, c. 28, 29) employs the same reasoning. "Is

Chiefly then through the stricter definition and limitation of the idea of Revelation, and partly through the need felt, in the controversies with the heretical and separating mind, of some infallible standard of appeal, did the authoritative character of the Scriptures come to be urged and established by the apologist of this Polemic period. Ever since this time, the Church has recognized the canonical books of the Old and New Testaments as the only *infallible* source of religious knowledge; ever refusing to attribute this characteristic to any other form of knowledge, however true and valid in its own province. The only exception to this is found in that portion of the history of the Roman Catholic Church in which tradition and ecclesiastical authority are placed upon an equality with Scripture. But this portion of Church History is the history of a corruption. For the doctrine of the infallibility of the Church is of the same nature, with that of the infallibility of the Pope. Both doctrines alike imply an absolute exemption from

it possible that so many churches, and so great ones, should have gone astray into the *same* erroneous belief? Never is there one result among many chances. In case the doctrinal system of the churches were error there must have been variety in its forms and statements. But where one and the same thing is found amongst many, this is not error but catholic tradition. . . . . Is it probable that a gospel of error was preached through the whole earth; that all mankind erroneously believed it; that so many thousands of thousands were baptized into error; that so many works of faith and miracles were wrought by error; and finally that so many martyrdoms in behalf of error were erroneously crowned?"

error, on the part of the finite mind,—a doctrine which belongs to the history of heresies.

4. A fourth characteristic of the Apologetic History of the period is the fact, that the Church did not array Revelation and Reason in hostility to each other. Careful and firm as the apologist was, in distinguishing revealed from natural religion, and scripture from the spontaneous teachings and operations of the human mind, he steadily refused to concede the position of his skeptical opponent, that Christianity is intrinsically irrational. It was one great aim of the skepticism of this age, as it has been in every age since, to establish if possible the fact of an inherent and necessary contradiction between the special revelation from God contained in the canonical scriptures, and those first principles of all reasoning which are involved in the rational understanding of man; and that consequently the alternative was either to accept Biblical Christianity in the face of all rational principles, or of rational principles in the face of Christianity. This alternative was not admitted. Neither horn of this dilemma was accepted by the Apologist. He denied that there is any inward and necessary contradiction between revelation and reason, or that the adoption of the evangelical system involves the rejection either of the first principles of ethics and natural religion, or of true philosophy. On the contrary he affirmed an inward harmony between the two, and bent the best energies of his intellect to

demonstrate it. The Church by this time had a philosophy of its own; and henceforward we find the most rational and truthful philosophical systems originating not in Heathendom but in Christendom. The cultivation of theological science proceeded along with that of philosophy; and down to the present day the Christian Apologist contends that any system of philosophy that is anti-Christian is *ipso facto* irrational,—an affirmation that implies an essential agreement between revelation and reason, and which cannot be made good without evincing this agreement. The assertion that whatever is contradictory to Christianity is irrational, necessarily implies that Christianity itself is reasonable.

Single passages may be quoted from the Fathers to show the carefulness with which they strove to identify the interests of theology with philosophy, and vice versa. Gregory of Nyssa and Epiphanius speak of a truth corroborated by the holy scriptures and right reason. Augustine denounces an error as unsupported by either the authority of scripture or the reasonableness of truth.[1] Single passages may also be quoted to prove that the Christian apologist disparaged reason and rep-

---

[1] GREGORIUS NYSSA (Contra Eunomium, I. p. 63. Ed. Par.): Ἀπὸ θείας φωνῆς ... ἐκ λογισμῶν ἀκολουθίαν. AUGUSTINUS (Gen. ad lit. VII. xxiv): Nulla scripturae auctoritas vel veritatis ratio; (De Civitate, VIII. i): Porro si sapientia deus est, per quem facta sunt omnia, sicut divina auctoritas veritasque monstravit, verus philosophus est amator dei. EPIPHANIUS (Haer. LXX. iii): Ἐκ θείων γραφῶν καὶ ὀρθοῦ λογισμοῦ.

resented it as inimical to revelation. But such passages must be read in their connection in the treatise, or the argument. Such expressions, disparaging the use of reason in religion, Baumgarten-Crusius remarks may be put into three classes: (1) Those in which reason is taken in its least extensive sense, to denote the reason of a particular system, party or school; (2) Those in which reason is taken in the sense of an arrogant private opinion which sets itself up against public sentiments, historical opinions, and authority generally; (3) Those in which reason is taken in the sense of a one-sided speculative disposition that is devoid of any profound religious feeling or want.[1] It is against reason in this narrow and inadequate signification, against which it is as much the interest of philosophy to inveigh as it is of revelation, that the disparaging remarks frequently found in Tertullian of the Apologetic period, and in Athanasius and Augustine of the Polemic, are leveled. But against the common reason of mankind, the unbiassed spontaneous convictions of the race, no such remarks are aimed. On the contrary, a confident appeal is made to them by these very Apologists;[2] while those systems of philosophy, and those intellectual methods that flow most legitimately and purely from them, are employed by the Christian Mind in developing and establishing the truths of revelation.

[1] BAUMGARTEN-CRUSIUS: Dogmengeschichte, II. § 15.

[2] Compare Tertullian's appeal, *ante*, p. 124.

The most powerful and grandest endeavour of the Apologetic Mind of this period to evince the harmony of revelation and reason is seen in the *De Civitate Dei* of Augustine. This is a treatise consisting of twenty-two books; the first ten of which contain a searching and extended critique of polytheism, in its principles and their influence, and the last twelve treat of Christianity as supernatural, and destined as the realized kingdom or city of God to overthrow all secular and earthly kingdoms and powers.[1] It is a work which merits the study of the modern theologian perhaps more than any other single treatise of the Ancient Church; whether we consider the range and variety of its contents, the depth and clearness of its views, and especially the thoroughly supernatural point of view from which everything is looked at.

§ 3. *Mutual relations of Faith and Science.*

We pass now to the second distinction which presents itself in the Apologetic History of the Polemic period,—the distinction, namely, between Faith and Scientific Knowledge.

In the Pagan world, faith was merely candour of mind, or a willingness to be convinced of the truth. In this sense, Aristotle remarks that, "it is necessary for one to believe, in order that he may

---

[1] See a synopsis of it in MILMAN: History of Christianity, III. x; and FLEURY: XXXIII.

learn."[1] This form of faith, though indispensable to the scholar, and the condition of all genuine intellectual culture, is very far from coming up to the Biblical idea of this grace. Faith, in the Christian system, is a positive and certain *conviction*. It differs from the Pagan conception by being more than a merely negative readiness to be convinced. It is an actual assurance of the mind; an inward certitude. Faith is the *substance* of things hoped for, the *evidence* of things not seen (Heb. xi. 1). It differs again from the inquiring temper of the secular mind by being accompanied with humility,—a virtue which was unknown to the Pagan ethics, and which is so generally expelled from the human mind by the conscious increase of knowledge, whose tendency it is to " puff up." In the scriptures, moreover, faith is described as a matter of the heart and will, of life and feeling. It is a practical, and not a speculative act of the mind. And this view of it was taken by the apologist of this period, and we may add of all periods.

During this Polemic age, the Church laid much stress upon the definition of faith given in Hebrews, xi. 1.: "Faith is the substance of things *hoped for*, the evidence of things *not seen*." It is an immoveable belief in the reality and paramount importance of the *future*, the *invisible*, and the *supernatural*. Says Augustine, "quod est fides, nisi credere quod

---

[1] Δεῖ πιστεύειν τὸν μανθάνοντα. Soph. El. I. ii.

non vides."[1] The object of faith is not cognizable by the senses; for this is the meaning of "invisible" in this connection. The eternal world with all its realities stands in no sort of relation to a sensuous organism, and is therefore inapprehensible by any or all of the physical media of knowledge. Faith therefore is the direct contrary of infidelity, which tests everything by a sensuous experience, and does not believe at all except upon a sensuous knowledge of objects. Faith is not a sensuous but an *intellectual* act, and as the etymology denotes, is *fidelity* to the future and eternal; is *fealty* to the invisible, the spiritual, and the supernatural. It is the positive certainty that these are the most real and important of all objects, notwithstanding that they do not come within the sphere of sensuous observation.

But while the Christian apologist of this period thus regarded faith as different in kind both from the cold and speculative belief of the intellect, and the warm but low certainty of the five senses, he maintained that it is a *rational* act and state of the soul. This is the second characteristic to be noticed. We find in this, as in the former instance, the same disposition on the part of the defender of Christianity to contend for the intrinsic reasonableness of revealed religion in all its parts and departments. This believing state of the soul, which Christianity insists so much upon, and which constitutes the

[1] Tractatus XL. in Joannem, Cap. ix.

very life and heart of this religion, is not the credulity of an ignorant and unthinking devotee. Hence the apologist sometimes represents faith as the most *natural* state of the soul. It is the foundation of human society, argues Augustine; we are born in faith, and shut up to it.[1] Origen presents the same view in his argument against the skepticism of Celsus.[2] Polycarp, in the very twilight of the controversy between faith and unbelief, calls faith "the mother of us all."[3] Nonnus, in similar phraseology, terms faith "the boundless mother of the world."[4] These expressions relate, it will of course be understood, to faith in its most general signification. They were not made with any direct reference to that more restricted and peculiar act of the soul by which the justifying work of the Redeemer is appropriated; though, it deserves to be noticed, they are not without a valid application to the doctrine of justifying faith itself. But these and similar statements of the defender of Christianity were intended to specify the nature of that general attitude of the mind towards revealed truth, and invisible things, which is required of man, in order that he may apprehend them. The apologist claimed that this recumbency of the soul upon the supernatural, the invisible, the specially revealed, was a most reasonable, and, in one sense of the

[1] De utilitate credendi, I. xii. xiv.
[2] Contra Celsum, IV. i. ii.
[3] Epist. III: Ἡ πίστις μήτηρ πάντων ἡμῶν.
[4] Ad Joann. i. 7: Ἀτέρμονα μητέρα κόσμου.

word, as Augustine teaches, a natural act and state of the human mind. Employing the term "natural" to denote what belongs to man's original, created nature,—to what belongs to his first unfallen nature, in distinction from his second apostate nature,—the Apologete maintained, in opposition to the skeptic, that Christian faith does no violence to the constitution of a rational spirit, but on the contrary falls in with its deepest wants and necessities, and is therefore a natural act and condition.[1] Faith, he said, corresponds to and satisfies the original needs of man and human society. It is the only safe and tranquil mental state for a creature who like man has not yet entered the eternal and invisible world, and who therefore must take eternal things for the present upon trust. And as matter of fact, so affirmed the defender of faith, we begin to exercise faith in some form or other, as soon as we begin to exist, either physically or morally. The child is the exhibitor and the symbol of this characteristic (Matt. xviii. 2–4); and in mature life those who cease from the trusting repose and faith of childhood, and become unbelieving and infidel, run counter to the convictions of the majority of mankind. In this sense, and by such and similar tokens, faith is perceived to be natural, and unbelief unnatural. The former consequently is

---

[1] A similar use of "nature" and "natural," in the sense of the created and normal, may be seen in CALVIN's Institutes, I. xv. 1, and II. i. 11.

rational, the latter irrational; so that the apparent contrariety between faith and reason disappears, as soon as a central point of view is attained.¹

The distinction itself between Faith and Science had already been formally made in the preceding Apologetic period, by the Alexandrine school. The great founder and head of this school, Origen, though one of the most speculative minds previous to the Schoolmen, was careful to lay down the position that faith precedes scientific knowledge in the order of nature. Though distinguishing so sharply between πίστις and γνῶσις as to lay the foundation for an exoteric and an esoteric knowledge in the Christian Church, thereby doing violence to the spirit of Christianity, which has no room within its communion, like the pagan philosophies, for a class of initiated persons,—though disposed to render to science its dues and more than its dues,—Origen steadfastly taught that the Speculative is grounded in the Practical, and not vice versa, and that it is impossible to build up Christian science out of any other materials than those which are furnished by revealed truth wrought into the Christian consciousness. Hence evangelical faith in the heart must precede the *philosophic* cognition of Christianity. It does not exist prior to any and every species of knowledge, but prior to *scientific*

---

[1] We find this same defence of faith, in substance, in all the more contemplative and religious philosophical systems. See PASCAL, JACOBI, and COLERIDGE, e. g. passim.

knowledge. Faith is an intelligent act, but not a *scientific* act. The statements of the Alexandrine school upon this subject are very clear and positive. "Faith," says Clement of Alexandria, "is more elementary than scientific knowledge; it is the foundation and rudimental material of science." In another place, according to the well-known Aristotelian dictum he terms it "the test and criterion of science."[1] And, on the other hand, science is represented by these highly adventurous and speculating Alexandrines as merely the developement and expansion of faith,—as the exact and logical opening up of what is contained potentially in the practical and living confidence of the mind in revealed truth and supernatural realities.

With these positions of Origen and his school, Augustine agreed entirely, as did the church generally, during the Polemic period. The same order of arrangement and degree of relative importance was affirmed to exist between faith and science, while there was far less of that disposition to extend the limits of Christian speculation beyond the powers and capacities of the finite mind which we perceive in Origen, and which in his pupils to a great degree, and in himself to no small degree, resulted in crude and irrational theories respecting the origin

---

[1] CLEMENS ALEXANDRINUS (Stromata, II. vi.): Στοιχειωδεστέρα ... τῶν ἀρητῶν τῆς γνώσεως ἡ πίστις .... κρηπὶς ἀληθείας; (Stromata, VII. x.): Κριτήριον τῆς ἐπιστήμης σύντομος γνῶσις. ORIGEN: (In Joannem, Tom. XIII. lii; XIX. i) presents the same view.

of the universe, the nature of matter, and above all the nature and origin of moral evil. Supernaturalism, says Hagenbach, in its most definite and intelligent opposition to rationalism, finds its ablest and most eloquent defender in Augustine. He postpones scientific knowledge to faith, and recognizes in Christianity the only absolute religion for mankind, to which he requires the human mind to submit itself; for faith in the object precedes the scientific cognition of the object. Reason, he says, would never have delivered man from darkness and corruption, if God had not accommodated himself to the finite, and "cum populari quadam clementia" humbled the Divine intellect even to the human nature and the human body.[1]

The following extracts from the great leader of opinions in the Western Church in this and succeeding ages, show the attitude of his mind towards the problems of faith and reason, and sound the key note to the harmony of philosophy and religion. "It cannot be that God hates that characteristic of reason in us, in respect to which he created us superior to the other animals. It cannot be, that we are to believe, in such a way as to preclude all use of our rational faculty. For we could not believe at all unless we had rational minds. It is therefore a reasonable act, when, in matters pertaining to salvation, which we are not able to completely understand as yet, but which we shall be able to

[1] Dogmengeschichte, § 116.

understand some time or other, our faith precedes our reason, and so purifies the heart that we become capable of the light of the perfect and supreme Reason. Thus it is reasonably said by the prophet (Is. vii. 9, Sept. Ver.): 'Unless ye believe ye shall not understand.' Without doubt he distinguishes here two things, faith and reason, and counsels us first to believe, that we may then be able to understand what we believe. .... Faith should precede philosophic intelligence (Fides intellectum precedere debet). Man as a believer should first inquire into the hidden and secret things of the kingdom of God, in order that he may understandingly perform them. For *faith is a species of intelligence;* but *scientific* intelligence is the reward of faith (Fides enim gradus est intelligendi; intellectus autem meritum fidei). The prophet plainly says this to all who hastily and prematurely require science and neglect faith. For he says: 'Unless ye believe ye shall not understand' (Is. vii. 9, Sept. Ver.). Ye desire to ascend, but overlook the steps by which it is to be done. How perverse is this! If, O man, I were able to show you here upon earth what is invisible, I should not exhort you to *believe*. ..... Although unless a man have *some* knowledge of God, he cannot believe in him, yet by this very faith itself his understanding is invigorated, so that it can obtain still more knowledge. For there are some things which we cannot believe in unless we understand them; and there are some things which we cannot understand unless we believe in them. For unless there are some things which we cannot understand antecedent to belief, the prophet (Is. vii. 9, Sept. Ver.) would not say: 'Unless ye believe ye shall not understand.' Our intellect, therefore, is of use for understanding what it believes, and faith is of use in believing what it understands."[1]

Whether faith is prior or posterior, in the order of nature, to science is the test question that determines the character of all philosophizing upon Christianity. If faith, in the phrase of Clement, be regarded as elementary, the test and epitome of science, there is little danger that the substance of scriptural Christianity will be evaporated in the endeavour to exhibit its reasonableness. If, on the other hand, the order is reversed, and scientific knowledge is made to precede belief; if the dictum is laid down, as it was by Abelard in the next period, that there is no believing antecedent to scientific understanding, and consequently that the degree of posterior faith depends upon the degree of anterior science; then the all-comprehending mystery and depth of revealed religion will be lost out of sight, and the whole grand system of Christianity will be reduced down to that "simple" religion desired by the French Director, which consists of "a couple of doctrines,"—viz: the existence of a God, and the immortality of the soul. As

---

[1] AUGUSTINE: Epistolarum CXX. 3 (Ed. Migne, II. 453); Sermonum CXXVI. (Ed. Migne, V. 698); Ennarratio in Ps. cxviii.

we follow the history of Apologies down to the present day, we perceive that leading minds have been supernaturalists or rationalists in their methods of defending and philosophizing upon Christianity, according as they have adopted or rejected the dictum first announced by Origen, repeated by Augustine, and most thoroughly expanded and established by Anselm,—the dictum, *fides precedit intellectum*. In the former class, we find the names of Origen, Augustine, Anselm, Calvin, Pascal. In the latter, the names of men like Scotus Erigena, Abelard, Raymund Lully, in whom the speculative energy overmastered the contemplative, and whose intuition and construction of Christian Doctrine was inadequate, and in some instances, certainly, fatally defective.

§ 4. *Mutual relations of the Supernatural and the Natural.*

The third distinction, by which we are aided in exhibiting the Apologetic History of this period, is that between the Supernatural and the Natural.

The same process went on in respect to this important distinction which we found took place in respect to the distinction between Revelation and Reason. The distinction became more clear and firm. The line that marked off the miracle from the ordinary course of nature grew more and more sharp, and distinguishing. In proportion as the Apologist insisted upon a special and peculiar revelation from the Divine Mind, was he led naturally to insist upon a special and peculiar working of the Divine Power. Indeed, all these fundamental distinctions by which we are examining and exhausting the doctrinal history of this period are so connected and sympathetic with each other, that the historic process is the same in reference to them all. Precision, science, and genuine developement affects them all alike; while looseness of conception, and heterodox or rationalizing notions are equally injurious to each and all of them.

The mind of the Church now insists that the Supernatural is so distinctive and peculiar, that it cannot be accounted for upon merely Natural principles. The miracle is not the common and ordinary working of the Deity, but his extraordinary and strange work. The miraculous is an intervention of Omnipotence into the sphere of the finite, precisely like the act of original creation; and not an evolution out of germes already in existence. The Apologist, looking at the subject from this point of view, set the Supernatural over against the Natural in the sharpest antithesis, and steadfastly refused to identify them as one and the same mode of the Divine Working. Each is a distinct and peculiar mode of the Divine efficiency, and neither one can be resolved or explained into the other. So positive and clear was the belief of the Christian Mind of this period, not only in the possibility but the reality of supernatural agency in the course of sacred history, that men like Ambrose and Augustine did not hesitate to affirm the continuance of such agency; though they were careful to distinguish between *biblical* and *ecclesiastical* miracles.[1] In this respect, the church of this period differed from the later Roman Church, which greatly multiplied the number of supposed miraculous occurrences in the lives of the saints, and what was of still more importance attributed a worth and authority to them greater than it attached to the scriptural supernaturalism itself.[2]

On the other side of the subject, we see in this instance, as we did in treating of the distinction between Revelation and Reason, the same disposition to *connect* the Supernatural with the Natural, so that the miracle shall not appear whimsical, but adapted to the end for which it is wrought; so that it shall not look like the arbitrary, capricious work of a merely magical agency.[3] The same God is the

---

[1] Upon ecclesiastical miracles, see MIDDLETON's Inquiry, CAMPBELL On Miracles, DOUGLASS On Miracles, NEWMAN's Essay, and GROTIUS on Mark xvi.

[2] Protestant writers have sometimes cherished the belief in a continued supernatural agency. Says LUTHER (Works XI. p. 1339, Ed. Walch), "how often has it happened, *and still does*, that devils have been driven out in the name of Christ; also by the calling of his name, and prayer, that the sick have been healed." QUENSTEDT (Theol. did. polem. Pt. I. p. 472) remarks: "Nolim negare Jesuitas in India et Japonica vera quaedam miracula edidisse."

[3] Among modern theologians, no one has been more successful than TWESTEN in cons'ructing a philosophy of miracles that preserves the strictest supernaturalism in union and fusion with the laws and elements of nature. See his Dogmatik, § 24.

author of the Supernatural and the Natural, and hence the desire to exhibit the relation between the two, and to show the point of contact between both, without however annihilating the distinction between them that had been seen, and firmly maintained. Hence the assertion, which is sometimes repeated in the Christian science of the present day, that the miracle is not contrary to *all* nature but only to nature as known to us, was made by the Apologist of this Polemic period. Says Augustine: " We are wont to say that all miracles and wonders are *contrary* to nature; but they are not. For how can that which occurs by the will of God be contrary to nature, when the will of God itself constitutes the nature of everything that exists? The miracle, consequently, does not take place contrary to universal nature, but contrary only to nature *so far as it is known to us;* although, even those things which occur in nature as known to us are not less wonderful, and stupendous, to those who would carefully consider them, were it not that men are accustomed to wonder only at things that are infrequent and rare. . . . . That miracle of our Lord Jesus Christ, by which he made the water wine, is not wonderful to those who know that it was GOD who performed it. For He who made wine on that marriage day, in those six waterpots which he commanded to be filled with water, *makes wine the whole year round in the grape vines.* But this latter we do not wonder at, because it occurs all the year round. By reason of the uniformity we lose our wonder."[1]

The Apologist could safely take this ground, and not run the hazard of explaining away the Supernatural into the Natural, because he had *started from the position of supernaturalism*. Had he, as has been done in some later periods, made the Natural the first, and from this as a point of departure endeavoured to construct a philosophy of miracles, he would have been likely to end with the annihilation of all that is truly and distinctively Supernatural. As in the former instance in which the relations of Revelation and Reason were concerned, so in regard to this distinction between the Supernatural and the Natural, all depends upon the point of departure. The truth is reached, and a genuine harmony is evinced between the Natural and the Miraculous, both of which are equally modes of the

---

[1] AUGUSTINE: De Civitate Dei, XXI. viii; Tractatus VIII. in Joannem (Ed. Migne, p. 1450).—This way of looking at miracles seems to be natural to the human mind. DR. JOHNSON, a profound believer in miracles, and even inclined to credulity as the story of the Cock Lane ghost evinces, thus expresses himself in his life of Sir Thomas Brown: "There is a sense undoubtedly in which all life is miraculous, as it is an union of powers of which we can image no connection; a succession of motions of which the first cause must be supernatural." This is not said from the position of science, for Johnson was no metaphysician, but it is a view that spontaneously suggests itself. COWPER gives expression to the same thought, in "The Task," Book VI.

. . . . "Should God again,
As once in Gibeon, interrupt the race
Of the undeviating and punctual sun,
How would the world admire! but speaks it less
An agency divine, to make him know
His moment when to sink, and when to rise,
Age after age, than to arrest his course?
*All we behold is miracle; but, seen
So duly, all is miracle in vain.*"

Divine efficiency, by first of all holding with firmness, and without any equivocation or mental reservation, to the possibility and the reality of a direct interference of the Deity in the ordinary course of natural phenomena, by which the old every-day course of events is sometimes stopped short off, sometimes wonderfully altered and modified, but in every instance a perfect domination and control over the laws and processes of the natural world is evinced and exercised. When the mind is convinced of the reasonableness of an *extraordinary* divine efficiency, it then becomes comparatively easy for it to detect that point of contact between the miracle and the common course of nature where both join together, and both co-operate towards the accomplishment of the end proposed by that Divine Being who is the author of both. The Christian apologist of this period was thus thoroughly convinced of the reality of the Divine supernatural intervention; so much so, that, as we have noticed above, he did not regard the age of supernaturalism as entirely past; and hence his attempts at a philosophy of Miracles were upon the whole as successful as any that are to be found in the history of Apologies.

It is deserving of notice however, that the controversy with the skeptic, in regard to miracles, did not reach its height of vehemence and acuteness until modern times. It was not until modern Deism made its appearance, that the Christian Apologist was compelled to his most elaborate defences in this respect. The Ancient World seems to have found it more easy than the Modern, to believe in the immediate operation of the deity in the course of nature; perhaps because it was two thousand years nearer the creative fiat, not very far off in time from such awfully miraculous displays as the deluge, and quite near to that continued series of supernatural events and agencies which accompanied the advent and ministry, the death, resurrection, and ascension of the Son of God. As a consequence, the ancient Apologete found a less unbelieving temper to contend with than his modern coadjutor does, in an age of the world which perhaps more than any other is inclined to that mere naturalism which puts the question: "Where is the promise of his coming? for since the fathers fell asleep, all things continue as they were from the beginning of the creation," (2 Pet. iii. 4).

§ 5. *Recapitulatory Survey.*

A brief and rapid recapitulation will serve to report the progress which has been made by the Church, in these apologetic endeavours of the Polemic age. We shall perceive that during this period of five centuries, the Ecclesiastical Mind gained a clearer understanding of certain subjects fundamental to the establishment and defence of Christianity, than it possessed during the Apologetic period.

1. In the first place, a more distinct and profound knowledge of the relation which exists between human Reason and divine Revelation was the consequence of the very great intellectual activity of this period. The difficulties and objections urged by the skeptic and the heretic compelled the Apologist to reflect more deeply, and to speak more precisely respecting the nature and functions of both of these correlated objects. That somewhat vague idea of revelation, which obtained in the Apologies of Justin Martyr, which left too little room for the distinction between natural and revealed religion, was now displaced by a more precise and scientific one, in which that which is attainable by the exercise of the unassisted finite faculty is distinguished from the products of the Supreme Reason. Here certainly is progress. It was a true and legitimate advance in Christian science to distinguish things that differ; to bring out into the clear light of knowledge, the exact difference there is between Revelation and Reason, and to state it in accurate and plain terms. It is not enough merely not to deny a fundamental distinction. Genuine science, be it Christian or secular, must positively affirm and establish fundamental distinctions. The earlier defenders of Christianity never *denied* the difference in kind between Revelation and Reason; but they did not discriminate and enunciate it with that scientific exactitude which is the result of sharp controversy. The peculiar form of infidelity which

they were called upon to combat did not lead them to do so, but on the contrary inclined them somewhat in the other direction. For the chief accusation brought against Christianity in the first two centuries was, that it was altogether alien to humanity, a new and peculiar religion wholly foreign and antagonistic to all that the world had heretofore known, and aiming to operate upon the mind and heart of man with a merely *magical* influence, and with no appeal to his reason. It was therefore the task of the Apologist of this period, to exhibit the *affinities* of Christianity with human nature; to show the point of contact between the human and Divine minds. He was led, consequently, to emphasize the *resemblance* that could be found in natural religion, as this had unfolded in the various systems of pagan philosophy and ethics, with the doctrines of Christianity, in order to win the attention and favour of the thoughtful and serious-minded pagan.

But when this ceased to be the state of the controversy, and the unbeliever now passed over to the opposite extreme, and asserted that Christianity contained nothing new or distinctively its own,[1] and

---

[1] "We,, also," says Celsus quoted by ORIGEN (Cont. Celsum, lib. VII), "can place a Supreme Being above the world, and above all human things, and approve of and sympathize in whatever may be taught of a spiritual, rather than material adoration of the gods; for with the belief in the gods worshipped in every land and by every people harmonizes the belief in a Primal Being, a Supreme God, who has given to every land its guardian, to every people its presiding deity. The unity of the Supreme Being, and

that all the truth necessary for man to know could be developed out of natural religion and ethics, it became necessary for the Christian philosopher to take another step, and while not denying the affinities between natural and revealed religion, exhibit the additional features, the divine and supernatural elements which the latter contained.[1] But in doing

the consequent unity of the design of the universe, remains, even if it be admitted that each people has its own gods, whom it must worship in a peculiar manner, according to their peculiar character; the worship of all these different deities is reflected back to the Supreme God, who has appointed them as it were his delegates and representatives. Those who argue that men ought not to serve many masters impute human weakness to God. God is not jealous of the adoration paid to subordinate deities; he is superior in his nature to degradation and insult. Reason itself might justify the belief in the inferior deities, which are the objects of the established worship. For, since the Supreme God can produce only that which is immortal and imperishable, the existence of mortal beings cannot be explained, unless we distinguish from him those inferior deities, and assert them to be the creators of mortal beings and of perishable things." Compare upon this point MILMAN's History of Christianity, Book II. Chap. viii.

[1] This same adroit method of the ancient skeptic was repeated by the English Deists of the 17th century. Says LELAND (Deistical Writers, Letter III), "It is to be observed that the learned writers who opposed Mr. Hobbs did not so much apply themselves to vindicate revealed religion, or the Christian system, as to establish the great principles of *all* religion and morality, which his scheme tended to subvert; and to show that they had a real foundation in reason and nature. In this they certainly did good service to religion; yet some of the enemies of revelation endeavored to take advantage of it, as if this showed that there is no other religion but the law of nature, and that any extraordinary revelation is needless and useless. Thus, on every supposition, these gentlemen resolved to carry their cause against Christianity. If there be no law of nature, no real difference in the nature of things between moral good and evil, virtue and vice, there is no such thing as religion at all, and, consequently, no Christian religion. On the other hand,

this, the Apologist unfolded the system of revealed truth more fully than had been done before. He traced the fundamental distinction between ethics and the gospel more profoundly and nearer to the centre, and thereby made a positive advance upon his less exact and scientific predecessors.

2. In the second place, the relation of Faith to Science was better understood and defined than it had been in the preceding period. The church had now wrought out a sounder philosophy of Christianity. The mind of Augustine manages the argument with the philosophical skeptic or the acute heretic, more successfully than had been done by the mind of Irenaeus, or even the mind of Origen. The apologetic writings of this period furnish more that can be used with advantage by the modern theologian, in the ever new and ever old conflict with infidelity, than he can derive from the more ardent and glowing, but less self-consistent and profound defences of Justin Martyr and Tertullian. Infidelity and heresy had now made themselves felt in their more acute and skilful forms of attack, and the defence and repulse evoked from the Church, a depth of reflection, and a power of logic which it had never before exhibited.

if it be proved that there is such a thing as the religion and law of nature, which is founded in the very nature and relations of things, and agreeable to right reason, then it is concluded that this alone is sufficient, and that it is clear and obvious to all mankind, and therefore they need no revelation to instruct them in it, or assure them of it."

3. And lastly, this same progress in the direction of a rational defence of Christianity brought along with it a clearer intuition of the difference in kind between the Supernatural and the Natural. This fundamental distinction, which had indeed been recognized in the Apologetic period, but which had not been reflected upon with that thoroughness of analysis and abstraction, which alone carries the mind to the inmost centre of an idea,—this distinction was now seen in its fulness of meaning, and asserted with a positiveness which all after Apologetics has only reiterated and heightened.

We perceive then, that during this second period in Apologetic History, the principal topics which constitute the subject-matter of Apologetics were discussed, and satisfactory positions were established respecting each of them. During the first seven centuries, skepticism from without, and heresy from within the church, had been instrumental in forming and fixing those fundamental distinctions upon which all successful defences of Christianity must ultimately rest. We shall not find very great advance upon the Apologetics of the Ancient Church, so far as the foundations of Christian evidences are concerned. That portion of the department, which consists of the evidences from physical nature, has indeed made great progress since this period. But this progress has occurred mostly within the last two centuries; inasmuch as it is the natural consequence of the remarkable advance which during this time has been made in the whole department of natural science. If then, we except the physico-moral argument, we may say as the conclusion of our survey that the evidences for the reasonableness of Christianity were in substance, enunciated and established during the Apologetic and Polemic periods.

CHAPTER III.

MEDIAEVAL DEFENCES OF CHRISTIANITY: A. D. 780—A. D. 1517.

§ 1. *Preliminary Statements.*

THE Mediaeval period, which includes 800 years from the first part of the 8th to the first part of the 16th century, was engaged chiefly in reducing the past results of theological investigation and controversy to a systematic form, and a scientific unity. Of this period, however, not more than four centuries witnessed any very great activity of the theological mind. Scotus Erigena, during the 9th century, shows signs of acute intellectual life, and by reason of his active and inquiring spirit becomes a striking object in that age of growing superstition and ignorance. Alcuin, the brightest ornament of the court of Charlemagne, and the soundest thinker between John of Damascus and Anselm, also throws a pure and serene ray into the darkness of the dark ages. It is not however until Scholasticism appears, that we perceive in the Church the reappearance of that same deep reflection which in Augustine settled the principal questions in Anthropology, and that same subtle analysis which in Athanasius constructed the Nicene Symbol. For two centuries, extending from Anselm to Aquinas (1075–1275), we find the theologians of the Church collectively endeavoring to rationalize Christianity and construct a philosophy of religion, with an energy and intensity of thinking that is remarkable. We shall mention only the more general tendencies and results of this mediaeval speculation, in their relation to the History of Apologies.

The old attacks upon Christianity by the Jews and Pagans had now ceased. Mohammedanism, which had come into existence, although it boasted of some learning, and made some few literary attacks upon Christianity, was far more formidable with the sword than with the pen. Defences were now called out mainly against skepticism and doubts *within* the Church itself. This skepticism was sometimes open and sometimes concealed; sometimes it was conscious and intended, and sometimes it was unconscious and unintentional. This latter species of skepticism, which is a very interesting form of unbelief, and exists more generally than appears at first sight in all ages of the church, springs out of an unsuccessful endeavour to fathom the depths of theology, and to construct a true philosophy of Christianity. The thinker sometimes supposes himself to have solved the problem, when he has in reality only undermined the doctrine. In attempting with perfect seriousness and good faith to rationalize religion, he has in reality annihilated it.

Some of the Schoolmen are a striking example of this. Minds like Amalrich of Bena, and David of Dinanto, in attempting to discover and exhibit the true nature of the deity, and the relation between creation and the creator, in reality enunciated a pantheistic theory of God and the universe. These men however were in and of the visible Church, and supposed that they were promoting the scientific interests of Christianity. There is reason to believe that they were sincere in this belief. They were unconsciously skeptical. Seeking to establish Christianity upon an absolutely scientific basis, they dug up the very lowest and most solid stratum upon which the entire structure rests,—the stratum of theism. On the other hand, Schoolmen like Anselm, Bernard, and Aquinas, more profound students of revealed truth, and possessing a deeper Christian experience, continued the defence of Christianity upon substantially the same grounds, and by the same methods, that we have seen to have been prevalent in the Ancient Church.

§ 2. *Apologetics of Anselm, Aquinas, and Bernard.*

Anselm's view of the relation of reason to faith agrees thoroughly with that of Augustine, and was unquestionably somewhat shaped by it. His two tracts, the Monologium and Proslogion, indirectly exhibit his opinions upon this subject with great clearness and power, and defend the supernaturalism of Christianity with a metaphysical talent that has never been excelled. In the Proslogion, he says, "I desire certainly to [scientifically] *understand* that truth which my heart believes and loves; yet I do not seek to understand that I may believe, but I believe that I may understand. For I believe the truth, because if I am unbelieving I cannot [philosophically] apprehend." Again he remarks, that "he who does not believe can have no experience, and he who has no experience cannot understand."[1] Unless there be a consciousness, there can be no scientific analysis of consciousness or philosophical construction of its contents; and there can be no consciousness without faith in the object of consciousness. Yet, on the other hand, Anselm is as careful as was Augustine to insist upon the intrinsic

---

[1] "Non tento, Domine, penetrare altitudinem tuam; quia nullatenus comparo illi intellectum meum, sed desidero aliquatenus intelligere veritatem tuam, quam credit et amat cor meum. Neque enim quaero intelligere, ut credam; sed credo, ut intelligam. Nam et hoc credo quia nisi crediderit, non intelligam." Proslogion, Cap. i. "Nimirum hoc ipsum quod dico, qui non crediderit, non intelliget. Nam qui non crediderit, non experietur; et qui expertus non fuerit, non intelliget. Nam quantum rei auditum superat experientia, tantum vincit audientis cognitionem experientis scientia: et non solum ad intelligendum altiora prohibitur mens ascendere sine fide et mandatorum Dei obedientia, sed etiam aliquando datus intellectus subtrahitur, et fides ipsa subvertitur, neglecta bona conscientia." De fide Trinitatis, Cap. ii.

rationality of Christianity, and to recommend the endeavour after a philosophical faith. In his tract upon the atonement, he assents to the assertion of his pupil Boso, that although the right order requires that we believe the profound mysteries of the Christian faith before we presume to discuss them upon grounds of reason, yet it is a neglect of duty, if after we are confirmed in our belief we do not study to understand what we believe.[1] If after we have obtained the inward experience and consciousness we do not then strive to interpret our own experience, and comprehend our own Christian consciousness, we are guilty of an indifference towards the truth that has in it far more of indolence than of grace, was the opinion of both Augustine and Anselm.

Aquinas takes the same general view of the relation of faith to scientific knowledge, though his intellectual tendency was more speculative than that of Anselm, and his theology has more of the Romish tone and spirit. He recognizes the fact that there are differences in the doctrines, some being more apprehensible than others, and in reference to such transcendent truths as the trinity, employs the phraseology so familiar in modern Apologetics, that though the Christian mysteries

---

[1] Sicut rectus ordo exigit ut profunda Christianae fidei credamus, priusquam ea praesumamus ratione discutere, ita negligentia mihi videtur, si postquam confirmati sumus in fide, non studemus quod credimus intelligere." Cur Deus Homo, Lib. I. Cap. ii.

are above reason, they are not against reason. In his defence of the catholic faith against the infidel,[1] he remarks, that "there are two classes of truths in the Christian system, respecting the being of God. First, those truths which transcend the entire power of human reason; such as that God is three and one. Secondly, those which even natural reason can attain to; such as that God is one, is infinite, is eternal, and such like, which even pagan philosophers have proved demonstratively, under the guiding light of natural reason." Yet even these latter truths, he says, need the corroboration and fuller unfolding of revelation, because this natural knowledge of God, when unaccompanied with the diffusing and realizing power of a supernatural dispensation gradually departs from the popular mind, and becomes confined to the schools of a few philosophers and sages; and because, furthermore, this philosophic knowledge in its best form is mixed with more or less of error.

That school of contemplative theologians, whom we have alluded to in a previous section under the designation of the Mystic Scholastics, also maintain the same view of the relation of faith to science, only with less regard for the scientific side. These men, because they were somewhat mystical in their intuition, were less inclined than the more scientific

---

[1] Summa catholicae fidei contra Gentiles. Lib. I. Cap. iii. HILDEBERT, Tractatus viii: "Fides non est contra rationem, sed supra rationem."

Anselm and Aquinas to care for the interests of reason and philosophy, though they by no means disregarded or overlooked them, as does the Mystic in the restricted signification of the term.

Bernard is the greatest and noblest representative of this class of minds; and an extract or two from him will serve to show his attitude towards Christian science in its relations to Christian faith. "Science," says St. Bernard, "reposes upon reason; faith upon authority. Both, however, are in possession of a sure and valid truth; but faith possesses the truth in a close and involuted form, while science possesses it in an open and expanded one. Scientific cognition not only possesses the truth, but the distinct comprehension of it. Faith is a sort of sure and instinctive (voluntaria) intimation [Germanicé, Ahnung] of truth that is not yet opened up before the mind in clear analysis and outline. How then does faith differ from science? In this, namely, that although faith is not in possession of an uncertain or an invalid truth any more than science is, yet it is in possession of an undeveloped truth, while science has the truth in an unfolded form. Science does not desire to contradict faith; but it desires to cognize with plainness what faith knows with certainty."[1] Hence, in another place, Bernard remarks

[1] "Intellectus rationi innititur, fides authoritati. Habent illa duo *certam* veritatem, sed fides clausam et involutam, intelligentia nudam et manifestam. ... Fides est voluntaria quaedam et certa praelibatio necdum propalatae veritatis. Intellectus est rei cujuscunque invisibilis certa et manifesta notitia .... Fides ambiguum non

of invisible and divine things, that "not disputation but holiness comprehends them."

Perhaps the relations of reason and faith have never been more concisely and accurately stated than in the pregnant and epigrammatic Latin of Anselm and Bernard. The practical belief of the truths of Christianity, according to these apologists, contains much that is latent and undeveloped. The Christian is wiser than he knows. The moment he begins to examine the implications and involutions of his own personal and certain consciousness, he finds that they contain the entire rudimental matter of Christian science. Faith, in the phrase of Clement of Alexandria, furnishes the στοιχεῖα, the elementary materials, of rational knowledge. The Christian, for illustration, believes in the one living and personal God. He possesses the idea of the deity by virtue of his creation and rational constitution. His faith holds it in its unexpanded form. But the instant he commences the analysis of this idea of ideas, he discovers its profound capacity and its immense involution. Again he believes in God incarnate. But when he endeavors to scientifically

---

habet: aut si habet, fides non est, sed opinio. Quid igitur distat ab intellectu? Nempe quod etsi non habet incertum non magis quam intellectus, habet tamen *involutum*, quod non intellectus." De Consideratione, Lib. V. Cap. iii. BERNARDI: Opera, p. 894. (Ed. Par. 1632).—Bernard in the above extract employs the word "voluntary," as the earlier English writers often do, in the sense of "spontaneous,"—as Milton, e. g. does when he defines poetry to be "thoughts that *voluntary* [spontaneously] move harmonious numbers."

analyse and comprehend what is contained in this doctrine and historical fact, he is overwhelmed by the multitude of its relations and the richness of its contents. His faith has actually and positively grasped these ideas of God and the God-Man. He is as *certain* of their validity as he is of any truth whatever. But his faith has grasped them, in the phrase of St. Bernard, in their undeveloped and pregnant form. If now, he would convert faith into science, and would pass from religion to philosophy, he has only to reflect upon the intrinsic meaning and substance of these ideas, until they open along the lines of their structure, and are apprehended philosophically, though not exhaustively. But in this process, faith itself is reinforced and deepened by a reflex action, while at the same time, the intellect is preserved reverent and vigilant, because the cognition, though positive and correct as far as it reaches, is not exhaustive and complete, only by reason of the immensity and infinitude of the object.[1]

---

[1] The distinction between a *positive* and an *exhaustive* conception has been overlooked in the recent discussions respecting the possibility of man's possessing a positive conception of the infinite. If by a positive knowledge is meant an infinite or perfect knowledge that exhausts all the mystery of an object, then man cannot have a positive knowledge of even any finite thing. But if by positive is meant true and valid as far as the cognition reaches,—if the term relates to *quality* and not to quantity,—then man's knowledge of the infinite is as positive as his knowledge of the finite. In this latter and only proper use of the term, man's conception of eternity is as positive as his conception of time, and his apprehension of divine justice is no more a negation than his apprehension of human justice. Man's knowledge of God, like his knowledge of the ocean, is a positive perception, as far as it extends. He does not exhaust

§ 3. *Apologetics of Abelard.*

In this scholastic and systematizing period, as we have before remarked, the priority of faith in the order was not acknowledged by all minds. Men of a speculative and rationalistic tendency like Abelard and Raymund Lully regarded the intellectual comprehension of the truths of Christianity as necessarily antecedent to all belief in them. The dictum of Abelard (Intr. ii. 3), "non credendum, nisi prius intellectum," is the exact reverse of Anselm's "credo ut intelligam." It ought however to be observed that Abelard, in the outset, endeavoured to provide for the interests and claims of faith by giving a somewhat wide meaning to the term "knowledge," or "intelligence." It is undoubtedly true, as Bernard himself concedes in describing the difference between the knowledge of faith and the knowledge of philosophy (ante, p. 183), that the human mind cannot believe a truth or a fact of which it has no species of apprehension whatsoever. Some degree of knowledge must ever be assumed, as simultaneous with the exercise of belief. The mind must at first know the object of its faith, by feeling

---

ively comprehend the ocean, but this does not render his knowledge of the ocean, as to its *quality*, a mere negation. But it is the quality and not the quantity of a cognition that determines its validity. There is for man no exhaustive or infinite knowledge of either the finite or the infinite. He finds it as impossible to give an all-comprehending definition of time as he does of eternity, of an atom of matter as of the essence of God.

(anticipatio, praelibatio), in distinction from conception; otherwise the object of faith is a nonentity for it. Had Abelard recognized this distinction, and thus guarded his statement that "knowledge is prior to faith," he might have come into agreement with his opponents. But, laying down his dictum as he did in terms exactly contrary to those of Origen, Augustine, Anselm, and Bernard, all qualifications were certain to be overborne by the logical proposition upon which he founded his method, and his school. The formal and theoretical precedence instead of postponement of knowledge to faith tended to rationalism in theology, and actually resulted in it. A position though erroneous, when held with moderation and qualifications, by its first author, may not be very injurious to the cause of truth. The element of truth which it contains may be prominent in the first stages of its history, while the elements of error recede from view and influence. But the tendency of the principle, after all, is to error, and as the course of its development goes on, the little truth that is contained in it is overborne, the principle itself is grasped more boldly and applied by a less moderate mind, until in the end it shows its real nature in the overthrow of all truth and belief. The class of men of whom we are speaking is an example. Abelard himself became more and more rationalistic in his views, until he passed the line that separates faith from unbelief, and the church, chiefly through the representations and arguments of the mild and tolerant, but devout and evangelical Bernard, formally condemned his philosophical and theological opinions.[1]

The most serious defect in the Apologetics of this Mediaeval period sprang from *the growing influence of traditional theology, at the expense of inspiration*. Even devout and spiritual theologians like Anselm and Bernard, whose views of truth, with the exception of their Mariolatry, were substantially scriptural, and whose religious experience had been formed and established by revelation, attributed too much weight to the opinions of distinguished church fathers, and to the decisions of Councils, *in comparison with the infallible authority of Scripture*. They by no means denied the paramount authority of revelation, and both in practical and theoretical respects are at a great distance from that distinctively Papal theology which received its first definite form and statement in the articles of the Council of Trent; yet it cannot be denied that their minds were not altogether unaffected by the influences of their time, and of their ecclesiastical connections. That direct and emphatic appeal to Scripture first of all, and only afterwards to authority, which is the characteristic of the Protestant theologian, and that constant renewal and revivification of scientific theology by fresh draughts at the fountain of theological knowledge, which has

---

[1] Abelard was condemned in nineteen articles of specification, at Soissons in 1121, and at Sens in 1140.

rendered Protestant science so vital and vigorous, is found in a too low degree in these men, who were yet the greatest and best minds of this systematizing period. In their successors, this tendency to exalt tradition increased with great rapidity, until error by its very excess brought about a reaction, and Protestantism once more set tradition and inspiration, historical theology and biblical doctrine, in right relations to each other.

CHAPTER IV.

MODERN DEFENCES OF CHRISTIANITY: A. D. 1517—A. D. 1850.

§ 1. *Preliminary Statements.*

THE Reformers themselves were too much occupied with stating and defending the Christian system in opposition to the corrupted theology of the Papal Church, to enter into a defence of it against the objections of skepticism. Hence the Reformatory age yields but little material of an apologetic character, and we pass directly to the most important section in the history of modern Apologetics, that, namely which relates to the *English Deism* of the 17th and 18th centuries.

The latter half of the 17th century was marked by great excitability and fermentation, both in the political and the religious world. England was passing through those revolutions which resulted in the restriction of the royal prerogative, the strengthening of the commonalty, and the settlement of the government in 1688 upon the basis of the Bill of Rights. Continental Europe was witnessing the great struggle by which the predominance of political power passed from the Southern to the Central nations,—from the Papal to the Protestant powers. Corresponding movements were occurring in the ecclesiastical world. The Lutheran church, at the close of the 17th century, was feeling an exciting influence of two very different kinds. The Pietists under the lead of Spener and Francke were infusing into the Old Lutheran orthodoxy some of the warmth and life that glowed in the Moravian Brethren; while, on another side, fanatical preachers and sectaries were breaking in upon the unity of the ancient ecclesiastical organization that had come down from the days of Luther. In the Reformed Church there was more or less reaction against the strict Calvinistic symbols; while in the Papal Church the Jansenists were attempting to revive the Augustinian orthodoxy which the council of Trent had covertly rejected, though pretending to receive it. Contemporaneously with this general excitement in the political and ecclesiastical world, there arose in England a class of minds, who with greater or less decision and bitterness rejected the Old and New Testaments as a revelation from God, and stood upon the principles of natural religion, though in some instances lapsing down from this position into that of sensualism and atheism.

§ 2. *Intellectual Deism of Herbert of Cherbury.*

Deism, the name given to the system of these men, is the general belief in a God, coupled with the disbelief in a written revelation, and of all those particular views of God and man which are taught in the Scriptures. In its best form it would, therefore, include the doctrine of the divine existence, of the divine unity, of the immortality of the soul, and of indefinite rewards and punishments hereafter; and it would reject the doctrines of the trinity, of the deity and incarnation of the Son, of the apostasy of man, of redemption, and of endless rewards and punishments. Deism appears in this highest form in the system of Lord Herbert of Cherbury († 1648), who may be regarded as the founder of the school of English Deists, though holding a much more elevated skepticism than any of his successors. After a survey of the various religions that have appeared, he reduces them to one universal religion, which he maintains is adequate to meet all the religious wants of mankind. This universal system consists of five articles: 1. That there is one supreme God. 2. That he is to be worshipped. 3. That piety and virtue are the principal part of his worship. 4. That man should repent of sin, and that if he does so, God will pardon it. 5. That there are rewards for the good, and punishments for the evil, partly in this life, and partly in a future state.[1] These articles Lord Herbert represents as sentiments inscribed by God on the minds of all men, and attempts to show that they have been universally acknowledged in all nations.

It is obvious, at the first glance, that this system is much in advance of the later forms of English infidelity. It contains a mixture of truth and error, so far as natural religion is concerned; but is erroneous so far as relates to revealed religion. That there is one Supreme Being, that he is to be worshipped, and that there are future rewards and punishments, are, indeed, truths that belong to the constitution of the human mind. But they have not been so generally acknowledged by all classes in all nations, as Lord Herbert represents. On the contrary, the recognition of these first truths of natural religion, like the recognition of the first truths of geometry, has been confined to a portion of mankind. They have been distinctly taught by only a few of the more thoughtful pagan philosophers, in different nations, and have constituted an esoteric system for particular schools. The great masses of the pagan world, on the contrary, have adopted the mythological religions, in which these theistic teachings of natural reason and conscience glimmer only here and there, and even these are contradicted or neutralized by polytheistic views and representations. With respect to the specific nature and extent of future rewards and punishments, there is

[1] HERBERT: De religione Gentilium, Caput I. Ed. Amstel. 1700.

indefiniteness in the views of many of the pagan writers; although, in some instances, as in that of Plutarch, there is great decision in the assertion of a fearful and awful vengeance upon the guilty.[1] And this indefiniteness appears in the representations of Lord Herbert himself, upon this important point.

The fourth tenet in Herbert's scheme, that of pardon upon repentance, is taught neither by natural nor revealed religion. For the light of nature gives no assurance that the deity will ever act upon any principles but those of justice. Hence the pagan religions were full of devices to *propitiate* justice; and yet they could never make it certain that justice had really been propitiated. With yet more emphasis than the inspired writer asserts it of the Jewish sacrifices, can it be said of all Pagan oblations, that they can never, though offered year by year continually, make the comers thereunto perfect in things pertaining to conscience (Heb. x. 1). The

---

[1] According to PLUTARCH (De sera numinis vindicta) there are three subordinate ministers of justice, under Nemesis the chief. The first, *Poena*, executes her office mainly in the present life, and is the author of the pains and penalties which are the more immediate effects of guilt. The second is *Dike* (Δίκη), who punishes in the future world those who have been but partially punished by Poena in this. Her inflictions are severer than those of Poena, and their duration depends upon the degree of guiltiness. The last and most terrible minister of Nemesis is *Erinnys*, or *Fury*, who punishes those who remain incorrigible after the other means have failed. She scourges her victims from place to place, and finally plunges them headlong into an abyss whose horrors no language can describe.

"universal consent" of mankind makes against the fourth article in Lord Herbert's creed rather than for it. The whole system of sacrifices in the pagan world, as well as the reasoning of some of the pagan philosophers, and particularly of the earlier Grecian poets, goes to prove that the pagan mind felt the natural incompatibility of pardon with justice, and by implication acknowledged the need of an atonement in order to its exercise.

The possibility of a special revelation from God Lord Herbert denies, except in its immediate form to each individual. This form he very singularly concedes, and claims for himself in the following remarkable passage from his very interesting Autobiography. Hesitating whether he should publish or suppress his principal work he says: "Being thus doubtful, in my chamber, one fair day in the summer, my casement being open towards the south, the sun shining clear, and no wind stirring, I took my book *De Veritate* in my hands, and kneeling on my knees, devoutly said these words: 'O thou eternal God, author of this light which now shines upon me, and giver of all inward illuminations, I do beseech thee, of thine infinite goodness, to pardon a greater request than a sinner ought to make: I am not satisfied enough, whether I shall publish this book; if it be for thy glory, I beseech thee give some sign from heaven; if not I shall suppress it.' I had no sooner spoken these words, but a loud, though yet gentle noise, came forth from the heavens (for it was like nothing on earth); which did so cheer and comfort me, that I took my petition as granted, and that I had the sign demanded; whereupon also I resolved to print my book. This, how strange soever it may seem, I protest before the eternal God, is true; neither am I any way superstitiously deceived herein; since I did not only clearly hear the noise, but in the serenest sky that ever I saw, being without all cloud, did, to my thinking, see the place whence it came."

The deism of Lord Herbert was evidently somewhat spiritualized by the Christianity in the midst of which it sprung up. He himself was the brother of the saintly George Herbert, whose religious poetry is among the purest expressions that have yet been made of the emotions and feelings of the penitent heart. And although the principles of his scheme, when logically carried out, conduct to the same conclusions to which the Tindals and Shaftesburys afterwards arrived, yet there is a serious and humane tone in the writings of Lord Herbert that elevates them much above the general level of deism.

§ 3. *Materialistic and Sensual Deism.*

Disbelief in revealed religion, and reliance upon natural religion as sufficient to meet the necessities of human nature, showed themselves most energetically in that political and religious reaction which followed the Cromwellian period. Deism in its most extreme forms now arises, and is characterized by bitter hatred of the church, both Established and Nonconforming, of the clergy, of theological science, and of the Scriptures as the source and support of all these. And inasmuch as the church in England was closely connected with the state, and the clergy were identified with the existing government, Deism was frequently found in alliance with the democratic, and sometimes the revolutionary, tendencies in the nation.

This was not always the case however. Thomas Hobbes († 1679) was a most servile advocate of kingly authority, and of the right of the state to coerce individual opinions. He is somewhat guarded in his treatment of the Scriptures, because the English state and church were founded upon them. Yet he expressly teaches that "we have no assurance of the certainty of scripture but by the authority of the church, and this he resolves into the authority of the commonwealth." Hobbes declares that until the sovereign ruler has prescribed them, "the precepts of scripture are not obligatory laws, but only counsel and advice"; Christians, he holds, are bound in conscience to obey the laws of an infidel king in matters of religion; "thought is free; but when it comes to confession of faith, the private reason must submit to the public, that is to say to God's lieutenant." Hence the subject, if commanded by the sovereign, may allowably deny Christ in words, if holding firmly in his heart the faith of Christ; for in that case "it is not he that denieth

Christ before men, but his governor and the laws of his country."

Hobbes acknowledges the existence of God, but denies that we know any more of him than that he exists; denies free will to man, and asserts that he is by creation a necessitated agent; asserts the materiality and mortality of the human soul, and represents the distinction between soul and body as an error contracted from the demonology of the Greeks; teaches that the belief in a future state is merely "a belief grounded upon other men's saying, that they knew it supernaturally, or that they knew those, that knew them, that knew others, that knew it supernaturally."[1] Thus in the general principles of his system, Hobbes falls far below Lord Herbert. Herbert is serious in maintaining the more important truths of natural religion, though rejecting revealed religion altogether, while Hobbes lays down positions that result in sheer materialism and atheism. And such in fact was the practical result of Hobbism. The licentious age of the second Charles was characterized by a large class of minds who had no belief in God, or in man's accountability.[2]

From Hobbes downward, English Deism grows more and more materialistic and sensual; for error like truth runs its own natural course of developement, and expands by its own internal law into more and more extreme forms. Shaftesbury (†1713),

---

[1] LELAND: Deistical Writers, Letter III. [2] MACAULAY: History of England, Chap. III.

in his work entitled "Characteristics of Man, Manners, Opinions, and Times," sets up ridicule as the test of truth, and labors hard to show the pernicious influence upon mankind of a belief in the doctrine of a future state, and of future rewards and punishments. Toland († 1722), a native of Ireland, in some of his works adopts the pantheism of Spinoza, and in others attempts to disprove the genuineness of the canonical scriptures by arguments built upon the apocryphal gospels and the forged writings of the first centuries. Collins († 1729) combats the proof for Christianity derived from the prophecies, which he represents as a species of mystical allegorizing peculiar to the Jewish mind. Woolston († 1733) seizes upon the allegorical method of interpreting the gospel narratives which many Christian writers had employed, and uses it as a medium of a coarse and ribald attack upon the person and character of Christ. Tindal († 1733) composed a work in which he argues against the very idea and possibility of revelation,—the earliest work of the kind, and written with more than ordinary ability and thoroughness. Tindal rejects from the Scriptures all that relates to man's apostasy and redemption, and regards the remainder as only the teachings of natural reason; so that "Christianity" is "as old as the creation," and the "Gospel" is only "a republication of the law of nature."[1] The scheme of

---

[1] His work is entitled: Christianity as old as the Creation, or the Gospel a Republication of the Law of Nature.

Tindal bears a close resemblance to that of Herbert. Morgan († 1743) follows Tindal in respect to his general principles, but devotes his attention mainly to an attack upon the Old Testament and the religion of Moses. Chubb († 1747) also takes the same position with Tindal and Morgan, so far as natural religion is concerned, and labors strenuously to show that true Christianity has been entirely misapprehended, and that it needs to be cleared of a class of doctrines which are foreign to it. In this reconstruction, or "True Gospel asserted," as he entitles his work, Chubb, as would be expected, reduces Christianity to Deism. Bolingbroke († 1751) constructed a scheme of which the following are the principal features: 1. There is one Supreme Being of almighty power and skill, but possessing no moral attributes distinct from his physical. He has no holiness, justice, or goodness, nor anything equivalent to these qualities as they exist in man; and to deduce moral obligations from these attributes, or to speak of imitating God in his moral attributes, is enthusiasm or blasphemy. 2. God made the world and established the laws of nature at the beginning; but he does not concern himself with the affairs of men, or at most, if he does, his providence extends only to collective bodies and not to individuals. 3. The soul is not a distinct substance from the body, and the whole man is dissolved at death. The doctrine of future rewards and punishments is a fiction, though a useful one to mankind. 4. The law of nature is sufficient, and therefore there is no need of a special revelation, and none has been made. 5. The Old Testament history is false and incredible, and the religion taught in it unworthy of God, and repugnant to his perfections. The New Testament contains two different systems contradictory to each other,—that of Christ, and that of Paul. Only the first is genuine Christianity, and may be regarded as a republication of the law of nature, or rather of the theology of Plato. Yet that portion of Christ's teaching which relates to the redemption of mankind by his own death, and to future rewards and punishments, is absurd and contrary to the attributes of God.[1]

The sentiments of these Deists penetrated the English literature of the 18th century to some extent, and exerted some indirect influence upon English theology itself. Alexander Pope, whose speculative opinions were very much shaped by Bolingbroke, his "guide, philosopher, and friend," has set forth natural religion and omitted revealed, in the most brilliant and polished poetry that has yet been composed. Jonathan Swift, a member of the ecclesiastical establishment, though opposed to Deism because Deism was opposed to the English church and state, has yet left nothing in his religious or theological writings that betokens any sympathy with New Testament Christianity. In these in-

[1] Compare LELAND: Deistical Writers; and LECHLER: Englisches Deismus.

stances, it would not be correct to charge an avowed adoption of deistical sentiments; for there was none in either. But the leaven of unbelief in the distinctively evangelical truths of Christianity, and the disposition to regard natural religion and ethics as sufficient for the religious necessities of mankind, had imperceptibly penetrated both the poet and the divine.[1]

The skepticism of England reached its full developement in the system of David Hume († 1776). The views of this writer are too generally known to need stating. It is sufficient to say respecting the speculation of Hume, that it is a system of universal doubt, like that of the Greek Pyrrho. As a consequence, the truths of natural religion, as well as of revealed, are invalidated. Hume concludes his "Natural History of Religion" with the remark: "The whole subject [of religion] is a riddle and an inexplicable mystery; doubt, uncertainty, suspension of the judgment, are the sole result of our close investigation of this subject." Deism could not continue to stand upon the comparatively elevated position of its English founder, Lord Herbert of Cherbury. It deteriorates by its own law of evo-

---

[1] HALLAM (Literature of Europe, II. 967, Harper's Ed.) remarks this same tendency in as influential a divine, as archbishop Tillotson. "What is most remarkable in Tillotson is his strong assertion, in almost all his sermons, of the principles of natural religion and morality, not only as the basis of all revelation, without a dependence upon which it cannot be believed, but as *nearly coincident with Christianity in its extent,*— a length to which few at present would be ready to follow him."

lution, as the latent elements are elicited one by one, and in its final form contains not even that small element of truth which is to be found in its earlier forms, and by means of which alone it could obtain any credence or acceptance among men. Had English infidelity made its first appearance in its last form; had the Pyrrhonism of David Hume, or the sensuality of Mandeville,[1] instead of the comparatively elevated and ethical system of Lord Herbert or Matthew Tindal, been the first form of English Deism, the national mind would have started back in alarm and disgust. But the process was a gradual one. The English infidel himself was prepared for the invalidation and rejection of *all* religion, only by the slow movement of more than a hundred years.

§ 4. *Replies to English Deism.*

A brief sketch of the principal *Apologetic Treatises composed in opposition to English Deism*, will properly follow this account of the English deistical writers.[2]

The views of Lord Herbert did not attract much

---

[1] MANDEVILLE († 1733) published a treatise entitled "Private Vices Public Benefits," in which he maintains that the luxury and voluptuousness of one class in society give employment and support to another class. It is the first attempt to found vice upon the principles of political economy, and justify it by a reference to the general welfare.

[2] Compare LECHLER: Englisches Deismus, pp. 54, sq.

attention in his own century. Cudworth and Locke merely allude to him as a writer of learning and talent, but enter upon no criticism of his religious system. Richard Baxter, in his apologetic treatise entitled "More reasons for the Christian religion, and no reason against it," cites some positions from Lord Herbert's work *De Veritate*, and controverts them. Baxter speaks with respect of Lord Herbert, and concedes that there is truth in what he says respecting the necessary nature of the doctrines of natural religion. The remark which Baxter makes, that he has replied to the positions of Herbert, lest "never having been answered, they might be thought unanswerable," would indicate that the writings of Lord Herbert had attracted but little attention.

The scheme of Herbert next received a criticism and reply from Thomas Halyburton, a professor in the Scotch university of St. Andrews. His work entitled "Natural religion insufficient, and revealed necessary to man's happiness," was published in 1714, and contains a detailed refutation of Herbert's sentiments. The following are Halyburton's principal positions: 1. Lord Herbert's five articles are not so *universally* acknowledged as he represents. 2. The clearness with which some pagans have perceived the truths of natural religion is not due solely to the workings of their own reason, but in part to the remnants of a primitive revelation. 3. Natural religion is not sufficient to secure the eternal welfare of man, because of man's apostasy and sinfulness. Human corruption is too deep and inveterate to be overcome by merely ethical principles. It requires a *redemptive* power and agency.

A learned and profound defence of the truths of natural religion, in opposition to the system of Hobbes, was made by two distinguished Platonists connected with the university of Cambridge; namely, Henry More († 1678), and Ralph Cudworth († 1688). The first-mentioned, in his "Antidote against Atheism," and tract upon the "Immortality of the Soul," presents both the *a priori* and *a posteriori* arguments for the divine existence, and the immateriality of the human mind, with great clearness and ingenuity. The "Intellectual System of the Universe," by Cudworth, aims to establish the doctrine of the divine existence, and the reality and immutability of the distinction between right and wrong upon an impregnable position; and in accomplishing this aim, the resources of a vastly learned, as well as profoundly contemplative intellect, are brought into requisition. The tenets of Hobbes and others are refuted, among other methods, by a most exhaustive citation of the views of pagan antiquity. The primary origin and source of natural religion was investigated by the learned Puritan, Theophilus Gale, in his work published 1669–1677 entitled, "The Court of the Gentiles." By a very extensive and minute examination of all the theism of the pagan world, he endeavours to show that what was correct in the religions of paganism sprang from sporadic portions of the Patriarchal and Jewish revelations,—that "Pythagoras's College, Plato's Academy, Aristotle's Peripatum, Zeno's Stoa, and Epicurus's Gardens were all watered with rivulets, which though in themselves corrupt were originally derived from the sacred fountain of Siloam;" and that "there was none that opened a more effectual door for the propagating of philosophical principle and light, than Moses, who laid the main foundations of all that philosophy, which first the Phenicians and Egyptians, and from them the Grecians, were masters of."[1]

[1] It is noteworthy that this reference of the theism of the elder pagan world to Hebrew sources has also been adopted by one of the most profound modern investigators of the philosophy of mythology. SCHELLING, in his Gottheiten von Samothrace, takes the following positions: 1. The names of the deities of Samothrace, as well as of the priests (who were named after the gods they served) were Phoenician, which language was substantially that of the Hebrews. Regard therefore must be had to the *Hebrew* archives and language, in investigating the Cabiric mysteries. 2. The esoteric religious system of the Greeks exhibits fragments of a system older than any that is to be found in the historical memorials of [pagan] antiquity, even the most ancient, and these fragments are not to be regarded as opening a fountain of knowledge absolutely new, but as parts of an earlier knowledge *confined to a definite portion of the race, and a particular locality*. This esoteric religious system of the Greeks must, therefore, be traced back to higher sources than Egyptian or Indian systems; and was drawn from a point nearer the original source of all religion, than the Egyptian, and Indian theogonies. 3. This esoteric doctrine, according to the Greeks themselves, came to them from the "barbarians;" but not necessarily from Egypt (nicht gerade eben aus Aegypten). This statement was in part only the tradition of the priests of Dodona, and in part a private opinion of Herodotus; and besides, many of the names in the Grecian religion can be explained

The celebrated natural philosopher Robert Boyle († 1691) left in his will a provision for an annual series of lectures, the object of which should be to defend the truth of the Christian religion against unbelievers of all kinds, viz: Atheists, Deists, Pagans, Jews, and Mohammedans. The first preacher upon this foundation was the renowned classical scholar Richard Bentley, who endeavoured to show the "Folly and Unreasonableness of Atheism," from the marks of design everywhere visible in the natural world. Bentley aimed more particularly at the sentiments of Hobbes. In the years 1704 and 1705, Samuel Clarke preached the Boylean lectures, and bent the whole force of his metaphysical mind and close logic, to a demonstration of the existence of God by the *a priori* method. In connection with this argument, he also endeavoured to demonstrate the immutable validity of the truths of natural religion, and the truth and certainty of Christianity. These arguments of Clarke enter as deeply into the first principles of all religion, as any that were called out by the English infidelity of the 17th and 18th centuries.

No portion of the English Deism, on the whole,

far more easily from the Hebrew than the Egyptian language. 4. If the poet, particularly Homer, in the naive and childlike play of the poet's fancy, presents a mythological world of divinities, he nevertheless does it with the reservation and understanding that the seriousness of the esoteric doctrine is to restore everything to its true relations again.—— CREUZER, on the other hand, in his Symbolik, traces this monotheism of the elder world to Egyptian and Oriental sources.

gave the Christian Apologist more trouble and taxed his resources more, than did those productions which earnestly asserted the validity of natural religion, but just as earnestly affirmed that revealed religion is for this very reason unnecessary. The position of Tindal,—that the religion of nature is absolutely valid and cannot be dispensed with, but that the Gospel is only a republication of the law of nature, and that Christianity is therefore as old as creation and the mind of man,—made it necessary for the Apologist to show, first, precisely what is the difference between natural and revealed religion, and, secondly, that the additional truths of the latter are not a mere expansion of data and elements contained in the former. Among the most successful treatises upon this subject, is that of John Conybeare,[1] in reply to the treatise of Tindal. It is characterized, says Lechler, by a distinctness in conception, a simplicity in the mode of presenting the subject, and a logical cogency in union with a dignified polemic attitude and a broad philosophic culture, that render it a masterly performance.

Conybeare, in the outset, directs attention to the two significations which the term "natural" may have, in the phrases "natural reason" and "natural religion." It may denote, first, that which

---

[1] A Defence of Revealed Religion against the exceptions of a late writer in his book entituled: Christianity as old as the Creation. London, 1732.

is *founded* in the nature and reason of things, or, secondly, that which is *discoverable* by the use of man's natural powers of mind.[1] It is by confounding the two significations, and passing from one to the other, that Tindal, he shows, is led to attribute "absolute perfection" to natural religion. Truth, as a matter of course, is absolutely perfect, but man's *perception* of it is not necessarily so. Hence Conybeare concedes a relative perfection, but not "absolute" perfection, to that body of truth which is reached by the natural operations of the human mind, and which goes under the name of natural religion. For the law of nature, or natural religion, in this sense of the word "natural," cannot be more perfect than the human mind is. But the human

[1] "This gentleman begins his second chapter with an explication of what he means by the religion of nature. 'By natural religion,' saith he, 'I understand the belief of the existence of a God, and the sense and practice of those duties which result from the knowledge we by *our reason* have of him and his perfections.' According to this account, natural religion can reach no further than natural light and reason can carry us. For it comprehends under it those duties only, which result from the knowledge we by *our reason* have of God.

"Yet notwithstanding this plain expression of his meaning, he immediately subjoins: 'So that the religion of nature takes in everything that is founded in the reason and nature of things.' What! doth the religion of nature take in everything that is founded in the reason and nature of things, when, according to this gentleman's own account it reaches no further than we by *our reason* are able to carry it? And if it reaches no further than we by *our reason* can carry it, doth it therefore follow, that it takes in *everything* which is founded in the nature and reason of things? I know but one way to get over this difficulty: viz. by asserting roundly that human reason is commensurate to all truth." CONYBEARE: Defence of Revealed Religion, p. 12.

mind is not absolutely perfect, since in this case it would be infallible and incapable of error. Natural religion, consequently, however much validity may be attached to it, cannot claim to be an *infallible* religion, inasmuch as it is liable to be vitiated by the medium through which it is apprehended,—viz: the powers of the human mind. Moreover, it must be remembered that this apprehension is itself only gradual and approximate. For we must distinguish between human reason as it is shared by all mankind, and human reason as it exists in single individuals. No individual, even of the highest capacities, has ever completely exhausted a single art or a single science. The same is true in morals. No merely human individual has ever yet published a perfect and complete code of morality, or completely fathomed the sphere of ethics. It is only through the successive and collective endeavours of many wise men, that even an approximate apprehension of the truths of natural religion is attained,—a completely exhaustive one being impossible.

In the second place, says Conybeare, there is required in order to the absolute perfection of a law, or a religion, perfect clearness and certainty in its sanctions; but in this respect the law of nature, or natural religion, is manifestly deficient. The effective power of law lies in the definite reward, or the definite penalty affixed to certain acts; in the good or evil consequences attending them. But in the actual course of events in this life, it often happens that the good are not rewarded, and the evil go unpunished. It was for this reason that the pagan philosophers postulated a retribution after death, to balance the scales of justice left unbalanced upon earth. With regard, however, to the manner and amount of this future punishment, natural religion could give no authentic and *infallible* information from the Supreme Judge who appoints it. That absolute sanction of the moral law which consists in a precise statement of the nature and quantity of the penalty affixed to it by its Author, the unassisted human mind is unable to specify, however bold and impressive may be its intimations and expectations of such a sanction.

In the third place, Conybeare directs attention to the fact of human apostasy as bringing man into a condition of guilt and corruption, and necessitating a species of knowledge for which natural religion makes no provision, because natural religion is adapted only to a state of innocency and holiness. Man is a transgressor, is obnoxious to penalty, and needs assurance of pardon on the one hand, and of purification on the other. The law of nature, or natural religion, can give him no assurance of mercy, but only of stark rigid justice; and the mere imperatives of conscience cannot subdue the will, or cleanse the heart.

In reference, then, to these three particulars,—an imperfect perception upon the part of the human mind, an imperfect sanction of the moral law, and the lack of provision for human apostasy,—Conybeare argues, in opposition to Tindal, that natural religion is inadequate, and needs to be supplemented and perfected by revealed. The Scriptures impart an "absolutely perfect" religion, because their contents are the teachings of the Supreme Mind, and are not liable to those vitiating influences from sense and earth, which so often, as the history of human opinions shows, modify and pervert even the best natural intuitions of the human intelligence. Revelation also imparts an absolute validity to the sanctions of natural religion, by authoritatively announcing in distinct and definite terms an endless penalty, or reward, and a final adjudication in the day of doom. And, lastly, the written revelation alone makes known a remedial plan adapted to that fallen and guilty condition of mankind, for which the "light of nature" has no remedy.

Nearly contemporaneously with the appearance of this vigorous and logical treatise of Conybeare, Joseph Butler († 1752) published his "Analogy of Religion, Natural and Revealed," in which he answers the objections of infidelity to revealed religion, by the negative method of pointing out equal or greater difficulties in natural religion. The argument is handled with great skill and fairness, and the work has had a more extensive circulation, and exerted a greater influence than any other apologetic treatise of the Modern Church. It supposes however that the objector concedes the truths of ethics and natural religion, and therefore is less effective as a reply to universal skepticism, or to such materialistic systems as those of Hobbes and Bolingbroke, than the work of Conybeare. The purely defensive attitude, moreover, which it assumes, in being content with merely showing that the same difficulty besets the religion of nature that lies against the religion of the Bible, imparts something of a cautious and timid tone to the work, though rendering it an exceedingly difficult one to be replied to.

The success with which the Christian Apologete conducted the controversy with the Deist depended very much upon the clearness and comprehensiveness of his views of revealed religion. In case he grasped with power the doctrines of the trinity, incarnation, apostasy, and redemption, it was a very easy task to show that revealed religion contains elements that are not to be found in natural religion, and ministers to moral wants for which natural religion has no supply. The assertion of the Deist, that Christianity is merely the republication of the law of nature, was easily disposed of by one who held, and could prove, that New Testament Christianity presupposes the fact of sin and guilt, and that its chief function is to provide an expiation for the one, and cleanse away the other. But if, as was the case sometimes, the Apologist himself adopted an inadequate and defective anthropology and soteriology, and his view of Christianity was such as to reduce it almost to the level of natural religion, it then became very difficult for him to show that it contains any additional elements, and thus to refute the most specious and subtle of all the positions of the skeptic. The 18th century was characterized by a low evangelical feeling within the English Church, and an indistinct apprehension of the doctrine of the cross. It is not surprising, consequently, that some of the defences of Christianity that were made at this time should possess but little value, so far as concerns the *distinctive* doctrines of revelation, inasmuch as they are occupied almost entirely with those truths which revelation presupposes indeed, but with which it by no means stops. Moreover, in being thus silent upon the distinguishing truths, there was an implication that these do not constitute the essence of Christianity; and in this way, while professing to defend Christianity, the Apologist was in fact merely defending natural religion, and conceding the position of one class of skeptics, that the law of nature and Christianity are one and the same thing. As an example of an Apologist of this class, may be mentioned Thomas Sherlock, who in a "Sermon before the Society for propagating the Gospel" took the ground, "that Christ came into the world not merely to restore the religion of nature, but to adapt it to the state and condition of man; and to supply the defects, not of religion, which continuated in its first purity and perfection, but of nature." This "adaptation" or reconstruction of the religion of nature, by the Author of Christianity, consisted according to the representations of this class of Apologists in a clearer statement of the doctrine of immortality, and of future rewards and punishments, together with the announcement of the doctrine of the resurrection from the dead. It is not difficult to see how upon this ground, and in this mode of defending Christianity, the intellectual and serious deist of Lord Herbert's school might come to fraternize with the Christian divine.

The attacks of some of the English Deists upon the authenticity and genuineness of the Scripture Canon elicited replies from some of the Apologists. The English infidel criticism of the 18th century, however, falls far behind the infidel criticism of Germany in the 19th, in respect to learning and ingenuity. Toland is perhaps the most learned of these critics, but his ignorance and mistakes were clearly exposed by Samuel Clarke, and Nathaniel Lardner. The latter, in his work entitled, "The Credibility of the Gospel History," evinces the genuineness of the New Testament Canon, and the spuriousness of the Apocryphal writings with which Toland had attempted to associate the received canonical scriptures, by a careful and learned exhibition of all the citations and references from the earliest authorities. Collins, in his "Discourse of Free Thinking," ventured, in one portion of it, upon a line of criticism upon the Canon, which called out a reply from Richard Bentley, in a tractate entitled "Remarks upon a late discourse of Free Thinking, by Phileleutherus Lipsiensis." This treatise of Bentley is a complete reply to the various positions of Collins, in his defence of skeptical thinking. The immensity and accuracy of the learning, the searching thoroughness of the analysis, the keenness and brilliancy of the retort, and the calm and conscious mastery of the whole ground, render this little work of the Master of Trinity College and the first classical scholar of his century, one of the most striking and effective in apologetic literature.

§ 5. *French Encyclopaedism, and German Rationalism.*

The Deism of England lies at the root of the Continental infidelity, and having examined the former with some particularity, a very rapid survey of the course of skeptical thought in France and Germany will be all that will be attempted.

The materialistic philosophy of Bolingbroke had more affinity with, and exerted more influence upon the French mind, than any other one of the English skeptical theories. But upon passing into the less thoughtful French nation, this type of infidelity immediately assumed an extremely superficial, but striking and brilliant form. Helvetius († 1771), and Condillac († 1780) were the philosophers for the party, and Voltaire († 1778), and Rousseau († 1778) were its litterateurs. The "Système de la Nature" published by Holbach in 1770 exhibits materialism in its grossest form. The distinction between mind and matter is annihilated; all intellectual and spiritual processes are represented as purely sensational, or, in the phrase of a stern critic of the theory, "as the liver secretes bile so the brain secretes thought." God is only a name for nature, and nature is a concourse of material atoms.

The application of these principles to social and political life, and the attempt to give them popular currency, was the task undertaken by the so-called Encyclopaedists, the chief of whom were d'Alembert († 1783), and Diderot († 1784). The "Encyclopédie ou Dictionnaire Universel," published in 1751 and onward, is an endeavour to construct a compendium of universal knowledge by the theories of materialism and atheism, and thereby to inject infidel ideas into all the history and products of the past. The literary treatment and decoration of this scheme fell into the hands of Rousseau and Voltaire; the former of whom by his fascinating sentimentality invested it with a strange charm for the young and dreaming visionary, while the latter, by the gayest of wit, and the sharpest and most biting of sarcasm, insinuated it into the hard and frivolous man of fashion, and man of the world.

This form of infidelity elicited hardly any reply

from the Christian Church. The old defences produced in the preceding century in England were the principal reliance, so far as a literary answer was concerned; but the great and stunning reply was in the utter demoralization of social and political life, and the chaotic horrors of the French Revolution.

The skeptical direction which the German mind took in the last half of the 18th and first half of the 19th century is a much more important phenomenon than the infidelity of France. Taken as a whole, German Rationalism has been learned and serious, comparing it with ancient and modern skepticism generally. In the philosopher Kant († 1804), it resembles the deism of the school of Herbert. In such theologians as Ammon († 1850), Wegscheider († 1848), Röhr († 1848), and Paulus († 1851), we observe the influence of Biblical education, and ecclesiastical connections in restraining the theorist, and holding him back from all the logical consequences of his principles. Yet this intellectual and ethical unbelief operated for a season all the more disastrously upon the interests of Christianity, from the very fact that, while it rejected the doctrines of sin and grace, and by a learned criticism attacked the canonical Scriptures, it maintained so loftily the ideas of God, freedom, and immortality, and urged so strenuously the imperatives of duty and the moral law. Had it taught the bald and sensual theories of Bolingbroke or Condillac, the popular mind of one of the most naturally devout and religious races would have revolted. But the substitution of an elevated ethics for the doctrine of Redemption was temporarily successful, by reason of the appeal that was made to conscience, and the higher religious aspirations. The secret of its final failure lay in the utter impotence of the human will to realize these ideas of the moral reason, which were so earnestly set forth as the only religion necessary for man. A system like Rationalism which holds up before mankind the ideal of virtue, while it rejects the only power by which that ideal can be made actual in character and life, is a ministry of condemnation. The principles of ethics and natural religion can become inward impulses of thought and action in the human soul, only through the regenerating influences of revealed religion. The serious and thoughtful Schiller, whose " muse was conscience" in the phrase of De Stael, and who presents one of the finest examples of a lofty and cultivated Rationalism, seems to have learned this truth after years of futile moral endeavour. In a letter to Goethe he thus enunciates the difference between morality and religion, ethics and the gospel: "The distinguishing characteristic of Christianity, by which it is differentiated from all other monotheistic systems, lies in the fact that it does away with the *law*, the Kantean *imperative*, and in the place of it substitutes a free and spontaneous *inclination* of the heart,"[1]—a sentiment coincident with the Pauline affirmation, that the Christian, as distinguished from the moralist, is "not under the law but under grace" (Rom. vi. 15).

[1] HAGENBACH: Kirchengeschichte des 18 und 19 Jahrhunderts, II. 120.

BOOK THIRD.

HISTORY

OF

THEOLOGY (TRINITARIANISM),

AND

CHRISTOLOGY.

> "O blessed glorious Trinity,
> Bones to philosophy, but milk to faith,
> Which as wise serpents, diversly,
> Most slipperiness, yet most entanglings hath."
>
> DONNE: The Trinity.

LITERATURE.

ATHANASIUS : Orationes contra Arianos, and Defensio fidei Nicaenae ; translated in the Oxford Library of the Fathers.
HILARIUS : De Trinitate.
AUGUSTINUS : De Trinitate ; Contra Maximinum Haereticum.
ANSELMUS : De Trinitate et Incarnatione ; De processione Spiritus Sancti.
PETAVIUS : De Theologicis Dogmatibus, Tomus II.
BULL : Defensio fidei Nicaenae ; translated in the Oxford Library of Anglo Catholic Theology.
PEARSON : Exposition of the Apostles' Creed.
WATERLAND : First and Second Defences, and Sermons.
HORSLEY : Belief of the first Ages in our Lord's Divinity.
BURTON : Testimonies of the Ante-Nicene Fathers to the Divinity of Christ.
HARVEY : The Three Creeds.
BAUR : Lehre von der Dreieinigkeit.
DORNER : Person Christi ; translated in Clark's Foreign Theological Library.
MEIER : Trinitätslehre.

CHAPTER I.

GENERAL DOCTRINE OF THE DIVINE EXISTENCE.

§ 1. *Name of the Deity.*

PRELIMINARY to the history of the doctrine of the Trinity, we shall cast a rapid glance at the doctrine of the Divine Existence in its more general aspects. Five topics will claim attention under this introductory division: viz., the name of the Deity; the amount of pantheism and dualism that has prevailed in connection with the development of the Christian doctrine of God; the species of arguments that have been employed by Christian theologians to prove the Divine Existence; the doctrine of the attributes; and the Pagan trinity.

In respect to the *name* of the Deity, as well as in respect to particular definitions of Him, the Christian church has always been distinguished by freedom of views and conceptions. In the Pagan world we find a superstitious feeling which led men to attach a magical meaning and power to certain names of the Deity, and a disposition to cling to some particular one. Christianity, on the contrary, has ever been free to adopt as the name of the Supreme Being that particular one which it found in current use in the nation to which it came; thereby indicating its belief that there is no particular virtue in a name, and still more that no single term is sufficiently comprehensive to describe the infinite plenitude of being and of excellence that is contained in God.[1] The latest missionary like the first takes the terms of the new language, and consecrates them to the higher meaning which he brings to the nation.

At the same time, however, it should be remarked that Christianity, on account of its connection with Judaism, prefers, and adopts when it can, that conception of the Godhead which denotes his necessary and absolute existence. The Hebrew Jehovah was translated in two ways in the Greek version of the Old Testament: ὁ ὤν, and τὸ ὄν. The personal and the impersonal forms were both employed; the former to denote the divine personality in opposition to pantheistic conceptions, the latter to denote an absolute and necessary being (οὐσία), in contradistinction to a conditioned and dependent γένεσις, or emanation. So far, conse-

---

[1] The Graeco-Roman, or classical name of the deity is derived from a natural attribute; θεός, deus, is from τίθημι, to dispose. The Gothic name comes from a moral attribute; God signifies the good.

quently, as the Church gave currency to the Old Testament name of God, through the medium of the Alexandrine Greek, it made use of the same idea and name of the Deity that were employed by the Deity himself in his self-manifestation to his chosen people.

§ 2. *Pantheism and Dualism in the Church.*

Respecting the amount and species of *Pantheism* that appears in connection with the development of the Christian doctrine of God, we remark the following.

The Church was not disturbed by any formal and elaborated Pantheism during the first eight centuries. Phraseology was, however, sometimes employed by orthodox teachers themselves, that would be pantheistic if employed by an acknowledged pantheist. Tatian, a convert and disciple of Justin Martyr, and one of the early Apologists, speaks of God as ὑπόστασις πάντων. Hilary uses the phrase, " deus anima mundi." Some of the hymns of Synesius are decidedly pantheistic in their strain. Hippolytus addresses the Christian as follows, in his Confession of Faith. " Thou wilt have an immortal body together with an imperishable soul, and wilt receive the kingdom of heaven. Having lived on earth, and having known the Heavenly King, thou wilt be a companion of God, and a fellow-heir with Christ, not subject to lust, or passion, or sickness. For thou hast become God (*γέγονας γὰρ θεός*). For whatever hardships thou hadst to suffer when a man, He gave them to thee because thou wast a man; but that which is proper to God [*παρακολουθεῖ*, what pertains to God's state and condition], God has declared he will give thee when thou shalt be deified (*ὅταν θεοποιηθῇς*), being born again an immortal."[1] Yet such expressions as these should be interpreted in connection with the acknowledged theistic and Christian character of their authors, and are to be attributed to an unguarded mode of expression, and not to a deliberate and theoretical belief.[2]

In the ninth century Scotus Erigena, the most acute mind of his time, in his speculations upon the mutual relations of the world and God, unfolded a system that is indisputably pantheistic.[3] A tendency to pantheism is also traceable in the scholastic age, in both the analytic and the mystical mind.

---

[1] BUNSEN: Hippolytus, I. 184.— It is evident from Hippolytus's own statement, that he does not mean to teach pantheism in these bold expressions, for the Christian is to have a "body together with an imperishable soul." The devout COWPER says:

.... " there lives and works
A soul in all things, and that soul is God."
—The Task, Book vi.

[2] The charge of pantheism was made by some of the fathers against the Sabellian doctrine of the trinity. It is noticeable that in the Modern Church the rejection of the hypostatical, and adoption of the modal trinity is sometimes found in alliance with a pantheistic tendency. The trinitarianism of Schleiermacher is an example of this.

[3] It is contained in his work De divisione Naturae, Ed. Gale, Oxford 1681. For an account of the Mediaeval Pantheism, see ENGELHARDT'S Dogmengeschichte, II. iii; and RITTER's Geschichte der Christlichen Philosophie, III. 206 –296.

Rationalizing intellects like Duns Scotus and Occam prepared the way for it, though their own speculations are not strictly chargeable with pantheism. But in Amalrich of Bena, and his disciple David of Dinanto, we perceive an arid and scholastic pantheism distinctly enunciated; while imaginative and mystical minds like Eckart and Silesius exhibit this system in a glowing and poetical form. Pantheism, however, was firmly opposed by the great body of the Schoolmen, and was condemned by councils of the Church, and bulls of the Pope.

The most profound and influential form of this species of infidelity appears in the Modern Church. It began with Spinoza's doctrine of "substantia una et unica," and ended with Schelling and Hegel's so-called ".philosophy of identity," in which Spinozism received new forms, but no new matter. Spinoza precluded the possibility of a secondary substance created de nihilo, by his fundamental postulate that there is only one substance endowed with two attributes, extension and thought. All material things are this substance, in the mode of extension; all immaterial things are this same substance, in the mode of cogitation. The first modification of the one only substance yields the physical world; the second, the mental world. There is but one Substance, Essence, or Being, ultimately; and this Being is both cause and effect, agent and patient, in all evil and in all good, both physical and moral. Schelling's system is Spinozism with a prevailing attention to the one only Substance as extended; i. e., to physical pantheism. Hegel's system is engaged with the one only Substance as cogitative, and yields intellectual pantheism.

The theology of Germany, since the middle of the 18th century, has been influenced by this system, to an extent unparalleled in the previous history of the Church; and from the effects of it, it has not yet recovered. Too many of the modes of contemplating the Deity, and of apprehending his relations to the universe, current in Germany, are rendered vague by the failure to draw the lines of theism with firmness and strength. The personality of God is not sufficiently clear and impressive for classes of theologians who yet ought not to be denominated pantheists; while, on the other hand, open and avowed pantheists have held position within the pale of the Lutheran Church. The English and American theologies have been comparatively little influenced by this form of error, so that the most consistent theism for the last century must be sought for within these churches.

The doctrine of the Divine Nature has experienced but little modification and corruption from *Dualism*. This is the opposite error to Pantheism. All deviations from the true idea of the Deity terminate either in a unity which identifies God and the universe in one essence, or a duality which so separates the universe from God as to render it either independent of him, or eternally hostile to him. But it was only the Ancient Church that was called to combat this latter form of error.[1] During the prevalence of the Manichaean and Gnostic systems, dualistic views were current, but since their disappearance, the Biblical doctrine of the Godhead has had to contend chiefly with the pantheistic deviation.

§ 3. *Evidences of the Divine Existence.*

The Ancient Church laid more stress upon faith, the Modern upon demonstration, in establishing the fact of the Divine Existence. This is the natural consequence of the increasing cultivation of philosophy. In proportion as science is developed, the mind is more inclined to syllogistic reasoning.

The Patristic arguments for the Divine Existence rest mainly upon the innate consciousness of the human mind. They magnify the internal evidence for this doctrine. Common terms to denote the species of knowledge which the soul has of God, and the kind of evidence of his existence which it possesses, are ἔμφυτον (Clemens Alex.), and ingenitum (Arnobius). Tertullian employs the phrase, "anima naturaliter sibi conscia Dei." The influence of the Platonic philosophy is apparent in these conceptions. They imply innate ideas; something kindred to Deity in the reason of man. The doc-

---

[1] Compare ATHANASIUS's Oratio contra Gentes, § 1–9, for a specimen of vigorous reasoning against the dualistic theory of evil.

trine of the Logos, derived and expanded from the gospel of John, strengthened the Early Fathers in this general view of God. God was conceived as directly manifesting himself to the moral sense, through that Divine Word or Reason who in their phraseology was the *manifested* Deity. In their view, God proved his existence by his presence to the mind. In the Western Church, particularly, this immediate manifestation and consequent proof of the Divine Existence was much insisted upon. Augustine in his Confessions implies that the Deity evinces his being and attributes by a direct operation,—an *impinging* as it were of himself, upon the rational soul of his creatures. "*Perculisti* cor, verbo tuo" is one of his expressions.[1]

But whenever a formal demonstration was attempted in the Patristic period, the *a posteriori* was the method employed. The physico-theological argument, derived from the harmony visible in the works of creation, was used by Irenaeus to prove the doctrine of the unity and simplicity of the Divine Nature, in opposition to Polytheism and Gnosticism,—the former of which held to a multitude of gods, and the latter to a multitude of aeons. The teleological argument, derived from the universal presence of a design in creation, was likewise employed in the Patristic theology.

---

[1] Confessions, X. vi. See Neander's Denkwürdigkeiten, I. 276–280, for a sketch of the method of the Early Fathers in handling the innate idea of the deity.

The *ontological* argument, which derives its force from the definition of an absolutely Perfect Being, was not formed and stated until the Scholastic age. It then received a construction and statement by Anselm, in his Monologium, and more particularly in his Proslogion, which has never been surpassed. It is no disparagement to the powerful *a priori* arguments that have characterized modern Protestant theology, to say, that the argument from the necessary nature of the Deity, is unfolded in these tracts of Anselm with a depth of reflection, and a subtlety of metaphysical acumen, that places them among the finest pieces of Christian speculation.

The substance of the Anselmic argument is to be found in the following positions taken in the Proslogion.[1]

The human mind possesses the idea of the most perfect Being conceivable. But such a Being is *necessarily* existent; because a being whose existence is contingent, who may or may not exist, is not the most perfect that we can conceive of. But a necessarily existent Being is one that cannot be conceived of as non-existent, and therefore is an actually existent Being. Necessary existence implies

---

[1] Cap. 2, and 4.—The Proslogion, and the objections of Gaunilo with Anselm's reply, have been translated by MAGINNIS, in the Bibliotheca Sacra, 1851. Both the Monologium and Proslogion have been translated into French by BOUCHETTÉ. Compare RITTER's Geschichte der Christlichen Philosophie, Th. III, 334 sq., and BAUR's Dreieinigkeitslehre, II. 374 sq., for a critique of Anselm's argument.

actual existence. In conceiving, therefore, of a Being who is *more perfect* than all others, the mind inevitably conceives of a real and not an imaginary being; in the same manner as in conceiving of a figure having three sides, it inevitably conceives of a figure having three angles.

The force of this argument depends entirely upon the characteristic of "*necessity* of existence."[1] This is an integral part of the idea of the most perfect Being, and *does not enter into the idea of any other being*. All other beings may or may not exist, because they are not the most perfect conceivable. Their existence is contingent; but that of the First Perfect is necessary. Hence the idea of God is a wholly *unique* idea, and an argument can be constructed out of it, *such as cannot be constructed out of the idea of any other being*. And one of its peculiarities is, that it must have an objective correspondent to itself. This is not the case with any other idea. When, for example, the mind has the idea of a man, of an angel, of a tree, or of anything that is not *God*, or the *most perfect* Being, there is

[1] "I am not unapprehensive that I might here indeed, following great examples, have proceeded in another method than that which I now choose; and because we can have no true, appropriate, or distinguishing idea or conception of deity which doth not include *necessity* of existence in it, have gone that shorter way, immediately to have concluded the existence of God, from his idea itself. And I see not but treading those wary steps which the incomparable Dr. Cudworth, in his Intellectual System, hath done, that argument admits, in spite of cavil, of being managed with demonstrative evidence." Howe: Living Temple, Pt. I. Ch. ii, § 8.

no certainty that there is a real man, angel, or tree corresponding to it. It may be a wholly subjective idea; a thought in the mind, without a thing in nature agreeing with it. And this, because the idea of a man, an angel, or a tree does not involve *necessity* of existence. In the instance, then, of any other idea but that of God, the mere idea in the mind is not sufficient to evince the actual reality of the object. But in the instance of the solitary and totally unique idea of the absolutely Perfect, the mere idea is sufficient for this, because it contains the element of necessity of existence. If therefore, argues Anselm, we concede as we must that the mind possesses the idea of the most perfect Being conceivable, and also, that perfection of being involves necessity of being, and yet, at the same time, treat it as we do our ideas of contingent and imperfect existences, and say that it may or may not have an objective correspondent, we contradict ourselves. "Surely," remarks Anselm,[1] "that, than which a greater cannot be conceived, cannot exist merely in the mind alone. For if we suppose that it exists only subjectively in the intellect, and not objectively in fact, then we can conceive of something greater; we can conceive of a being who exists objectively, and this is greater than a merely mental existence. If, therefore, that than which a greater cannot be conceived exists only in the conception or intelligence, and not outwardly in fact, then that very thing than which a

[1] Proslogion, Cap. 2.

greater cannot be conceived is something than which a greater can be conceived,—which is self-contradictory. There exists, therefore, beyond doubt, both in the mind, and in reality, a Being than which a greater cannot be conceived."

Anselm goes a step further, and argues that the mind *cannot conceive of the non-existence of God*, without a logical contradiction.[1] Here, again, the difference between the idea of the Supreme Being, and that of all other beings is apparent. There is nothing self-contradictory in supposing the non-existence of man, of angels, of trees, or of matter universally, because their definition does not imply that they must exist of necessity. But to suppose that a Being who is in his nature necessarily existent is not in existence is absurd. We can, therefore, think the creation out of existence, but we cannot even in thought annihilate the Creator. In the fourth chapter of the Proslogion, Anselm argues this point in the following manner. "A thing is conceived, in one sense, when the mere words that designate it are conceived; in another sense, when the thing itself is in its own nature understood and comprehended. In the former sense, God can be conceived not to exist; in the latter sense he cannot be. For no one who understands what fire is, and

---

[1] ANSELM maintains that any being who can logically be conceived as non-existent is by this very fact proved not to be the most perfect being conceivable. "Et quod incipit a non esse, et potest cogitari non esse .... id non est proprie et absolute." Proslogion, c. 22.

what water is, can conceive that fire is water; though he may conceive this as to the mere sound and meaning of the words. In like manner, no one who understands what God is, and clearly comprehends that he is a necessarily existent Being, can conceive that God is non-existent,—although, like the Psalmist's fool, he may say in his heart the words, 'There is no God.' For God is that, than which a greater cannot be conceived. He who properly understands this, understands therefore that this something exists in such a mode, that it cannot even be conceived of as non-existent. He therefore who understands that God exists as the most perfect Being conceivable, cannot conceive of him as a non-entity. Thanks be to Thee, O Lord, thanks be to Thee, that what I at first believed through thine own endowment, I now understand through thine illumination; so that even if I were unwilling to believe that thou art, I cannot remain ignorant of thine existence."

Anselm's argument was assailed by a monk Gaunilo, in a little work entitled, *Liber pro insipiente* (A plea for the fool); in allusion to Anselm's quotation from the Psalms: 'The fool hath said in his heart, there is no God.' His principal objection is, that the existence of the idea of a thing does not prove the existence of the thing. "Suppose," he says,[1] "that we have the idea of an island more perfect than any other portion of the earth; it does

[1] Liber pro insipiente, in ANSELMI Opera, Ed. Migne, I. 246.

not follow that because this island exists in the mind, it therefore exists in reality." This objection started by Gaunilo has been frequently urged since. The mere idea of a griffin, or of a chimaera, it has been said, does not evince the actual existence of a griffin or a chimaera. But an objection of this kind fails to invalidate Anselm's argument, because there is no logical parallelism between the two species of ideas. It overlooks the fact that the idea of the Deity is wholly solitary and unique; there is no second idea like it. As Anselm remarks in his reply to Gaunilo, if the island abovementioned were *the most perfect thing conceivable*, then he would insist that the existence of the idea in the mind would be evidence of the existence of the island itself.[1] But the idea of the island does not, like the idea of God, contain the elements of *absolute perfection* of being, and *necessity* of being. And the same is true of the idea of a griffin, or of a chimaera, or of any imaginary or contingent existence whatever. The idea of a man, or an angel, does not carry with it that the man, or the angel, cannot but exist, and that his non-existence is inconceivable. But the idea of God, as a Being totally *different* from all created and contingent beings, does carry with it the property of necessary existence; and therefore

[1] "Fidens loquor; quia si quis invenerit mihi aliquid aut reipsa, aut sola cogitatione existens, praeter quo majus cogitari non possit, cui aptare valeat connexionem hujus meae argumentationis, inveniam, et dabo illi perditam insulam *amplius non perdendam*." ANSELMI Opera, Ed. Migne, I. 252.

an objection like that of Gaunilo, drawn from the province of contingent existences, does not hold. It is an instance of what Aristotle denominates μετάβασις εἰς ἄλλω γένος,—a transfer of what is true of one species to a species of totally different nature. As if one should transfer what is true of the idea of matter, to the idea of mind ; or should argue that because a solid cube is capable of being measured and weighed, therefore the invisible soul of man can be also. According to Anselm, the idea of God is wholly unique. It is the only idea of the species. No other idea, consequently, can be a logical parallel to it; and therefore all these arguments from analogy fail. The idea of every other being but God contains the element of contingent existence, and therefore can afford no logical basis upon which to found an argument against an ontological demonstration that rests upon the element of necessary existence contained in the idea of the most perfect Being, who of course must be the only being of the kind.[1]

[1] The nature of this argument of Anselm may be seen by throwing it into the following dialogue. "*Anselm.* I have the idea of the most perfect being conceivable. *Gaunilo.* True : but it is a mere idea, and there is no being corresponding to it. *Anselm.* But if there is no being answering to my idea, then my idea of the most perfect being conceivable is that of an *imaginary* being; but an imaginary being is not the most perfect being that I can conceive of. The being who corresponds to my idea must be a real being. If therefore you grant me my postulate, namely, that I have the idea of the most perfect being conceivable, you concede the existence of an *actual* being correspondent to it."

Another a priori argument for the Divine Existence might be

The a priori mode of proving the Divine Existence was the favorite one in the Scholastic age, for two reasons. In the first place, it harmonized most with the metaphysical bent of the time, and afforded more scope for subtle thinking, and close reasoning. In the second place, the low state of natural science, and the very slight knowledge which men had of the created universe, left them almost destitute of the materials of a posteriori arguments. Arguments from the order, harmony, and design in

constructed in Anselm's method by selecting *actuality* of existence, instead of necessity of existence, as an element in the idea of the most perfect Being. Thus: "I have the idea of the most perfect being conceivable; but the most perfect being conceivable cannot be an imaginary one. The idea of an absolutely perfect being implies an objective correspondent, as necessarily as the idea of a figure bounded by three straight lines implies a figure containing three angles. Three-sidedness in a figure implies triangularity of necessity. In like manner, if the idea of the most perfect being conceivable be granted, then that of an actually existent being is conceded by necessary implication, because the perfection of being must be an actual being.——Two objections, not urged by Anselm's opponents in his own day, but by modern critics of his argument, are worthy of notice. The first is, that the argument makes mere existence an *attribute* of the most perfect being, when in fact it is being itself. But this is an error. Anselm does not build his argument upon the notion of mere existence, but of *necessity* of existence. And this is an attribute or characteristic quality, as truly as contingency of existence. The second objection is, that Anselm's argument amounts only to the hypothetical proposition: "*If* there be a necessarily existent being, of course there is an actually existent one." But as the most perfect being conceivable is one who cannot be *conceived of* as existing contingently, it is as illogical to employ the subjunctive mode in reference to him, and speak of him as possibly non-existent, as to employ the hypothetical mode in reference to the mathematical proposition that two and two make four.

the universe, cannot be successfully constructed, unless that order, harmony, and design are apparent. But this was impossible in an age when the Ptolemaic astronomy was the received system,—the earth being the centre of the solar system, and the starry heavens, in Milton's phrase,

> "With centric and eccentric scribbled o'er,
> Cycle and epicycle, orb in orb."

The *moral argument* for the Divine Existence is found in its simplest form, in the very earliest periods in the Church. God is known by being loved; love then, or a right state of the heart, implies and contains a proof of the reality of the Divine Being that is incontrovertible certainly to the subject of the affection. The more elaborate form of this argument is not found until the time of Kant, who elevated it in his system to a high degree of importance.

In the modern Protestant theology, both the a priori and a posteriori methods of demonstrating the divine existence have been employed. The progressive development has been confined mostly to the a posteriori arguments. The cultivation and advancement of natural science has furnished both matter and impulse to the evidences from design, order, and harmony in creation. Progress in the a priori argument depends so much upon purely metaphysical acumen, while the scope for variety in the construction and statement of the demonstration is so very limited, that the ontological argument remains very nearly as it was when Anselm formed it.

§ 4. *The doctrine of the Attributes.*

The Church early recognized the distinction between the *essence* and the *attributes* of the Deity. The former, in and by itself, was regarded as unknowable by the finite mind. The theologians of the first two centuries sometimes distinguished between the unrevealed and the revealed Deity. By the former, they meant the simple substance of the Godhead apart from the attributes, of which it was impossible to affirm anything, and which consequently was beyond the ken of the human mind. They intended to keep clear of that vague idea of an abstract Monad without predicates, which figures in the Gnostic systems under the name of the *Abyss* ($Bυθός$), and which has re-appeared in the modern systems of Schelling and Hegel, under the names of the *Urgrund*, and *Das Nichts*, but they did not always succeed. Their motive was a good one. They desired to express the truth that the Divine Nature is a mystery which can never be fathomed to the bottom by any finite intelligence; but in their representations they sometimes ventured upon the dangerous position, that the Godhead is above all essence, and without essence ($ὑπερούσιος$, and $ἀνούσιος$). As theological science advanced, however, it was perceived that the essence of the Deity cannot safely be contemplated apart from his attributes. The essence is *in* the attributes, and the attributes *in* the essence, and consequently Christian science must seize both ideas at once, and hold them both together. This led to the examination and exhibition of the Divine attributes, as *real* and *eternal* characteristics of the Deity.

We cannot follow out the developement of thought upon the Divine attributes; for this would require their being taken up one by one, and their history exhibited through the various periods. A single remark, only, can be made at this point. In proportion as the attributes have been discussed in connection with the essence of the Deity, has the doctrine of God been kept clear from pantheistic conceptions. In proportion, on the contrary, as speculation has been engaged with the essence of the Godhead, to the neglect or non-recognition of the attributes in which this essence manifests itself, has it become pantheistic. It is impossible for the human mind to know the Deity abstractly from his attributes. It may posit, i. e. set down on paper, an unknown ground of being, like the unknown x in algebra, of which nothing can be predicated, and may suppose that this is knowing the absolute Deity. But there is no such dark predicateless ground; there is no such Gnostic abyss. The Divine Nature is in and with the attributes, and hence the attributes are as deep and absolute as the Nature. The substance and attributes of God are in the same plane of being. Neither one is more aboriginal than the other. Both are equally eternal, and equally necessary. Christian science, consequently, has never isolated them from each other. It distinguishes them, it is true, in order that it may form conceptions of them, and describe them, but it is ever careful to affirm as absolute and profound a reality in the Divine attributes as in the Divine essence. It never recognizes a Divine essence without attributes, any more than it recognizes Divine attributes without a Divine essence. The Gnostic and the Pantheistic speculatist, on the contrary, has bestowed but little reflection upon the personal characteristics of the Deity. He has been inclined to contemplate and discuss the bare predicateless Essence or Being,—τὸ ὄν rather than ὁ ὤν.[1] Attributes like personality, unity, immutability, and, still more, moral attributes like holiness, justice, truth, and mercy, enter little, or none at all, into the ancient Gnostic, and the modern Pantheistic construction of the doctrine of God. Yet these constitute the very divinity of the Deity; and hence the Christian theologian made them the object of his first and unceasing contemplation. These attributes are personal qualities, and thus it is easy to see, that theism is inseparably and naturally connected with the developement of the doctrine of the Attributes.

[1] The use of the phrase, "The Absolute," in Hegel's system, is an example of this predicateless abstraction.

§ 5. *The Pagan Trinity.*

Some of the theologies of pagan antiquity contain intimations of trinality in the Divine Being. The writings of Plato, particularly, in Occidental philosophy, and some of the Oriental systems, such as the Hindoo, contain allusions to this mode of the Divine Existence. But the Pagan trinity is one of figurative personification, and not of interior hypostatical distinctions in the Divine Essence constituting three real persons who may be addressed in supplication and worship. It is commonly constructed in one of two ways. Either the Triad is made out, by personifying three of the more fundamental faculties and attributes of God,—as Goodness, Intellect, and Will,—which is Plato's method;[1] or else

---

[1] CUDWORTH attempts to find a hypostatical trinity in Plato. MORGAN (Trinity of Plato and Philo) concedes the monotheism of Plato, but denies that the Christian or hypostatical trinity is to be found in his writings.

The following passage from the Epinomis (986. d, Ed. Tauchnitz, VI. 495) has been supposed to teach the doctrine of the Logos: "Each [of the eight heavenly powers (δυνάμεις) residing in the sun, moon, &c.] goes through its revolution, and completes the order (κόσμον) which reason (λόγος), the most divine of all, has appointed to be visible." Here, says MORGAN (Trinity of Plato, p. 6),

"Plato is speaking merely of the law of harmony which prevails in the material universe; and the word λόγος is without the article. The connection shows conclusively, that he is speaking of an abstract principle, and not of a person."

Another passage which Cudworth and others suppose teaches the doctrine of a hypostatical trinity is found in Plato's second Epistle to Dionysius (Opera VIII. 118, Ed. Tauchnitz). "As regards the king of all, all things are his, and all are for his sake, and he is the cause of all beautiful things. And there is a *second*, in respect to secondary things,

by personifying three of the powers of nature,—as the creating, preserving, and destroying forces of the Hindoo Trimurti. In these schemes, the facul-

and a *third*, in respect to tertiary things."

According to CUDWORTH (Intellectual System, II. 364 sq. Tegg's Ed.), Plato held a hypostatical trinity, consisting of τὸ ἀγαθον, νοῦς, and ψύχη. These, he thinks, are what Plato meant by his "king of all," "second," and "third," in his Epistle to Dionysius. Respecting the first and second hypostases, he contends that there can be no doubt that Plato held them to be *uncreated* and *eternal* subsistences. Respecting the third, the so-called "mundane soul," he concedes that there "may be some more reason to make a question" whether Plato held to its eternity. He is himself of the opinion that Plato "held a double Psyche, or Soul; one mundane, which is, as it were, the concrete form of this corporeal world [the plastic principle in nature]; another, supermundane, which is not so much the form as the artificer of the world." This latter, Cudworth contends is the third hypostasis in the Platonic trinity, and is uncreated and eternal.

The Platonic and Pythagorean trinity, CUDWORTH (Intel. Syst. II. 333, 339, 340) holds to be a "theology of Divine tradition, or revelation,—θεοπαράδοτος θεολογία, a Divine cabala,—amongst the Hebrews first, and from them afterwards communicated to the Egyptians, and other nations." He also distinguishes the genuine Platonic from the pseudo-Platonic trinity of the later Platonists. This latter consisted in deifying with the first universal Mind, many secondary particular minds,—namely, all particular souls above the human. In this way, they "melted the deity by degrees, and bringing it down lower and lower, they made the juncture and commixtion betwixt God and the creature so smooth and close, that where they indeed parted was altogether undiscoverable." In this way, they "laid a foundation for infinite polytheism, cosmolatry (or world-idolatry) and creature worship."—THEODORET (De affect. II. 750) remarks, that "Plotinus and Numenius, explaining the sense of Plato, say, that he taught three Principles, beyond time, and eternal: namely Good, Intellect, and the Soul of All." PLOTINUS (4 Ennead, iv. 16) says of this trinity: "It is as if one were to place Good as the centre, Intellect like an immovable circle round, and Soul a movable circle, and movable by appetite."

The Hindoo trinity is a combination of three powers,—that of creation (Brahma), preservation

ties, attributes, and functions of the Deity take the place of interior and substantial distinctions in his Essence. There is, therefore, when the ultimate analysis is made, no true and proper tripersonality. There is merely a personification of three impersonalities. The Pagan trinity, consequently, is only a figurative and nominal one.

This examination of the Pagan trinitarianism refutes the assertion of Socinus that the Church derived the doctrine of the trinity from the writings of Plato. The two doctrines are fundamentally different. At the same time, however, they have just sufficient resemblance to each other, to justify the assertion, that the Biblical doctrine of the trinity cannot be so utterly contrary to the natural apprehensions of the human mind, as its opponents represent, inasmuch as the most elaborate and thoughtful of the pagan philosophies and theologies groped towards it, though they did not reach it. An inadequate and defective view of truth is better than none at all; and although it is insufficient for the purposes of either theory or practice, it is yet a corroboration, so far as it reaches, of the full and adequate doctrine. Both the copy and the counterfeit are evidences of the reality of the original.

(Vishnu), and destruction (Siva). And these three are emanations from the original Monad (Brahm).

The Persian worship recognizes two great principles, Ormusd and Ahriman, both subordinate to Mithra, the great Primal Cause, or Time without bounds. "The dualism of Persia made the two antagonist powers to be created by, or proceed from, the One Supreme or Uncreated." MILMAN: History of Christianity, p. 200, Harper's Ed.

CHAPTER II.

ANTE-NICENE TRINITARIANISM.

§ 1. *Preliminary Statements.*

THE early history of the Doctrine of the Trinity shows that Christian faith may exist without a scientific and technical expression of it. This ability comes in only as those heresies arise which necessitate the exact and guarded statements of systematic theology. Waterland, in alluding to the severity of the criticisms which Photius makes upon the trinitarianism of the Ante-Nicene writers, justly remarks, that he did not "consider the difference of times, or how unreasonable it is to expect that those who lived before the rise and condemnation of heresies should come up to every accurate form of expression which long experience afterwards found necessary, to guard the faith."[1] Many a man in the very bosom of the church at this day cherishes a

---
[1] WATERLAND: Preface to Second Defence, p. 17.

belief in the triune God, that involves a speculative definition of the three persons and their mutual relations, which in his present lack of theological discipline he could no more give with exactness, and without deviation towards Sabellianism on the right hand, and Arianism on the left, than he could specify the chemical elements of the air he breathes, or map the sky under whose dome he walks every day. The same fact meets us upon the wider arena of the Universal Church. The Christian experience is one and the same in all ages and periods, but the ability to make scientific statements of those doctrines which are received by the believing soul, varies with the peculiar demands for such statements, and the intensity with which, in peculiar emergencies, the theological mind is directed towards them. We do not, therefore, find in the first two centuries of the history of Christian Doctrine, so much fullness and exactitude of technical definition as in after ages, though there was undoubtedly full as much unity of internal belief. The Primitive Christians received the doctrines in the general form in which they are given in Scripture, and were preserved from the laxness of theory, and the corruption of experience and practice so liable to accompany indefinite and merely general views, by the unusual vitality and vigour of the divine life within their souls. General statements of Christian doctrine satisfy two extremes of religious character. They are sufficient for a warm and glowing piety, which, because it already holds the truth in all its meaning and comprehensiveness within the depths of a believing spirit, can dispense with technical and scientific statements. They are satisfactory to a cold and lifeless religionism, which, because it rejects the essential truth in the depths of an unbelieving spirit, prefers an inexact phraseology, because of the facility with which it may be twisted and tortured to its own real preconceptions and prejudices. The absence of a scientific phraseology is characteristic, consequently, either of the most devout, or the most rationalistic periods in Church History.

The difference between the mental attitude of each of these two classes towards the truth is perceived in the difference in the feeling exhibited by each, respectively, when a systematic and technical statement is made. The catholic mind accepts the creed when constructed, because it sees in it only an exact and full statement of what it already holds in practical experience. The heretical mind, on the contrary, rejects the creed-statement when made, because it knows that it does not receive the tenets taught by it, and because the logical and technical articles of the creed preclude all equivocation or ambiguity. The Catholic welcomed, therefore, the explicit trinitarian statements of Nice, but the Arian rejected them. A recent writer exhibits the connection between the practical faith of the common believer, and the scientific statements of the theologian, in the following exceedingly clear and truthful manner. "No one professes to maintain that the disciples of St. John habitually used such *words* as 'hypostatic,' 'consubstantiality,' &c.—What proportion of the whole multitude of perfectly orthodox believers on earth, even at *this* hour, habitually use them, or have ever used them? It may be further admitted, that when a doctrine has come to be *intellectually* analysed and measured, certain relations may be seen to be involved in it, the distinct expression of which may become thenceforth useful, and even necessary; and that until circumstances, usually heresy, have led to this close intellectual survey, these relations, though involved in the existing belief, and logically deducible therefrom, may not occupy a prominent position in the common expositions of the faith. In what precise *degree* this holds in such a statement of the doctrine of the trinity as the Athanasian Creed is another question; the *principle* is exemplified in every stage of the history of theology. Those,—not even to investigate their expressed dogmatic belief,—who were taught to equally *worship* the mysterious Three into whose single Divine Name they had been baptized,—to look on them habitually as Protecting Powers equally because infinitely above them, separate in their special titles, offices, and agency, and so a real Three, yet One (as the very act of supreme worship implied),—would probably see little in even that elaborate creed beyond the careful intellectual exhibition of truths necessarily involved in that worship. They would easily see that to *con-tradict* explicitly any proposition of that creed would be directly or indirectly to deny the faith; while at the same time they may have held, as the infinite majority of the Christian world have since held, the pure faith of Father, Son, and Holy Ghost, without perpetually retaining a distinct explicit recollection of all the separate propositions that creed contains. . . . . In short, that creed gives us, as it were, the intellectual *edition* of the doctrine held from the beginning,—the doctrine expressed (as mathematicians say) 'in *terms* of' the pure intellect.

"It would probably illustrate this process, if any one were to reflect upon the quantity of minute and refined thought, and the extreme accuracy of expression, required to fix and secure, so as at once to discriminate them from all rival hypotheses, some of those elementary and fundamental notions of *simple theism*, which yet no one doubts to be the real belief, not merely of all classes of Christians, but of the greater portion of the civilized world. For example, to fix the precise and formal notion of creation out of nothing (so as to distinguish it absolutely from, e. g., the hypothesis of emanation); to state the precise relation of the Divine Power to the Divine Rectitude,—such, that the *Almighty* God *can* never do but what is right; to deliver with accuracy liable to no evasion the exact relation of the Divine Omnipotence and Goodness to the existence of moral evil, &c. On all such subjects, every ordinary Christian has a sufficiently decisive practical belief, a belief which would at once be shocked by any express assertion of its contradictory: he tells you; 'God made all things from nothing;' 'God can never do wrong;' 'God makes no man sin, it is the devil who tempts him, it is man's own corrupt choice to do evil:' and yet it is easy to conceive how very different an aspect these simple but profound truths would assume in an *Athanasian creed* of theism; how novel might *appear* doctrines, before almost too universally recognized to be laboriously insisted on, if it became necessary to exhibit them guarded at all points against the subtlety of some Arius or Sabellius of *Natural* Theology."[1]

But although the doctrine of the trinity, like other doctrines of the Christian system, did not obtain a technical construction in those first two centuries and a half, during which the Church was called chiefly to a general defence of Christianity, rather than to define its single dogmas, it would be a great error to infer that there were no results in this direction. The controversies that were necessitated by the Gnostic heresies led indirectly to some more exact statements respecting the doctrine of the trinity; but the defective and inadequate trinitarianism of certain men of this period, some of whom were excommunicated because of their errors, while

[1] ARCHER BUTLER: Letters on Romanism, p. 224.

some still remained within the pale of the church, either because of the comparative mildness of their heterodoxy, or because a less vigorous and scientific spirit prevailed in those portions of the church to which they belonged, contributed far more than any other cause, to the scientific and technical enunciation of the doctrine of the three Persons in the one Essence.

Some writers have attempted to prove that the Ante-Nicene Church held only the most vague and shadowy species of trinitarianism. But a church that was capable of grappling with the emanationism of the Gnostic, and saw the fatal error in the modal trinitarianism of the Patripassians,—the most subtle, and also the most elevated of all the forms of spurious trinitarianism,—must have possessed an exceedingly clear intuition of the true doctrine. The orthodoxy of the Primitive Church is demonstrated by the heterodoxy which it combatted and refuted. "Had we no other ways to know it," says Sherlock, "we might learn the faith of the catholic Church, by its opposition to those heresies which it condemned." We shall therefore, first specify and delineate those heterodox theories of the Apologetic period which elicited the clearest counter statements, and thereby contributed in a negative way, to the early orthodox construction of the dogma whose historical development we are describing.[1]

---

[1] "Improbatio quippe haereticorum facit eminere quid ecclesia tua sentiat, et quid habeat sana doctrina. Oportuit enim et hae-

§ 2. *Classes of Anti-Trinitarians.*

In the course of the first three centuries, three sects were formed, with varieties of view and phraseology, all of whom were characterized by an erroneous apprehension of the doctrine of the trinity; owing, in most instances, to an attempt to fathom the depths of this mystery by a process of speculation, instead of by a comprehensive reflection upon the Biblical data for its construction.[1] As we examine them, we shall perceive that the mind looked at only one side of the great truth, and dwelt upon only a single one of the several representations in the revealed word. Some sought to affirm, and that very strongly, the doctrine of the deity of Christ; but denied his distinct personality. Christ, they held, was God the Father himself, in a particular aspect or relationship. Essence and Person were identical, for them; and as there was but one Essence there could be but one Person. Others denied the proper deity of Christ, assumed only an extraordinary and pre-eminent connection of the man Jesus with the Divine Essence, and made two divine powers ($\delta v v \acute{\alpha} \mu \epsilon \iota \varsigma$), not persons ($\acute{v}\pi o \sigma \tau \acute{\alpha} \sigma \epsilon \iota \varsigma$),

reses esse, ut probati manifesti fierent inter infirmos (1 Cor. xi. 19)." AUGUSTINUS: Confessiones VII. xix.

[1] In some instances, probably, there was a desire to explain the doctrine and relieve it of its mystery. The modal trinity, for example, is quite intelligible. It is a significant remark of HOOKER (Eccl. Pol. I. 586), that "the Scripture doctrine of the Trinity is more true than plain, while the heretical doctrine of the Trinity is more plain than true."

of the Son and the Holy Spirit. Others still, held Christ to be a mere man. Anti-Trinitarians of this period were, consequently, of three classes; namely *Patripassians* or *Monarchians*, *Nominal Trinitarians*, and *Humanitarians*. The Church, however, engaged in controversy with only the first two; because the third class did not pretend to hold the doctrine of the trinity in any form, while the others claimed to teach the true Biblical trinitarianism.

I. The first class of Anti-Trinitarians were denominated *Patripassians* or *Monarchians*, because they asserted the Monad and denied the Triad. They asserted the deity of Christ, but held the church doctrine of three persons to be irreconcilable with that of the unity of God. Hence they affirmed that there is only one divine Person. This one only Person conceived of in his abstract simplicity and eternity was denominated God the Father; but in his incarnation, he was denominated God the Son. Sometimes, a somewhat different mode of apprehension and statement was employed. God in his concealed unrevealed nature and being was denominated God the Father, and when he comes forth from the depths of his essence, creating a universe, and revealing and communicating himself to it, he therein takes on a different relation, and assumes another denomination: namely, God the Son, or the Logos.

In their Christology, the Patripassians taught that this single divine Person, in his form of Son or Logos, animated the human body of Christ; and denied the existence of a true human soul in the Person of Jesus Christ. It was, consequently, the divine essence itself in alliance with a physical organization and nature, that suffered for the sin of mankind; and hence the term Patripassians was given to the advocates of this doctrine.

The principal Patripassians were the following:[1]

1. *Praxeas* of Asia Minor, originally, who appears at Rome about the year 200, and was opposed by Tertullian in his tract *Adversus Praxean*. The opening sentences of this treatise are characteristic. "The devil is jealous of the truth in various ways. Sometimes he affects it, in order by defending, to overthrow it. He maintains one only supreme Lord, the omnipotent former of the world, in order to construct a heresy out of this unit (unico). He says that the Father descended into a virgin, was himself born of her, himself suffered, and finally that the Father himself is Jesus Christ."

2. *Noetus* at Smyrna, about 230, was excommunicated on account of heresy. His principal opponent was Hippolytus in his tractate, *Contra haeresin Noëti*.[2]

3. *Beryl*, bishop of Bostra in Arabia, about 250. He was tried for heresy by an Arabian Synod, in 244, and by the arguments of Origen, whom the

---

[1] Compare GUERICKE: Church History, §56.

[2] See WORDSWORTH's Hippolytus, pp. 243, 261 sq., 281 sq.,—a more reliable work than that of BUNSEN, in regard to the doctrinal opinions of Hippolytus, and the Ante-Nicene period generally.

synod had called to their aid, was convinced of his error, and renounced his Patripassianism. According to Jerome, he sought further instruction from Origen, in a correspondence with him upon the doctrine of the trinity.

II. The second class of Anti-Trinitarians, whom we denominate *Nominal Trinitarians*, conceded no proper deity to Christ, but only a certain species of divinity. The distinction between deity and divinity is important in the history of Trinitarianism. The former is an absolute term, and implies essential and eternal godhood. The latter is relative, and is therefore sometimes applied to a created essence of a high order, and sometimes to human nature itself. This second class, who attributed divinity but denied deity to Christ, held that the concealed unrevealed God,—corresponding to the Father in the Patripassian theory,—reveals himself by means of two Powers which stream forth from him, as rays of light are rayed out from the sun: one an illuminating Power, the other an enlivening. The illuminating Power is the divine Wisdom, or Reason, or Logos, which exists in two forms: first, the indwelling reflective reason of the Deity, whereby he is capable of rational intelligence ($\lambda \acute{o} \gamma o \varsigma \; \acute{\epsilon} \nu \delta \iota \acute{a} \vartheta \epsilon \tau o \varsigma$); secondly the outworking self-expressive reason of the Deity, whereby he creates, and makes communications to his creation ($\lambda \acute{o} \gamma o \varsigma \; \pi \rho o \varphi o \rho \iota \varkappa \acute{o} \varsigma$). The enlivening Power is the Holy Spirit. With the divine Logos, or the illuminating Power,—which is not an hypostasis, but only an emanation issuing from the essential Deity,—the man Jesus was united from his birth in a pre-eminent manner, and in a degree higher than the inspiration of any prophet; and as a man thus standing under this pre-eminent illumination and guidance of the Logos, he is called the Son of God.

1. A representative of this second class of Anti-Trinitarians, is Paul of Samosata, bishop of Antioch for some time after 260, a man of great vanity and love of show. He was pronounced heretical by two Antiochian synods, in 264 and 269, and deposed from his bishopric by the last synod, but found powerful support from Queen Zenobia, and continued to discharge the functions of his office. On the conquest of the queen by the emperor Aurelian, the synodal decree of deposition was carried into execution, after a new preferring of charges by the bishops of the region, and the urgent co-operation of the bishop of Rome.[1]

2. A second representative of this second class of Anti-Trinitarians is Sabellius, presbyter of Ptolemais in Pentapolis, 250–260; though he stands somewhat between the first and second classes. He belongs to the second class, so far as he understands by the Logos and the Holy Spirit two Powers ($\delta \upsilon \nu \acute{a} \mu \epsilon \iota \varsigma$) streaming forth from the divine Essence, through which God works and reveals himself;[2]

---

[1] EUSEBIUS: Eccl. Hist., VII. 27–30.
[2] Sabellius seems to have regarded the Monad as *antithetic*

but departs from this class and approximates to the Patripassians, in denying that Christ was merely an ordinary man upon whom the divine Logos only exerted a peculiar influence, and affirming that the Logos-Power itself belonged to the proper personality of Christ, and thereby determined and shaped his personal consciousness during the period of his earthly life. The Logos entered into *union* with Christ's humanity, and not merely inspired it. But this more exalted view of the Person of Christ is immediately depressed again to the humanitarian level of the second class, by the further assertion, that this divine Logos-Power, which had thus issued forth from God, and united itself with a human body, and formed one communion of life and consciousness with it during the period of Christ's earthly existence, was at the ascension of Jesus again withdrawn into the depths of the Divine

to the Triad, thus introducing four factors into the problem. Whether he regarded the Father as the Monad, or supposed the Father to stand in the same relation to the Monad, that the Logos and Spirit do, is uncertain. NEANDER (I. 595) is of opinion that Sabellius held the Father as unrevealed to be the Monad, and as revealed to be the Father properly so called. He employed the following comparison to illustrate his view of the Trinity. "As in the sun we may distinguish its proper substance, its round shape, and its power of communicating heat and light, so in God we may distinguish his self-subsistent essence ($\mu\acute{o}\nu\alpha\varsigma$), the illuminating power of the Logos, and the enlivening energy of the Holy Spirit in the hearts of believers." NEANDER (I. 596) also remarks that Sabellius employed the catholic phrase, "three Persons," but in the sense of personifications, or characters which the one essence assumed according to varying occasions. Compare EUSEBIUS: Eccl. Hist. VII. vi; EPIPHANIUS: Haereses, LXII.

Nature.[1] Sabellianism maintained itself down into the 4th century, chiefly at Rome and in Mesopotamia.

III. The third class of Anti-Trinitarians, whom we denominate the *Humanitarians*, were those who asserted the mere and sole humanity of Christ, and denied his divinity in any and every sense of the term; some of them holding, however, to an extraordinary humanity in Christ, and others only to an ordinary.[2] The views of this class were so palpably in conflict with the representations of Scripture that the Church became engaged in no controversy with them. It was only with those parties who held a

---

[1] Sabellius's trinity, says NEANDER (I. 598-9), is transitory. When the purposes of its formation are accomplished, the Triad is resolved again into the Monad. Sabellius did not apply the name of Son to the Logos; but only to the Person resulting from the union of the Logos with the man Jesus. He maintains, that in the Old Testament no mention is made of the Son of God, but only of the Logos.

[2] We group under this general name of Humanitarians all those sects, such as the Ebionites, Theodotians, Artemonites, and Alogi, who denied both the deity and the divinity of Christ. WATERLAND, upon the strength of a statement of Epiphanius, maintains that the doctrine that Christ was only a mere and ordinary man was not taught until Theodotus (A. D. 196) broached it. The earlier heretics, like the Ebionites, Cerinthus, and Carpocrates, all held to a species of connection between Christ and a superior being, which made his humanity an *extraordinary* one. These sects held that upon the mere and ordinary man Jesus, who was born by ordinary generation of Joseph and Mary, the aeon Christ descended at his baptism, investing him with miraculous powers, but left him again at the time of his death. All these representations were rejected by Theodotus, who held that Christ was in every respect an ordinary mortal man (ψιλός ἄνθρωπος). NEANDER (I. 580), on the contrary, quotes Theodotus's explanation of Luke i. 31 to show that he did not deny the supernatural character of Christ's nativity.

species of trinitarianism that the catholic mind entered into earnest and prolonged discussion.

Criticising the first two classes, in reference to whom the term Anti-Trinitarian has its weightiest application, it is obvious that the Patripassians or Monarchians approached nearer to the revealed doctrine of the absolute deity of Christ than did the Nominal Trinitarians. According to them, God in his *essential being* was in Christ. The Logos was not a mere emanation from the divine nature, but was the very divine nature itself. Their conception of Christ as to his deity was elevated, and hence, as Neander remarks, "the more profound pious feeling in those of the laity who were not well indoctrinated seems to have inclined them rather to that form of Monarchianism which saw in Christ nothing but God, and overlooked and suppressed the human element, than towards the other."[1] In respect to Christology, the emanationism of the second class was further from the truth, than was the monarchianism of the first class. But in respect to Trinitarianism, the Patripassians admitted no interior and immanent distinctions in the Godhead. Their Supreme Deity was a monad,—a unit, without any inward and personal subsistences. This unit was only *expanded* or *metamorphosed*.[2] A trinality in

---

[1] NEANDER: Church History, I. 577.

[2] ATHANASIUS (Contra Arianos, IV. 14, 22), describes the Monarchian theory in the following phraseology: ἡ μονὰς πλατυνθεῖσα γέγονε τριάς· ἐπλατύνθη ἡ μονὰς εἰς τριάδα. Again (Cont. A. IV. 6) he describes the Sabellian trinitarian process as a "dilatation

the Divine Nature itself was denied. The Nominal Trinitarians, on the other hand, approached nearer to the truth, so far as concerns the doctrine of a Trinity in the Unity. They admitted three distinctions of *some* sort. But they diverged again from the common faith of the church, in holding that these were only modal distinctions. The Logos and the Holy Spirit possessed no essential being. The only *essence* was the monad,—the Father. The Logos and the Holy Spirit were merely *effluences, radiations, powers, energies* streaming out like rays from the substance of the sun, which might be and actually were retracted and re-absorbed in the Divine Essence. Tested rigorously, indeed, both classes held a common view. Both alike denied a trinity of *essence*, and affirmed only a monad without hypostatical distinctions, or persons in it. But having regard only to phraseology, it may be said, that Patripassianism approached nearest to orthodoxy upon the side of Christology; Nominal Trinitarianism nearest, upon the side of Trinitarianism.

§ 3. *Trinitarianism of the Apostolic, and Primitive Fathers.*

The foundation of the doctrine of the trinity in the Primitive Church was the baptismal formula, and the doxologies in the Epistles, together with

and contraction," an "expanding and collapsing" of the Divine Essence. See BAUR: Dreieinigkeitslehre, I. 257 sq.

the Logos-doctrine of the apostle John. The creed-statement of the dogma did not go beyond the phraseology of these. The catechumen upon his entrance into the Christian Church professed his faith in " God the Father almighty, and in his Son Jesus Christ, and in the Holy Ghost." This is the formula employed in the so-called Apostles' Creed, and is as definite a statement of the doctrine of the trinity as was made in any public document, previous to those Sabellian and Arian controversies which resulted in the more exhaustive and technical definitions of the Nicene Symbol.

The construction of the doctrine of the trinity started not so much from a consideration of the three Persons, as from a belief in the deity of one of them, namely the Son. This was the root of the most speculative dogma in the Christian system. The highly metaphysical doctrine of the trinity, as Guericke[1] remarks, "had its origin, primarily, in a *living belief;* namely, in the practical faith and feeling of the primitive Christian that Christ is the co-equal Son of God." For if there is any fact in history that is indisputable, it is that the Apostolic and Primitive Church *worshipped* Jesus Christ. This was the distinctive characteristic of the adherents of the new religion. Pliny's testimony is well known, that the Christians as a sect were accustomed to meet before day-break, and sing a responsive hymn (carmen dicere secum invicem) to

[1] Church History, § 56.

Christ, as to God (Christo quasi Deo).[1] The earliest liturgies are full of adoration towards the sacred Three, and particularly towards the second and middle Person. The liturgy of the Church of Alexandria, which in the opinion of Bunsen[2] was adopted about the year 200, and the ground plan of which dates back to the year 150, teaches the "People" to respond: "One alone is holy, the Father; One alone is holy, the Son; One alone is holy, the Spirit." The religious experience of the Primitive Church was marked by joy at the finished work of redemption; and this joy was accompanied with profound and thankful adoration towards its Author. If regard be had to the emotional utterances and invocations of the first generations of Christians, there is full as much evidence for the deity of the Son as of the Father. The religious feeling in all its varieties terminated full as much upon the second Person of the trinity, as upon the first, in that early period in the history of Christianity that was nearest to the living presence and teachings of its Founder. The incarnation of the Logos,—God becoming man,—is the great dogmatic idea of the first Christian centuries, and shapes the whole thinking and experience of the Church. This accounts for the absence of such technical terms as appear in the Nicene Symbol; and explains why it was, that

---

[1] PLINIUS: Ep. x. 96.
[2] BUNSEN: Analecta Ante-Nicaena, III. 23. Compare EUSEBIUS (Eccl. Hist. V. 28), for the proofs that the deity of Christ was constantly asserted from the beginning, and constantly claimed to be the apostolical doctrine.

the general, and purely Biblical language of the Apostles' Creed was sufficient for the wants of the Apostolic and Primitive Church. The actual and reverent worship of the believer was constantly going out towards the Son equally with the Father and the Spirit; and in this condition of things, metaphysical terms and distinctions were not required. The faith and feeling of the catholic heart were sufficient. Until pretended and spurious forms of trinitarianism arose, that compelled it, there was no necessity of employing in the creed for the catechumens, a rigorous and exact trinitarian nomenclature,—no use for the terms "essence" and "hypostasis," "generation" and "procession." Hence the Ante-Nicene Church contented itself with embodying its reverence and worship of the Eternal Three, in hymns and liturgical formularies, and with employing in its creed statements the general and untechnical language of the Scriptures.[1]

The *Apostolic Fathers* lived before the rise of the two principal Anti-Trinitarian theories described in a previous section, and hence attempted no spec-

[1] "It hath been the custom of the Church of Christ to end sometimes prayers, and sermons always, with words of glory (gloria Patri); wherein, as long as the blessed Trinity had honor, and *till Arianism had made it a matter of great sharpness, and subtlety of wit, to be a sound believing Christian*, men were not curious what syllables or particles of speech they used." HOOKER Eccl. Pol. V. xliii.—HOOKER adds, that Basil, because he sometimes employed the words "*with* the Son," and "*by* the Son, *in* the Spirit," felt compelled to allay the suspicions which he thereby had unintentionally awakened in some minds, by writing his tracts upon the Trinity.

ulative construction of the doctrine of the trinity. They merely repeat the Biblical phraseology, without endeavouring to collect and combine the data of revelation into a systematic form. They invariably speak of Christ as divine; and make no distinction in their modes of thought and expression, between the deity of the Son and that of the Father. These immediate pupils of the Apostles enter into no speculative investigation of the doctrine of the Logos, and content themselves with the simplest and most common expressions respecting the trinity. In these expressions, however, the germs of the future scientific statement may be discovered; and it is the remark of Meier, one of the fairest of those who have written the history of Trinitarianism, that the beginnings of an immanent trinity can be seen in the writings of the practical and totally unspeculative Apostolic Fathers.[1]

The following extracts from their writings are sufficient to indicate the freedom with which the Apostolic Fathers apply the term God ($\Theta\epsilon\acute{o}\varsigma$) to the second Person, who is most commonly conceived of as the God-man, and called Jesus Christ by them.

"Brethren," says *Clement of Rome* (Ep. II. c. 1), "we ought to conceive of ($\varphi\rho o\nu\epsilon\tilde{\iota}\nu \; \pi\epsilon\rho\grave{\iota}$) Jesus Christ as of God ($\acute{\omega}\varsigma \; \pi\epsilon\rho\grave{\iota} \; \vartheta\epsilon o\tilde{\upsilon}$), as of the judge of the living and the dead." *Ignatius* addresses, in his greeting, the church at Ephesus, as "united and elected by a true passion, according to the will of

[1] Meier: Geschichte der Trinitätslehre, pp. 47, 54.

the Father, and of Jesus Christ our God" ('Ἰησοῦ Χριστοῦ, τοῦ θεοῦ ἡμῶν). Writing to the church at Rome, he describes them, in his greeting, as "illuminated by the will of Him who willeth all things that are according to the love of Jesus Christ our God" (τοῦ θεοῦ ἡμῶν); and desires for them "abundant and uncontaminated salvation in Jesus Christ our God" (τῷ θεῷ ἡμῶν). He also urges them (c. 3), to mind invisible rather than earthly things, for "the things that are seen are temporal, but the things that are not seen are eternal. For even our God, Jesus Christ (ὁ γὰρ θεὸς ἡμῶν, Ἰησους Χριστὸς) being in the Father, [i. e. having ascended again to the Father] is more glorified" [in the invisible world than when upon earth]. He enjoins it upon the Trallian Church (c. 7), to "continue inseparable from God, even Jesus Christ" (θεοῦ Ἰησοῦ Χριστοῦ); and says to the Smyrnaean Church, (c. 1), "I glorify Jesus Christ, even God (Δοξάζω Ἰησοῦν Χριστὸν τὸν θεὸν), who has given you such wisdom."[1]

---

[1] MEIER, a recent critic, contends for the genuineness of the "longer recension" of the Ignatian Epistles, rather than the "shorter recension," because the latter he thinks contains the distinct *Nicene* statement of Christ's deity, while the former enunciates the doctrine of Christ's deity in the more general form of the Ante-Nicene trinitarianism. To which Hefele replies, in favor of the "shorter recension," "Verum acrior utriusque recensionis inspectio docet, *longiorem* quoque octies decies Christum *Deum* nominare, eam magis definite de persona Spiritus Sancti loqui, pleniorique formula Trinitatis esse usam; quo fit, ut merito posterioribus sit temporibus tribuenda," HEFELE: Patrum Apostolicorum Opera (Prolegomena, xlv.).

The following allusions to the trinity occur in the Apostolic Fathers. *Clement of Rome*, in his first epistle to the Corinthians (c. 46), asks: "Have we not one God, and one Christ? Is there not one Spirit of grace, who is poured out upon us, and one calling in Christ?" *Polycarp*, according to the Letter of the Smyrna Church (c. 14), closed his prayer at the stake with the glowing ascription: "For this, and for all things, I praise thee, I bless thee, I glorify thee, together with the eternal and heavenly Jesus, thy beloved Son; with whom to thee, and the Holy Ghost, be glory, both now, and to all succeeding ages. Amen." *Ignatius*, in his epistle to the Magnesians (c. 13), places the Son *first* in the enumeration of the three Persons in the trinity: "Study, that whatsoever ye do, ye may prosper both in body and spirit, in faith and charity, in the Son, and in the Father, and in the Holy Spirit,"—following in this particular St. Paul in 2 Cor. xiii. 13. *Barnabas* (Epist. c. 5) finds the trinity in the Old Testament. "For this cause, the Lord endured to suffer for our souls, although he was Lord of the whole earth, to whom he [the Father] said before the making of the world: 'Let us make man after our own image and likeness.'"[1]

---

[1] HEFELE: Patrum Apostolicorum Opera, in locis. The question of authenticity cannot be examined, of course, in such a work as this. The reader will find in the edition of Hefele a compact account of the course of criticism upon these earliest Christian writings, after the close of the Canon; and a defence of their genuineness that accords substantially with the results of the in-

Those of the *Primitive Fathers* who speculated at all upon the trinity confined their reflections mostly to the relations of the first and second Persons. Justin Martyr († 163), and Clement of Alexandria († about 220), whose literary activity falls between 150 and 250, represent the Greek trinitarianism of the second century; and Irenaeus († about 202), Hippolytus († 235), and Tertullian († about 220), represent the Latin trinitarianism of the same time. An examination of the writings of these Fathers will evince that they held the two fundamental positions of catholic trinitarianism: namely, *unity of essence* between the Father and Son, and *distinction of persons*.[1]

Justin Martyr affirms that the Person who spoke to Moses out of the burning bush was the Logos or Son, and not the Father. This Being, who then

---

vestigations of English and Continental scholars, in the 17th, 18th, and 19th centuries. That the Epistles of Ignatius have undergone no interpolations is far from the truth; but that they are spurious down to every paragraph and letter, is still farther. The learning of such scholars as Usher, Vossius, Pearson, Bull, Mosheim, Neander, Gieseler, Rothe, and Dorner,—all of whom affirm the genuineness of the "shorter recension" of the seven Ignatian Epistles mentioned by Eusebius, though some of them, as Mosheim and Neander, contend for considerable interpolation in them, much outweighs the learning of those who have affirmed the spuriousness. Even Baur, while disputing their genuineness, concedes to them a very early origin; regarding them as a "Pauline product of the second half of the 2d century." Compare GUERICKE: Church Hist., § 57; and SCHAFF: Church Hist., § 119.

[1] The text John x. 30 enunciates unity of essence with distinction of persons: ἐγὼ καὶ ὁ πατὴρ ἕν (not εἷς) ἐσμεν; I and my Father are one being (not one person).

and there styled himself the self-existent I AM, or The Eternal, he maintains became incarnate in Jesus Christ. In his First Apology to the emperor, he argues this position with great earnestness in the following manner. "'And the angel of God spake unto Moses in a flame of fire out of the midst of a bush, and said, I am that I am, the God of Abraham, the God of Isaac, and the God of Jacob, the God of your fathers, go down into Egypt and bring up my people from thence.' .... These words were spoken to demonstrate the Son of God and Apostle, to be our Jesus Christ, who is the very pre-existing Logos; who appeared sometimes in the form of fire, sometimes in the likeness of angels, and in these last days was made man by the will of God, for the salvation of mankind, and was contented to suffer what the devils could inflict upon him, by the infatuated Jews; who, notwithstanding that they have these express words in the writings of Moses: 'And the angel of the Lord spake with Moses in a flame of fire out of the bush, and said, I am that I am, the self-existent, the God of Abraham, the God of Isaac, and the God of Jacob;' notwithstanding this, I say, they affirm these words to be spoken by God the Father and Maker of all things. For which oversight the Prophetic Spirit thus charges them: 'Israel hath not known me, my people have not understood me;' and as I have said, Jesus taxed them again for the same thing, while He was amongst them: 'No man hath known the Father but the Son, nor the Son, but those to whom the Son will reveal Him.' The Jews, therefore, for maintaining that it was the Father of the universe who had the conference with Moses, when it was the very Son of God who had it, and who is styled both angel and apostle (Heb. iii. 1), are justly accused by the Prophetic Spirit, and Christ himself, for knowing neither the Father nor the Son; for they who affirm the Son to be the Father, are guilty of not knowing that the Father of the universe has a Son, who, being the Logos, and first-begotten of God, is God ($\varkappa\alpha\grave{\iota}\ \vartheta\varepsilon\grave{o}\varsigma\ \dot{\upsilon}\pi\alpha\varrho\chi\varepsilon\iota$). And He it is who heretofore appeared to Moses and the rest of the prophets, sometimes in fire, and sometimes in the form of angels; but now under your empire, as I mentioned, was born of a virgin, according to the will of his Father, to save such as believe in Him."[1]

Respecting the nature and dignity of the Logos, Justin remarks that "God in the beginning, before all creation ($\pi\varrho\grave{o}\ \pi\alpha\nu\tau\tilde{\omega}\nu\ \tau\tilde{\omega}\nu\ \varkappa\tau\iota\sigma\mu\acute{\alpha}\tau\omega\nu$), begat from himself a certain rational Power ($\gamma\varepsilon\gamma\acute{\varepsilon}\nu\nu\eta\varkappa\varepsilon\ \delta\acute{\upsilon}\nu\alpha\mu\iota\nu\ \tau\iota\nu\grave{\alpha}\ \dot{\varepsilon}\xi\ \dot{\varepsilon}\alpha\upsilon\tau o\tilde{\upsilon}\ \lambda o\gamma\iota\varkappa\grave{\eta}\nu$), who is called by the Holy Spirit, the Glory of the Lord, sometimes the Son, sometimes the Wisdom." "This rational Power," he says in another passage, "was generated from the Father by his energy and will, yet without

---

[1] JUSTIN MARTYR: Apologia I. 63 (Ed. Cong. St. Mauri. Par. 1742). See BURTON's Testimonies of Ante-Nicene Fathers, pp. 38, 39, for a list of the passages in the Early Fathers, in which this same view of Christ as the Jehovah of the Old Testament is taught.

any abscission or division of the essence of the Father."[1] In these passages Justin teaches the Nicene doctrine of eternal generation, as distinguished from creation. For in asserting that God the Father begat the Son from *Himself* (ἐξ ἑαυτοῦ), he teaches that the Son's constitutional being is identical with that of the Father. If the Father had created the Son *de nihilo*, the Son's substance or constitutional being would not have been ἐξ ἑαυτοῦ, but would have been an entirely new and secondary one. Such phraseology is never applied either by Justin Martyr, or any of the Fathers, to the act of pure creation. Justin's idea of eternal generation, like that of Athanasius, is the direct contrary to that of creation. That which is eternally generated cannot be a created thing, because it is ἐκ θεοῦ ἑαυτοῦ,—in and of His own substance. And that which is created *de nihilo*, at a certain punctum temporis, cannot be an eternal generation, because it is a new substance willed into being from absolute nonentity. The statement that the Logos was generated from the Father "by his will" is one that appears occasionally in the writings of some of the Post-Nicene trinitarians, and is capable of an explanation in harmony with the doctrine of the absolute deity of the second Person. For it is qualified by the explanation, that the generation occurs without " any abscission or division of the

[1] JUSTIN MARTYR: Dialogus cum Tryphone, 61, 128 (Ed. Cong. St. Mauri, Par. 1742).

essence of the Father." It must therefore be an immanent act in the Divine Essence; yet voluntary, in the sense of not being necessitated *ab extra*. The generation is by both nature and will, which in the Godhead are one.

Concerning the distinct personality of the Logos, Justin makes the following statement: "This rational Power is not, like the light of the sun, merely nominally different [from the Father], but really another numerically (οὐκ ὡς τὸ ἡλίου φῶς ὀνόματι μόνον ἀριθμεῖται, ἀλλὰ καὶ ἀριθμῷ ἕτερόν τι ἐστί).[1] In this passage, Justin teaches that the second Person does not merely sustain the relation to the Divine Essence that a sunbeam does to the sun. He is numerically distinct, ἕτερόν τι, a subsistence, and not a mere effluence or emanation. The pre-existence and eternity of the Logos are asserted by Justin in the following passages: "The Son of the Father, even he who is properly called his Son, the Word, was with him, and begotten of him before the creation (πρὸ τῶν ποιημάτων), because he in the beginning made and disposed all things." "This Being who was really begotten of the Father, and proceeded from him, existed before all creatures (πρὸ πάντων ποιημάτων) with the Father, and conversed with him."[2] Justin also repeatedly denominates the Logos, God. The passage

---

[1] JUSTIN MARTYR: Dialogus cum Tryphone, 128, 129 (Ed. Cong. St. Mauri, Par. 1742).

[2] JUSTIN MARTYR: Apologia, I. 31; Dialogus cum Tryphone, 129 (Ed. Cong. St. Mauri, Par. 1742).

in the First Apology (c. 63) has already been cited, in which he says that " the Logos is the First-Begotten of God, and he is God" (καὶ θεὸς ὑπαρχει). In the Dialogue with Trypho, Justin remarks concerning Joshua, that he distributed to the Israelites an inheritance which was not eternal, but only temporal, "forasmuch as he was not Christ who is God, nor the Son of God" (ἅτε οὐ Χριστὸς ὁ θεὸς ὤν, οὐδὲ υἱὸς θεοῦ).[1]

Justin's recognition of the trinity appears in the following extracts. Defending the Christians against the charge of atheism, he says : " We worship the creator of this universe. . . . . . . Again, we have learned that he who taught us these things, and who for this end was born (γεννηθέντα), even Jesus Christ, who was crucified under Pontius Pilate the procurator of Judea in the time of Tiberius Caesar, was the Son of him who is truly God; and we esteem him in the second place (χώρᾳ). And that we with reason honor the Prophetic Spirit in the third rank (τάξει), we shall hereafter shew."[2] Again he says, " We bless the creator of all, through his Son Jesus Christ, and through the Holy Ghost. . . . . . We confess, indeed, that we are unbelievers in such pretended gods, but not of the most true God, the Father of righteousness and temperance, and of all other virtues, in whom is no mixture of evil. . But we worship and adore Him, and his Son

[1] Dialogus cum Tryphone, 113 (Ed. Cong. St. Mauri, Par. 1742).   [2] Apologia I. 13 (Ed. Cong. St. Mauri, Par. 1742).

who came out from him, and has taught us respecting these things, and respecting the host of the other good angels who follow him, and are made like unto him; and [we worship and adore] the Prophetic Spirit; honoring them in reason and truth." Justin also represents baptism as administered in the church, "in the name of God the Father and Lord of all, and of our Saviour Jesus Christ, and of the Holy Spirit."[1]

Clement of Alexandria asserts unity of essence between the Father and the Logos in the most explicit manner. Speaking of the Father and the Son, he says: "The two are one, namely God." ($ἕν\ γὰρ\ ἄμφω,\ ὁ\ θεός$.) Speaking of the Son, he describes him as "the Divine Word who is most manifestly true God ($οντῶς\ θεός$), who is equalized ($ἐξισωθεὶς$) with the Lord of the universe, because he was his Son, and was the Word of God. . . . . . . There is one Unbegotten Being, even God, who rules over all ($παντοκράτωρ$); and there is one First-Begotten Being, by whom all things were made."[2]

The following extracts from Clement contain very plain statements of the trinality in the Godhead: "There is one Father of the universe; there is also one Word of the universe; and one Holy Spirit, who is everywhere." "Be propitious to thy

---

[1] Apologia I. 67, 6, 61 (Ed. Cong. St. Mauri, Par. 1742).
[2] CLEMENS ALEXANDRINUS: Paedagogus, III. 12; Cohortatio ad Gentes, p. 68; Stromata, Lib. VI. (Ed. Potter).

children, O Teacher, Father, Chariot of Israel, Son and Father both One, O Lord" (*υἱὲ καὶ πατήρ, ἓν ἄμφω, κύριε*). "Let us give thanks to the only Father and Son, Son and Father, our Teacher and Master, together with the Holy Spirit, one God through all things, in whom are all things, by whom alone are all things .... to whom be glory now and forever, Amen."[1]

These early Greek Trinitarians, as did the early Latin to some extent, made use of figures and analogies borrowed from external nature, and from the mind of man, to *illustrate*, but not to explain, the personal existence of the Logos, and his relation to the Father. They asserted that the Son was not created a new essence from nonentity, but was generated out of an eternal essence; and this generation they sought to render intelligible by a variety of images. The human logos, or word, they said, is uttered, is emitted from the human soul, without the soul's thereby losing anything from its essence. In like manner, the generation of the Son, or Logos as he was more commonly termed, left the Divine Nature unimpaired, and the same. The ray of light streams forth from the substance of the sun, without any waning or loss in the luminary itself. In like manner the Reason, or Wisdom, of God

---

[1] CLEMENS ALEXANDRINUS: Paedagogus, I. 6; Paedagogus, sub fine. For other extracts to the same effect from Clement, see BULL: Defensio Fidei Nicaenae, II. 6; WATERLAND: Second Defence, Query II.

manifests and mediates God's absolute essence, without any subtraction from it.

It is evident that these analogical illustrations were not adequate to a complete statement of the doctrine of the trinity. They would serve for only one part of the dogma: that viz. of the unity of essence. Such illustrations would suffice to show how the generation of the Son did not infringe upon the oneness of the Divine Nature; but they would convey an inadequate notion of the hypostasis, or personal distinction. The word uttered from the lips of a human being does not, indeed, diminish anything from his soul; but then this word has no distinct *subsistence* like his soul. The ray from the sun is not a luminous centre like the orb itself. These figures, consequently, would not afford a just and full analogon to the personal distinction; for this, though discriminated from the Divine Essence, is yet substantial enough to possess and wield all the attributes of the Essence. Yet, so long as the distinct and real personality of Father and Son was not called in question, such illustrations as these were naturally and safely employed to guard against the notion, that the generation of the second Person implied abscission or division of the one eternal Essence of the Godhead.[1] These figurative repre-

---

[1] Upon the use of these illustrations by the Early Trinitarians, WATERLAND (Second Defence, Query VIII.) makes the following remarks. "The comparisons of fountain and stream, root and branch, body and effluvia, light and light, fire and fire, and such like, served more peculiarly to signify the *consubstantiality;* but

sentations, moreover, prepared the way for the conceptional and technical statement of the doctrine of the trinity. They implied, and, so far as it could be done in this manner, they explained, that the Son is, in respect to *constitutional substance*, identical with the Father, and yet in a certain other respect, is different from the Father. And these two positions constitute the substance of the doctrine of the trinity. But as trinitarian science advanced, under the pressure from Patripassianism and Arianism, distinct metaphysical conceptions of "essence" and "hypostasis" were formed, and were expressed in a technical nomenclature and dialectical propositions; and under these circumstances, the figurative representations of Justin and Tertullian gave way to the analytic and carefully guarded clauses of the Nicene and Athanasian Creeds.

The trinitarian positions of *Tertullian* were called out by the Patripassian theory, and have reference chiefly to that heresy. As his opponents strongly asserted the doctrine of the unity of essence, and of the deity of Christ, there was no special necessity for him to discuss this side of the subject. Tertullian's main force is devoted to the

those of mind and thought, light and splendour (ἀπαύγασμα), were more peculiarly calculated to denote *co-eternity*, abstracting the notion of consubstantiality. For thought is not anything *substantial*. I know not whether splendour (ἀπαύγασμα) was ever taken to be so, by the ancient Fathers. It is certain that sometimes it was looked upon as a mere energy or quality (Justin Martyr, Eusebius, Damascene). I say then, that co-eternity was more fitly represented by those similitudes, than consubstantiality."

doctrine of the distinct personality of the Son and Spirit. In so doing, he makes a real contribution to the scientific construction of the trinitarian dogma. In affirming sameness of essence between Father and Son, the church had from the first denied that the Son is a creature. The Patripassian also affirmed this, but at the expense of the Son's distinct personality. Tertullian grasps both conceptions, and while maintaining that the Father and Son are one in one respect, contends that they are two in another respect. The positiveness with which Tertullian defends the doctrine of unity of essence between the Father and Son, together with that of a personal distinction between them, is apparent in the following extracts from his writings. Having employed the examples of a river which is never separated from its source, and of a ray which is never separated from the sun, in order to illustrate the doctrine of the unity of the Divine Nature, he then proceeds to argue for the distinction of Persons in the following manner. "Wherefore, in accordance with these examples, I assert that there are *two*, God and his Word, the Father and his Son. For the root and the trunk are two things, but conjoined; and the fountain and stream are two phenomenal appearances (species),[1] but undivided; and the sun and ray are two forms (formae), but

[1] The reader will observe how Tertullian labors to find terms in the rude Punic Latin, to express the trinitarian conceptions with which his mind was full. The terms taken singly, and by themselves, are inadequate, like any and every other term; but the

coherent. Everything that issues from another thing (prodit ex aliquo) is a second thing in relation to that from which it issues; but it is not for that reason *separate* from it. But where there is a second thing, there are two things; and where there is a third thing, there are three. For the third is the Spirit, from God and the Son; as the fruit from the trunk is third from the root, and the canal (rivus) from the stream is third from the fountain, and the scintillation (apex) from the ray is third from the sun. Nevertheless nothing becomes foreign to the source whence it derives its properties. In like manner the trinity (trinitas) flowing down (decurrens) from the Father, through continuous and connected gradations, interferes not with the Divine monarchy, and preserves the status of the Divine economy (monarchiae nihil obstrepit, et οἰκονομίας statum protegit) ...... I say that the Father is one, the Son is another, and the Spirit another. Nevertheless the Son is not another than the Father by diversity [of essence], but by distribution [of essence]; not another by division [of essence], but by distinction [of essence]; because the Father and Son are not one and the same [person], but one differs from the other in a certain special manner" (modulo).[1]

whole connection of thought evinces plainly, that like the Nicene trinitarians he is endeavoring to hold in one intuition, unity of essence with distinction of persons.

[1] TERTULLIANUS. Adversus Praxean, Cap. 8, 9, 13.—Tertullian's "distribution" [of essence] is the same as the Nicene "communication" of essence.

On the other side of the subject, namely the unity of essence, Tertullian is equally explicit. "They [the Monarchians, or Patripassians] assume that the number and disposition of the trinity is a division of the unity; whereas the unity deriving the trinity out of itself is not destroyed, but is administered by it (quando unitas, ex semet ipsa derivans trinitatem, non destruatur ab illa, sed administretur) . . . . I who derive the Son not from a foreign source (aliunde), but from the substance of the Father,—a Son who does nothing without the will of the Father, and has received all power from the Father,—how is it possible that I destroy the Divine monarchy? On the contrary, I preserve it in the Son, delivered to him from the Father. . . . . In this way, also, One is All, in that All are One; by unity of substance, that is. Whilst, nevertheless, the mystery of the economy (οἰκονομίας) is guarded, which distributes the unity into a trinity, placing in their order three [persons], the Father, the Son, and the Holy Ghost,—three, however, not in condition (statu), but in degree (gradu); not in substance, but in form; not in power, but in aspect; *yet of one substance, and of one condition* (status), *and of one power.*"[1]

Tertullian also anticipates an argument for the doctrine of the three Persons in the one Nature, which we shall find employed by Athanasius,[2] and

[1] TERTULLIANUS: Adversus Praxean, Cap. 3, 4, 2.
[2] ATHANASIUS: Nicaenae Fidei Defensio, Cap. iii.

others of the Nicene trinitarians. It is the argument that the eternity of the *first* person is conditioned by that of the second, and vice versa. If there be a time when there is no second Person, there is a time when there is no first Person. First and second are necessarily correlated to each other. Father and Son have no meaning except in coexistence and correlationship; and the same argument that disproves the eternity of the Son, disproves the eternity of the Father. "It is necessary," says Tertullian, "that God the Father should have God the Son, in order that he himself may be God the Father; and that God the Son should have God the Father, that he himself may be God the Son. Yet it is one thing to *have*, and another thing to *be*" (aliud est autem habere, aliud esse).[1]

Dorner, in summing up respecting Tertullian's trinitarianism, remarks that the fact that Tertullian distinctly teaches an *essential* trinity is very significant and important in the history of Trinitarianism, and exerted much influence upon the subsequent developement of the doctrine. "Seine Trinität fällt nicht in die Sphäre des Werdens, ohnehin nicht der γεννητά, sondern in die ewige Sphäre. Der Sohn ist ihm ewige Hypostase; Gott ist ihm statu, nicht erst gradu dreieinig."[2]

---

[1] TERTULLIANUS: Adversus Praxean, Cap. 10.

[2] DORNER : Person Christi, I. 641. Dorner, however, is mistaken in this last remark. Tertullian's language is, "tres autem, non statu, sed gradu, nec substantia, sed forma, nec potestate, sed specie, unius autem substantiae, et unius status, et unius potestatis, quia unus deus est." Adv. Praxean, Cap. 2.

Irenaeus, partly from his practical spirit, which inclined him to adopt traditional views, and partly from his abhorrence of Gnostic speculations, is disposed to accept the doctrine of the trinity as one of pure revelation. He affirms the eternal pre-existence of the Logos; regards him as the Jehovah of the Old Testament, agreeing in this with Tertullian,[1] and Justin Martyr; attributes deity to him as to his essence; and represents him as an object of worship. He also distinctly teaches the doctrine of three Persons in the Godhead. The following extracts from his great work, written in defence of the Christian system, in opposition to the heretical theories of his time, will exhibit the general character of Irenaeus's trinitarianism.

Irenaeus argues for the *eternal pre-existence* of the Son as follows: "Having shown that the Word who existed in the beginning with God, by whom all things were made, and who was always present to the human race, has in these last times become a patible man, ... the objection is excluded of those who say: 'If Christ was born at that time,

---

[1] IRENAEUS: Adversus Haereses, III. vi. 1 (Ed. Harvey). "In eversione Sodomitarum scriptura ait 'Et pluit Dominus super Sodomam et Gomorrham ignem et sulfur a Domino de coelo.' Filium enim hic significat, *qui et Abrahae collocutus sit*, a Patre accepisse potestatem judicandi Sodomitas propter iniquitatem eorum." TERTULLIAN: De Praescriptionibus, c. 13. "Id Verbum Filius ejus appellatum, in nomine Dei, *varie visum patriarchis, in prophetis semper auditum*, postremo delatum ex spiritu Patris Dei et virtute in virginem Mariam, etc." —See other extracts from the Primitive Fathers, to the same effect, in the Oxford Library of the Fathers, TERTULLIAN's Works, I. 447. (Note).

then before that time he did not exist.' For we have shown that because he always existed with the Father, he did not at that time begin to be the Son of God..... Wherefore, in the beginning, God formed Adam, not as though God needed man, but that he might have one upon whom he could bestow benefits. For not only before Adam, but before all creation (ante omnem conditionem), the *Word* was glorifying his Father, being immanent (manens) in Him; and He himself was glorified by the Father, as he himself says: 'Father, glorify thou me with the glory which I had with thee before the world was.' .... The Jews departed from God, because they did not receive his Word, but supposed that they could know the Father alone by himself, without his Word, that is his Son; not knowing God who spake in a visible form (figura) to Abraham, and again to Moses, saying: 'I have seen the affliction of my people in Egypt, and have come down to deliver them.'" After remarking that God does not need either men or angels as the medium by which to create, Irenaeus assigns as the reason, that He has as his medium, "his own offspring (progenies), and his own image (figuratio), viz: the Son and Holy Spirit, the Word and Wisdom; to whom all angels are servants and subject."[1]

The *trinality* in the Godhead is taught by

---

[1] IRENAEUS: Adversus Haereses (Ed. Harvey), III. xix. 1; IV. xxv. 1; IV. xiv.—Compare also Adv. Haer. IV. xxxiv. 7; II. xxxvii. 3; II. xlvii. 2; and Index, sub voce Logos.

Irenaeus, in the following statements. "But if we are not able to find solutions of everything that is required in the Scriptures, we ought not to seek another God than him who is God. For this is the highest impiety. But we should commit such things to God who made us, and gave us accurate knowledge because the Scriptures are perfect, since they were uttered (dictae) by the Word of God, and his Spirit..... In the name Christ [Anointed] is implied, He who anoints, He who is anointed, and the Unction with which the anointing is made. The Father anoints, but it is the Son who is anointed, in the Spirit, who is the unction; as the Word (Sermo) says by Isaiah, 'The Spirit of God is upon me, because he hath anointed me.'..... Man is a tempering together of the spirit and flesh, formed after the similitude of God, and shaped by his hands, that is by the Son, and Holy Spirit, to whom he also said: 'Let us make man.'..... There is one God the Father, in all and through all, and one Word, and one Son, and one Spirit, and one salvation to all who believe in Him."[1]

Irenaeus testifies to the *worship* of Christ by the church, and against the Papal doctrine of saint-worship, in the following passage, which is only one of multitudes in his writings. "The Church does nothing by angelic invocations or incantations,

---

[1] IRENAEUS: Adversus Haereses (Ed. Harvey), III. xli. 1; III. xix. 3; IV. xi. 5.—Compare also, Adv. Haer. IV. xxxiv. 1, 5, 6, 12; IV. xliii. 2; V. i. 2; and Index, sub voce Trinity.

... but directing its prayers purely and openly to the Lord who made all things, and invoking the name of the Lord Jesus Christ, performs miracles for the benefit of mankind, but not for their seduction" [as do the Gnostics].[1]

Tertullian and Irenaeus differ from Justin Martyr, in more frequently employing the term Son, in the discussion, and thereby introduce more of the personal element into the doctrine. Distinguishing, as they generally do, the second person in the Godhead by the name Son, rather than Logos, they prepared the way for that distinct enunciation of hypostatical or personal distinctions in the Divine Nature, which we find in the Polemic period.[2] For the terms Logos, Reason, and Wisdom, while they direct attention to the eternity and essentiality of the second distinction in the Godhead, are not so well adapted to bring out the conception of conscious personality, as the term Son. Hence we shall find one great difference between the trinitarian writings of Justin Martyr in the middle of the 2d century, and those of the Nicene period, to consist in the comparative disuse of the term Logos, and the more common use of the term Son, to designate the second hypostasis.

Hippolytus, the disciple of Irenaeus, also, explicitly teaches the doctrine of the trinity, and argues for the catholic doctrine of interior distinc-

---

[1] IRENAEUS: Adversus Haereses (Ed. Harvey), II. xlix. 3.   [2] DORNER: Person Christi, I. 600.

tions, in opposition to the modalism of Noëtus. Having affirmed that Christ is the Word by whom all things were made, and having quoted the beginning of John's gospel in proof of this, he proceeds to say that, "we behold the Word incarnate in Him; we understand the Father by him; we believe the Son; we worship the Holy Ghost."[1] He then encounters the argument of the Noëtians, who charged the orthodox with belief in two Gods, because they maintained that the Father is God, and the Son is God, and replies: "I will not say two Gods, but one God, and two Persons. For the Father is one; but there are two Persons, because there is also the Son, and the third Person is the Holy Ghost..... The Word of God, Christ, having risen from the dead, gave therefore this charge to his disciples, 'Go and teach all nations, baptizing them in the name of the Father, and of the Son, and of the Holy Ghost,' showing that whosoever omits one of these, does not fully glorify God. For through the trinity, the Father is glorified. The Father willed, the Son wrought, the Holy Spirit manifested. All the scriptures proclaim this." Hippolytus likewise affirms the deity of the Son, and carefully distinguishes between generation out of the Divine Essence, and creation from nothing. "The Word alone is God, of God himself. Wherefore he is God; being the substance of God. But the world is of nothing; wherefore it is not God.

[1] HIPPOLYTUS: In Noet. c. 12.

The world is liable to dissolution, also, when He who created it, so wills,"—ὁ Λόγος μόνος ἐξ αὐτοῦ· διὸ καὶ θεός, οὐσία ὑπάρχων θεοῦ. Ὁ δὲ κόσμος ἐξ οὐδενός· διὸ οὐ θεός.[1]

We close this survey of the trinitarianism of the principal Ante-Nicene Fathers, with the following particulars mentioned by Waterland, which cannot be invalidated, and which prove conclusively that they held the same trinitarianism with the Nicene and Post-Nicene divines.

1. The Ante-Nicene Fathers employed the word God in the strict sense of signifying the Divine *substance*, and applied it to the Son in this sense. 2. They admitted but one substance to be strictly Divine, and rejected with abhorrence the notion of inferior and secondary divinities. 3. They confined worship to the one true God, and yet worshipped the Son. 4. They attributed eternity, omnipotence, and uncreatedness to the Son, and held him to be the Creator and Preserver of the universe. 5. Had the Ante-Nicene Fathers held that the Son was different from the Father in respect to substance, eternity, omnipotence, uncreatedness, &c., they would certainly have specified this difference in the Sabellian controversy; for this would have proved beyond all dispute that the Son and Father are not one Person or Hypostasis. But they never did.[2]

[1] WORDSWORTH: Hippolytus, pp. 175, 176, 287.
[2] WATERLAND: First Defence, Query XXV.

§ 4. *Origen's Trinitarianism.*

The speculations of Origen mark an epoch in the history of the doctrine of the Trinity, and we shall, therefore, examine them by themselves.

Origen joined on where his cautious and practical predecessors Tertullian and Irenaeus had left off; but seeking to unfold the doctrine by a speculative method, in which the scriptural data did not receive sufficient examination and combination, he laid the foundation for some radical errors, which it required a whole century of discussion to distinctly detect, explicitly guard against, and condemn.

Origen seized upon the idea of Sonship, which had shaped the views of his predecessors, and which it must be acknowledged is a more frequent idea in the New Testament than the Logos-idea, with great energy. This idea led him to discuss the doctrine of the *eternal generation* of the second Person in the trinity, which was afterwards authoritatively taught by the Nicene Symbol, and which enters into that construction of the doctrine of the trinity in the most thorough manner.

So far as Origen's *general trinitarian position* is concerned, it is past all doubt that he was himself sincerely concerned for the orthodox statement of the doctrine of the trinity, as it had been made in the Apostles' Creed. He was the most intellectual and ablest opponent that the Monarchianism of his day had to contend with, and we have already noticed the fact, that by his logic and learning he brought off Beryl from his Patripassian position. At the same time he was always ready to attempt the difficult task of reconciling opposing views, and particularly of detecting and conceding the element of truth in the mass of heterodoxy, in order to conciliate the errorist, and carry him up to that higher orthodox position where the whole truth is to be seen without the mixture of foreign and contradictory opinions. Origen belonged to that enterprising and adventurous class of theologians, who attempt more than they accomplish, and more, perhaps, than the human mind is able to accomplish. In all his controversies,—and his whole life was a controversy,—he seems to have been actuated by a single steady theological endeavour,—the endeavour, namely, to exhibit the doctrinal system of the Church as the solvent, not only for all the problems that press upon the general human mind, but for all the doubts, difficulties, and errors of heresy itself. He strove with an energy of intellect, and a wealth of learning, that made him the greatest man of his century, to show the heretic that the scattered atoms of truth in his radically defective apprehension of Christianity were to be found in greater fulness, in the orthodox system, and, what was of still more importance, in juster proportions and more legitimate connections; and that only in the common faith of the *church*, was that all-comprehending and organic unity of system to be found, in which truth receives a developement in all legitimate directions, while no single constituent part is so magnified or distorted as to become, virtually, the sum-total.

That Origen did not succeed in this grand and noble endeavour, is evident from the fact that both parties claimed him as their authority.[1] Arius insisted that the doctrine of the eternal generation of the Son, which Origen urged so earnestly, when fully unfolded, involved the constituent doctrine of his own scheme,—namely, that the Son is finite and created. The opponents of Arius, on the other hand, affirmed that Origen intended, equally with the Nicene theologians who also maintained the doctrine of eternal generation, to distinguish between generation and creation in such a manner as to uphold the true and proper deity of the Son; and that even if he were not entirely successful, the will should be taken for the deed. Athanasius claims Origen, as teaching the same doctrine with

[1] "Athanasius, Gregory Nazianzen, Basil (though Basil thought Origen not altogether accurate respecting the Holy Ghost), claimed Origen as against the Arians. Jerome at first defended him, but afterwards attacks his writings as unsound; in which attack he was joined by Epiphanius, Theophilus, Anastasius of Rome. Gregory Nyssen and Chrysostom defend him. Augustine (Haereses, xliii.) appears doubtful, but leans to the severer side." See WATERLAND'S recital, in his Second Defence, Qu. xii. pp. 352–357.—The trinitarianism in Origen's work Contra Celsum, is better than that in his other works; and Bull maintains his orthodoxy chiefly by citations from it. It has been supposed that Origen's writings have been corrupted by interpolations, by latitudinarian hands.

that which he is himself maintaining.[1] But we shall find the difference to be a marked one, between the Athanasian and the Origenistic definition of "eternal generation;" and it is a difference of the utmost importance in the history of the doctrine of the trinity.

In order to form a just estimate of Origen's scheme, it is necessary to consider the point from which he started, and the position from which he viewed the whole subject. Inasmuch as Monarchianism, and the denial of the hypostases, was the form of error to which the catholic statement of the doctrine of the trinity was most exposed in the time of Origen, it was natural that his speculations should take form from his endeavour to refute, and guard against this. Monarchianism, or Patripassianism, affirmed the unity, and denied the trinality, in the divine essence. The hypostatical *distinctions* in the nature of the Godhead would consequently be the side of the subject that would be most considered, and urged by an opponent of Monarchianism. Origen's great endeavor, consequently, was to defend the real *personality* of both the Father and the

---

[1] De decretis synodi Nicaenae, Cap. vi. § 27. Athanasius, however, implies that Origen had said some things that appeared to conflict with the Nicene doctrine. For he remarks: "Let no one take as expressive of Origen's own sentiments what he has written as though inquiring, and exercising himself (ὡς ζητῶν καὶ γυμνάζων); but as expressive of parties who are disputing in the investigation. Only what he distinctly declares is to be regarded as the sentiment of the labour-loving (φιλοπόνος) man."

Son, the strict hypostatical character of each, against that confusion and mixture of subsistence which leaves for the mind, only a single essential Person in the Godhead. It was his aim to show, that the Son was as truly and distinctly a *hypostasis* as the Father, and that the personal pronouns could be applied as strictly and properly to one as to the other. In this particular, he made a positive advance upon the views of his teacher Clement of Alexandria, and upon the general views of this school, by more sharply distinguishing three hypostases,—an expression that had not previously been employed,[1]—and rejecting every identification of the Logos with the Father, as if he were only a power proceeding from him, and working in Christ, as the Holy Spirit does in the believer. In Clement, the hypostatical distinction, though asserted, is not so *definitely* and *energetically* asserted, but that the Logos, somewhat as in the trinitarian writings of Justin Martyr, runs some hazard of evaporating into the conception of the Universal Reason.[2] Origen is not satisfied with any vagueness upon this side of the doctrine of the trinity, and firmly announces that the Father and Son are two *real* hypostases, or personal subsistences.

[1] Origen very seldom denominates the three hypostases a triad. The Greek word τριάς is found only twice: Tom. in Joann. vi. 133; in Matt. xv. 698,—though the translation by Rufinus employs *trinitas* oftener than this.

[2] "Clement sometimes fails to distinguish carefully between the Son and Spirit, though reckoning them as two Persons in the trinity." MÜNSCHER-VON CÖLLN: Dogmengeschichte, I. 183.

But how is the unity of the Godhead to be maintained in consistence with this trinal distinction, was a question which must be answered. The attempt to answer it introduced a radical defect into the Origenistic construction of the doctrine of the trinity. In opposing the Monarchianism which fixed its eye too exclusively upon the unity of the Divine Essence, Origen, while doing a valuable work for Christian trinitarianism, in forming and fixing the doctrine of hypostatical distinctions, at the same time, by his inadequate statements, laid the foundation for the Arian heresy of a created Son of God.

Origen endeavoured to harmonize the doctrine of three Persons, with the doctrine of one Essence, by employing the idea of *eternal generation*, suggested by the term Son, which is so generally used in the New Testament to designate the second distinction in the trinity. In so doing, he took the same method with the Nicene theologians. But unlike the Nicenes, he so defined this phrase as to teach the subordination of the second to the first hypostasis, *in respect to essence.* He explained his view in the following manner. It is necessary, he said, to distinguish between $\vartheta εός$ and $ὁ \vartheta εός$. The Father alone is $ὁ \vartheta εός$; the Son is $\vartheta εός$. The Son is not God in the primary and absolute sense; and hence the apostle John omits the article (John i. 1), when he denominates the Logos God, but employs it when speaking of the absolute God, in the same verse.[1] The Son does not participate in the self-subsistent substance of the deity, and therefore it is not proper to denominate him consubstantial (ὁμοούσιος) with the Father. He is God only by virtue of the communication of a *secondary* grade or species of divinity, which may be termed θεός, but not ὁ θεός. The first Person in the trinity, alone, possesses the absolute and eternal essence of the Godhead. The eternal generation does not communicate this to the second Person. That which is derived by the Father to the Son, in the eternal generation, is of another essence than that of the Father,—ἕτερος κατ' οὐσίαν καὶ ὑποκείμενον ἐστίν ὁ υἱός τοῦ πατρός.[2] Accordingly, Origen sometimes denominates the Son θεός δεύτερος.[3] He will call the Son αὐτοσοφία, αὐτοαλήθεια, etc., but will not call him αὐτόθεος. God the Father of the Truth is greater than the Truth itself, and God the Father of Wisdom is greater than Wisdom itself.

A few extracts will exhibit Origen's mode of reasoning upon this distinction so fundamental in his scheme, and so fatal to the co-equality of the second Person. "*Αὐτόθεος* is God per se, God with the article. Wherefore the Saviour, in his prayer

---

[1] ORIGENES: In Joann. Tom. II. p. 271. Ed. Basil. "When the term God is employed in reference to the unbegotten (ingenitus) Author of all, he [John] uses the article, omitting it when the Word is denominated God."

[2] ORIGENES: De Oratione, 222.

[3] ORIGENES: Cont. Celsum, V. 608. For further citations upon this point, see REDEPENNING: Origenes, II. 304 sq.; BAUR: Dreieinigkeitslehre, I. 197 sq.; THOMASIUS: Origenes, 118 sq.; GUERICKE: De Schola Alexandrina, 201 sq.

to the Father, says: 'That they may know thee, the only true God.' But whatsoever is deified (deificatum) over and beside him who is denominated αὐτόθεος or God per se, by a participation and communion of that divinity, is not to be denominated God with the article, but more properly God without the article; which latter designation belongs to the First-Begotten of every creature, because inasmuch as he first attracted divinity to himself, he is more honourable than the other gods who exist besides himself; according as it is said: 'God the Lord of gods spake and called the earth.'"[1]

" Him [Jesus], we affirm to be the Son of God, of God, I say, whom (to employ the phrase of Celsus) we worship supremely (magnopere); and his Son we acknowledge as exalted (auctum) by the Father, by the greatest honours. Grant that there are some, as might be expected in so great a multitude of believers, who differing from the others, rashly affirm that the Saviour himself is God the Lord of the universe: we certainly do not do this, for we believe the Saviour himself when he says: 'My Father is greater than I.' Wherefore we do not subject him whom we denominate the Father, to the Son of God, as Celsus falsely alleges.... For we plainly teach that the Son of the Creator who formed this sensible world is not mightier than the Father, but inferior. This we affirm, on the authority of the Son himself, who says: 'The Father who sent me is

[1] ORIGENES: In Joannem, Tom. II. p. 272, Ed. Basil.

greater than I.' Nor is there any one of us so demented as to say, that the Son of Man is the Lord of God. Yet we ascribe divine authority (imperium) to him as the Word, Wisdom, Justice, and Truth of God, against all who are suspicious of him under this name, but not against God the omnipotent Father of all."[1]

At the same time, Origen denied that the Son is a creature. In his treatise against Celsus, he maintains that the second Person in the trinity is not to be numbered with the γενητά, or created existences, but "he is of a nature midway between that of the Uncreated, and that of all creatures,"— μεταξὺ τὴν τοῦ ἀγενήτου καὶ τῆς τῶν γενητῶν πάντων φύσεως.[2] As such he is higher than the whole series of creatures from the lowest to the highest. For Origen held to the existence of "a world of spirits, who, as they are allied to the absolute deity by nature, are also by their communion with him deified, and raised superior to the limitations of a finite existence. By virtue of this divine life, the more exalted of these spirits may be denominated in a certain sense *divine beings, gods*."[3] The difference

---

[1] ORIGENES: Cont. Celsum, Lib. VIII. pp. 793, 794. Ed. Basil. From these passages, it would seem that Celsus supposed the Christians to subordinate the Father to the Son. Origen in correcting this error, however, distinctly teaches the subordination of the Son to the Father. And that the subordination is not that of order and relationship merely, as the Nicenes themselves held, but of *essence*, is proved by his distinction between Θεός and ὁ Θεός.

[2] ORIGEN: Contra Celsum, III. 34, p. 469 (Ed. La Rue).

[3] NEANDER: Church History, I. 587. Neander also adds, that Or-

between the Son and the created universe lies in the fact, that the Son derives his (secondary) divinity *immediately* from the absolute deity (ὁ θεός), while the created universe, including the highest celestial spirits or "gods," derives its existence *mediately* through the Son, from the Father, who is the first ground and cause of all things.[1] The Logos is the creator of the universe, in Origen's theory, because, according to his citation of Christ's words, God the Father has given to God the Son, to have life *in himself*, and he who has life *in himself* is capable of creating.[2]

[1] This position was afterwards taken by the Arians. ATHANASIUS (Nic. Def. III. 7) represents them as explaining the application of the term Only-Begotten to the Son as follows: "We consider that the Son has this prerogative over others, and therefore is to be called Only-Begotten, because he alone was brought into existence by God alone, and all other things were created by God through the Son."

[2] BAUR (Dreieinigkeitslehre, I. 197 sq.) makes the following points in his summary of Origen's trinitarianism. 1. Origen starts with the fact of *difference* between Father and Son; in other words, igen argued for a certain necessity for polytheism, or the worship of these "gods," as one step in the religious education of man, ordained by God from the hypostatical character. 2. This difference is marked by the Apostle John, in the first verse of his Gospel, by the use of the article when the Unbegotten is meant, and its omission when the Begotten is signified. 3. This difference implies the subordination of the Son to the Father, as to essence; for though he calls the Son αὐτοσοφία, αὐτοαλήθεια, etc., he will not call him αὐτόθεος; he interprets Matt. xix. 16 to mean that only God in the absolute sense, and not God the Son, is "good;" and holds that the sphere in which the Son acts is second to that in which the Father acts, and that of the Holy Ghost is second to that of the Son,—the Father's sphere being all-comprehending, including those of the Son and the Spirit,—the Son's being comprehensive only of crea-

1. In this distinction between ὁ θεός and θεός, lies the first defect in Origen's construction of the doctrine of the trinity. Two species of divinity are sought to be maintained; two grades of divine existence are attempted to be established. That idea of deity, which is the simplest, as it is the most profound of all ideas, is made a complex notion, so as to include species under a genus. The distinction between the finite and infinite is annihilated; so that there is a variety of grades and a series of gradations of existence, in the sphere of the infinite and eternal, as there is in that of the finite and temporal. Instead of leaving the conception of Godhood in the pure and uncompounded form in which a true theism finds it and leaves it, Origen, in reality, though without intending it, brought over into the sphere of Christian speculation a polytheistic conception of the deity. Godhood, in his scheme, as in polytheism, is a thing of degrees. The Father possesses it in a higher grade than the Logos; and the nature of Logos again, is more exalted than that of the descending series of the heavenly hierarchies.[1] The gulf between the finite and infinite is filled up by an interminable series of intermediates; so that when this theogony is subjected to a rigorous logic and examination, it is

---

tion, and the Holy Spirit's agency being limited to the minds of the holy. 4. Origen reduces the triplicity to a unity, not by means of unity of essence, but of moral harmony of will.

[1] THOMASIUS: Origenes, pp. 120, 121.

found not to differ in kind from the pagan emanation-scheme itself.

2. The second defect in Origen's construction of the doctrine of trinity is the position, that the generation of the Son proceeds *from the will of the Father*. There is some dispute among writers whether Origen did actually adopt this view; but the great preponderance of opinion is in favour of the affirmative. Neander remarks that Origen "affirmed that we are not to conceive of a natural necessity in the case of the generation of the Son of God, but, precisely as in the case of the creation, we must conceive of an act flowing from the divine will; but he must have excluded here all *temporal* succession of the different momenta. From this view of the subject, Origen was also led to object emphatically to the notion of a generation of the Son out of the essence of the Father."[1] Neander takes the ground, that the doctrine of the unity of essence of the Son with the Father, was the distinctive peculiarity of the Western theology, and that the subordination-theory, which, he thinks, denied unity of essence and affirmed only similarity of essence,[2] was peculiar to the Eastern, and that

---

[1] NEANDER: Church History, I. 589.

[2] Origen's conception of "participation" is indicated in the following extract from De Principiis, IV. 381. "Every being who participates in any particular with him who is a participant in the same thing, is without doubt of one substance and one nature with him. Every mind which participates in intellectual light is, without doubt, of one nature with every other mind that

Origen's writings were the principal source of this view. Ritter thinks that Origen held to a generation by the will of the Father, but out of his essence. Baur is of opinion that Origen really wavered in his own mind, between the doctrine of a generation out of the divine essence, and a generation by the divine will,—an opinion which certainly has something to support it, in the apparently contradictory statements of this mind so desirous of reconciling opposing views, and of bringing all partial statements into the full comprehensiveness of an all-embracing theological system. Meier agrees with Neander in his judgment; while Dorner differs from all these authorities, and by a minute examination of Origen's positions, and an ingenious specification of subtle distinctions, endeavours to establish the position that Origen did not hold that the existence of the second hypostasis is dependent upon the will of the first. Yet after all his investigation, Dorner himself is compelled to acknowledge that Origen's scheme does in reality make the Father the Monad,—not merely one of the three hypostatical distinctions, but the Godhead itself in its original and absolute unity, in respect to which the second and third hypostases have only a relative existence. Comparing Origen's opinions with those of the later Semi-Arian party, who unquestionably

---

in like manner participates in intellectual light."—But this is plainly similarity, and not sameness of essence; ὁμοιούσιος, not ὁμοούσιος. Compare REDEPENNING: Origenes, II. 345.

drew their opinions in a great measure from Origen's writings, Dorner concedes, that as the Semi-Arians made the Father more than a single member of the trinity,—in their phraseology, ῥίζα πάσης θεότητος,—so Origen regards the Father alone the πηγὴ πάσης θεότητος, while the Son is πηγὴ θεότητος only for the world, or creation.[1]

[1] DORNER: Person Christi, I. 663. REDEPENNING (Origenes II. 302) also inclines to the position that Origen's trinitarianism agrees with that of the Church. After quoting the passage, οὗτος δέ ὁ υἱὸς ἐκ ϑελήματος τοῦ πατρὸς γεννηϑείς (Fragm. l. iv. De Princ. 5. p. 80), he adds: "Origenes behauptet nicht direct die Erzeugung des Sohnes aus dem Wesen des Väters, aber sucht doch hier, mehr, als eine Erzeugung durch einen einzelen Willensact desselben, ein Erschaffen. So schwankt er denn nicht, wie Baur, in der Geschichte der Lehre von der Dreieinigkeit, I. 204, es angiebt: er will nur jede Emanation beseitigen. Und wenn er sagt, der Wille des Väters genüge zur Hervorbringung des Sohnes (De Princip. I. 112), so ist ihm da der Wille,—in der That das concentrirteste Geistesleben,—eben Wesenheit Gottes selber."—But by "will," Origen here means a volition, and not the voluntary faculty itself. His statement in Rufinus's version is: "filius utique natus ex patre est, velut quaedam voluntas ejus ex mente procedens." (De Princip. I. 112). There is a passage in the De Principiis (I. ii. 4) that seems to teach the doctrine of consubstantiality: "Non per adoptionem spiritus filius fit *extrinsecus*, sed *natura* filius est." But this "nature" was not, in Origen's view, the absolute and primary nature of God. It was a secondary nature, indicated by the omission of the article. Yet it was a real nature, and not an effluence or emanation, and a highly exalted one; so that Christ was the Son of God by more than a mere "adoption" of an ordinary human nature. Origen, from his position, could energetically reject the low theory of adoption, and yet not accept the high theory of consubstantiality. BULL (Fid. Nic. Sec. III. cap. iii) attempts to prove that Origen was orthodox according to the Nicene standard. He relies chiefly upon the fact, that Origen clearly and often asserts the *eternity* of the Son. But this is not sufficient in Origen's case, because he also asserted the eternity of creation. Nothing but the assertion of *consubstantiality* would be sufficient to prove Ni-

But the decisive evidence that Origen did not clearly see, and firmly assert the doctrine of an immanent trinity, so far as the true and proper deity of the second hypostasis is concerned, is found in the fact of his opposition to the fundamental position that the Son is *of the same essence*, ὁμοούσιος, with the Father.[1] It is indeed true, that he opposed the doctrine of an identity of essence between the Father and the Son, primarily because he deemed it to be Sabellian, and incompatible with hypostatical distinctions in the Deity; but it was the duty of a scientific theologian, as it ever has been the problem of scientific theology, to rise above this erroneous supposition, and evince the logical consistency of three personal distinctions in one and the same essence. While, therefore, due weight is to be given to the motive that impelled Origen to oppose

cenism, and this is wanting.—Waterland (Second Defence, Qu. XVII.) also endeavours to explain the following passage from Origen in accordance with the Nicene trinitarianism: "All supplication and prayer, and intercession, and thanksgiving are to be sent up to the God over all, by the High Priest, who is above all angels, being the living Word, and God. And we may also offer supplications to the Word himself, and intercession, and thanksgiving, and prayer; *if we can understand the difference between prayer literally, and prayer figuratively*" (προσευχῆς κυριολέξεως καὶ κατα- χρήσεως). His explanation is, that prayer is most commonly addressed to the first Person, and that this is what Origen means by prayer "literally." Neander (I. 591) interprets a similar passage in Origen's treatise De Oratore (c. 15), in the opposite and obvious manner. Compare Thomasius: Origenes, p. 128.

[1] "It appeared to Origen something like a profanation of the first and supreme essence, to suppose an equality of essence, or a unity between him and any other being whatever, not excepting the Son of God. As the Son of God and the Holy Spirit are incom-

the catholic doctrine of the consubstantiality of the Son with the Father, his scientific merits must be judged of by the results at which he actually arrived, and the critical estimate which came to be put upon his views, as the developement of the revealed dogma proceeded.

Origen's views respecting the third Person in the trinity were still farther removed from the catholic type of doctrine. Those who would defend his orthodoxy in regard to the Son, hesitate to do so in regard to the Spirit. "Basil," remarks Waterland,[1] "thought Origen's notion of the Holy Ghost not altogether sound." Redepenning, who we have seen is inclined to maintain the orthodoxy of Origen in respect to the deity of the second Person, remarks that in Origen's scheme, "the Holy Ghost is the first in the series of creatures, but it is peculiar to him to possess goodness by nature;" and that "the Holy Ghost is a creature in the literal sense of the term, the first creature made by the Father through the Son,"—τάξει πάντων (lege πρῶτον) τῶν ὑπο τοῦ πατρὸς διὰ Χριστοῦ γεγενημένων (Tom. in Joann. II. 60).[2]

We close this sketch of Origen's trinitarianism, by summing up in the words of Meier. "The

parably exalted above all other existences, even in the highest ranks of the spiritual world, so high and yet higher is the Father exalted even above them." NEANDER: I. 590.

[1] WATERLAND: Second Defence, Query XII.
[2] REDEPENNING: Origenes, II. 317, 311. Compare also, GUERICKE: De Schola Alexandrina, p. 197 sq.

meaning and importance of Origenism, in the history of the doctrine of the trinity, does not lie in the intrinsic worth of the system, so much as in its connections, and relations, and general influence. If the system itself is followed out with rigour, it conducts to a deity who is involved in a constant process of developement,—a doctrine which is utterly incompatible with an immanent and eternal trinity in the Godhead. Its chief value consists in its connection with the antecedent trinitarianism of Tertullian and Irenaeus; first, by its frequent use of the term Son, as well as Logos, to denote the true personality of the second distinction, and, secondly, by its strenuous resistance of the Sabellian doctrine of only one Person, and its assertion of real hypostatical distinctions."[1]

[1] MEIER: Trinitätslehre, 109, 110.—The views of DIONYSIUS, bishop of Rome, 260, are of much value as indicating the condition of trinitarianism in the time of Origen, and the state of the question. Dionysius of Alexandria, in opposing Sabellianism, had made the distinction between the Father and Son so wide as to lead him to some statements that implied diversity in essence between them. Dionysius of Rome made a statement that combined unity of essence, with distinction of persons, in such a clear and satisfactory manner that Dionysius of Alexandria accepted it in the place of his own. A fragment of this letter of the Roman Dionysius has been preserved by Athanasius (De sententia Dionysii; and De decretis synodi Nic.), from which it appears that there were four hypotheses in existence at the time when he wrote; of which, three are rejected by Dionysius as heretical, and not received by the church. The *first* theory was the Sabellian, which made the Son the Father, and the Father the Son. The *second* was the theory of those who, in their opposition to Sabellianism, made τρεῖς ἀρχὰς, three Principles, and, consequently, τρεῖς ὑποστάσεις ξένας ἀλλήλων παντάπασι κεχωρισμένας, three in-

dependent separate Hypostases unallied to each other, and not united in one Substance or Nature. This is condemned as tritheism. A *third* opinion, which also arose in opposition to Sabellianism, made the Father alone the one God, and reduced the Son and Spirit to the condition of creatures. The *fourth* view is that which Dionysius holds, and defends, as the faith of the church, in the following phraseology: "Therefore it concerns us by all means, not to divide the venerable Divine Unity or Monad (μονάδα) into three deities (θεότητας), nor to diminish the preëminent majesty and greatness of our Lord by making him a creature; but to believe in God the Father Almighty, and in Christ Jesus his Son, and in the Holy Ghost; and that the Word is united (unified, ἡνῶσθαι) with the God over all: For he says, 'I and my Father are one;' and, 'I am in the Father and the Father in me.' So shall the Divine Trinity (ἡ θεία τριὰς), as also the sacred doctrine of the Unity (μοναρχία) be preserved." In another passage, preserved by Athanasius, Dionysius remarks that: "The Divine Word must of necessity be united (unified) with the God of the universe (ἡνῶσθαι γὰρ ἀνάγκη τῷ θεῷ τῶν ὅλων τον θεῖον λόγον); and it is necessary that the Holy Spirit abide and be immanent in God; and the Divine Trinity (τριάδα) be gathered together, and united into One, as into a certain Head (κορυφήν), viz: the God of the universe, the Almighty." See WATERLAND'S Second Defence, Query II.

CHAPTER III.

NICENE TRINITARIANISM.

§ 1. *Preliminary Statements.*

WE pass now to the examination of that more completely scientific statement of the doctrine of the trinity which was the consequence of the Arian controversy, and was fixed in a creed-form in the *Nicene Symbol.*

Origen, we have seen, rejected the doctrine of identity of essence between the Father and Son (ὁμοούσιον), and took the ground that the Son is of *another* essence, or nature, than the Father.[1] In

---

[1] De Oratione, c. 15: κατ' οὐσίαν καὶ καθ' ὑποκείμενόν, ἐστιν ὁ υἱὸς ἕτερος τοῦ πατρός.—In the Apologia Pamphili pro Origine (ORIGENIS Opera, I. 767, Ed. Bas. 1571), the term ὁμοούσιος is accepted, but illustrated by the "vapour" or "effluence" that radiates from any substance. The Son is ὁμοούσιος with the Father, "enim aporrhoea ὁμοούσιος videtur, id est unius substantiae cum illo corpore ex quo est vel aporrhoea vel vapor." Origen himself (De Princ. I. c. ii. Ed. Bas. 1571. I. 671) employs the same terms "vapor" and "aporrhoea" in illustrating the relation of the

his scheme, "eternal generation" is the communication of a *secondary* substance. The Son, consequently, does not participate in the Father's primary essence. The nature of the second Person is not identical or equal with that of the first. It is another nature, and inferior to that of the Father, the αὐτοθεός, though highly exalted above the nature of creatures. Upon this notion of a secondary essence, *Arius*, a man of less devout spirit and less profundity than Origen, seized, and, contending with logical truth that there can be no third species of essence midway between that of God and that of the creature, deduced the doctrine that the Son is not divine in *any* sense, but is strictly a creature, though the very highest and first of all.[1]

The opposition to Arianism began at Alexandria, from Arius's own bishop Alexander. This theologian contended for the true and proper deity of the Son, at the same time maintaining the doctrine of eternal Sonship, or generation. He agreed with Origen in respect to the latter point, but differed from him, by asserting that eternal generation is a communication, not of a secondary essence, but of the identical and primary substance of the Father,

---

Son to the Father. Such phraseology would place Origen in the class of Nominal Trinitarians, who made the Son an *effluence*, and not a hypostasis.

[1] Arius held that the Son of God was a κτίσμα ἐξ οὐκ ὄντων, and that ἦν ποτέ, ὅτε οὐκ ἦν. These were phrases that were in continual use during the whole controversy, as the exact contraries of the orthodox γέννεσις ἐκ τῆς οὐσίας.

and that, consequently, there must be a perfect equality between the first and second hypostatical distinctions. Furthermore, as Arius had advanced the doctrine, never advanced it should be observed by Origen, that the Son has only a *temporal* nature and existence, though running back indeed ages upon ages into the past eternity, Alexander insisted very fully upon the eternity of the Logos. The Son as Logos, he says, must be eternal, otherwise the Father must originally have been ἄλογος,—a being without reason. This is a form of argument which we find often employed in the controversy.

The views of Arius were condemned by the Synod of Alexandria in 321; but so many difficult questions were involved in the whole subject, that it was impossible for a provincial synod to answer them all, or still more to construct a creed that should secure the confidence of the universal Church, and be generally authoritative. This led to the summoning of an oecumenical council at Nice, in 325; composed of upwards of three hundred bishops.

§ 2. *Problem before the Nicene Council.*

The problem to be solved by the Nicene council was to exhibit the doctrine of the trinity in its *completeness;* to bring into the creed statement the *total* data of Scripture upon the side of both unity and trinity. Heresy had arisen, partly, from incomplete exegesis. Monarchianism, or Patripassianism, had seized only upon that class of texts which teach the unity of God, and neglected that other class which imply His *real* and not modal trinality. This led to an assertion of the consubstantiality of the Son, at the expense of his distinct personality. Origenism and Arianism, at the other extreme, following the same one-sided exegesis, had asserted the distinct personality of the Son, at the expense of his unity of essence, and equal deity with the Father. It now remained for the catholic scientific mind, to employ an all-comprehending exegesis of the Biblical data, and assert *both* consubstantiality and hypostatical distinction; *both* unity and trinity.

In doing this, the Nicene Council made use of conceptions and terms that had been employed by both of those forms of error, against which it was their object to guard. Sabellianism had employed the term $\dot{o}\mu oo\dot{v}\sigma\iota o\varsigma$, to denote the conception of consubstantiality. The Monarchians were strong in their assertion that God is one Essence or Being. On the side of the Divine Unity, they were scriptural and orthodox. The Nicene trinitarians recognized this fact, and hence adopted their term. Athanasius insisted as earnestly as ever Sabellius did, that there is but one *Essence* in the Godhead; that there is but one Divine *Substance*, or *Nature*, or *Being*. Hence the Nicene Council adopted that very term $\dot{o}\mu oo\dot{v}\sigma\iota o\varsigma$, which the orthodox mind one hundred years before, in the controversy with Paul of Samosata and the Anti-trinitarianism he represented, had rejected as a distinctively heretical term. The persistence with which Athanasius sought to establish the doctrine that the Son is of the *very same* substance with the Father, evinces the depth and subtlety of that remarkable mind, which exerted so great an influence upon the scientific construction of the Trinitarian creed of the church.[1] Two creeds, one by Eusebius of Nicomedia, and another by Eusebius of Caesarea, were introduced, which conceded everything except the single position that the Son is of the *very same* and *identical* substance with the Father. The position of Eusebius of Caesarea was, that the Son is of "*similar*" essence (ὁμοιούσιος) with the Father; he is "God of God, Light of Light, and begotten of God the Father before all worlds."[2] But the

---

[1] Upon the logical inconceivableness of a nature *midway between* the uncreated and the created, which was the vice of Origenism, see GUERICKE's Church History, pp. 318 and 324 (Notes). Athanasius argued, that because there is no middle essence, the Son must be God absolute; and the Eunomians, or extreme Arians, argued that because there is no middle essence, the Son must be man merely, and simply. AUGUSTINE (De Trinitate, I. vi.) also argues the same point with Athanasius, in the following terse style: "Unde liquido apparet ipsum factum non esse per quem facta sunt omnia. Et si factus non est, creatura non est: si autem creatura non est, ejusdem cum Patre substantiae est. *Omnis enim substantia quae Deus non est, creatura est; et quae creatura non est, Deus est.*"

[2] EUSEBIUS employs the following phraseology regarding the Son, in his Demonstratio Evangelica (IV. ii.): "This offspring, He [the Father] first produced from Himself, as a foundation of those things which should follow, the perfect *handi-work* (δημιούργημα) of the Perfect, and the wise *structure* (ἀρχιτεκτόνημα) of the Wise." This phraseology looks in the direction of the doctrine that the Son is a κτίσμα,—only of

essence of the human soul is "*like*" that of the Deity, and, consequently, there was nothing in the term ὁμοιούσιος that would imply that the essence of the Son differs in kind and grade from that of any finite spirit made after the likeness of Deity. The time had now come, when silence on the highly metaphysical but vitally fundamental point of the *substance* of the second Person in the trinity could not be allowed. It was now necessary to employ a technical term that *could not by any possibility* be explained or tortured into an Arian signification. The term ὁμοούσιος could not by any ingenuity be made to teach anything but that the essence of the Son is one and identical with that of the Father; and this placed him in the same grade of *uncreated* being with the Father, and made him αὐτοθεὸς.[1]

the highest order of creatures, fabricated as an instrument to the creation of the lower creatures. In his Demonstratio Evangelica (IV. i.), Eusebius denies that any being whatever is "from nothing." "God," he says, "proposed his own will and power, as a *sort of matter and substance* of the production and constitution of the universe, so that it is not reasonable to say that anything is 'out of nothing.' For what is from nothing cannot be at all. How, indeed, can nothing be to anything a cause of being? But all that is takes its being from One who only is, and was, and who also said, 'I am that I am.'"

Again, Eusebius (Eccl. Theol. I. ix), speaking of the Son, remarks: "He who was from nothing would not truly be Son of God, *as neither is any other of things generate.*"—This reasoning, to say the least, certainly does not tend to *discriminate* the substance of the Son from that of the creation, or to demonstrate that his essence is one and identical with that of the Father

[1] "Unable to resist the clear testimonies of the Scriptures, Arius confessed Christ to be God, and the Son of God; and, as though this were all that was necessary, he pretended to agree with the church at large. But at the same

The two Eusebiuses, and many of the Oriental bishops, were Origenistic in their views upon this part of the doctrine. With some of this party,

time he continued to maintain that Christ was created, and had a beginning like other creatures. To draw the versatile subtlety of this man from its concealment, the ancient Fathers proceeded further, and declared Christ to be the eternal Son of the Father, and *consubstantial* with the Father. Here impiety openly discovered itself, when the Arians began inveterately to hate and execrate the name ὁμοούσιος. But, if in the first instance, they had sincerely and cordially confessed Christ to be God, they would not have denied him to be consubstantial with the Father." CALVIN: Institutes, I. xiii. 4. "The Arians, those eminent masters of pretence and dissimulation, did not reject any one form of speech, which the Catholics had adopted and used, either out of Scripture or from tradition, with the sole exception of the word ὁμοούσιος; as being a word of which the precision and exactness precluded all attempt at equivocation. When they were asked, whether they acknowledged that the Son was begotten of the Father Himself? they used to assent, understanding, as is plain, the Son to be of God in such sense as all creatures are of God, that is, have the beginning of their existence from him. When the Catholics enquired of them, whether they confessed that the Son of God was God, they forthwith answered, 'Most certainly.' Nay more, they used of their own accord openly to declare that the Son of God is true God. But in what sense? Forsooth being *made* true God, He is true God; that is, He is true God who was truly *made* God. Lastly, when they were charged by the Catholics with asserting that the Son of God is a creature, they would repel the charge, not without some indignation, with the secret reservation of its being in this sense, that the Son of God is not *such* a creature as all other creatures are,—they being created by God *mediately* through the Son, not immediately as the Son himself. The word ὁμοούσιος, "of one substance," was the only expression which they could not in any way reconcile with their heresy." BULL: Def. Fid. Nic. II. i. 12, 13.

The Arians at Antioch (A. D. 349) altered the Gloria Patri, substituting prepositions for the conjunction; so that instead of glorifying the Father, *and* the Son, *and* the Spirit, they glorified the Father *by* the Son, *in* the Spirit. THEODORET: Eccl. Hist. II. xxiv.

which was considerably numerous, and, as it afterward appeared, able to re-open the subject, and involve the church in another controversy, the difficulty was a speculative one, certainly to some extent. They were afraid of Sabellianism,[1] and supposed that by affirming a unity and sameness of essence between the Father and the Son, they necessarily denied the distinction of persons between them. This portion, consisting of the more devout minds, who practically

---

[1] It is with reference to this class of Semi-Arians, who finally passed over to Nicenism, that Athanasius (De Synodis, § 41) makes the remark: πρὸς δὲ τοὺς ἀποδεχομένους τὰ μὲν ἄλλα πάντα τῶν ἐν Νικαίᾳ γραφέντων, περὶ δὲ μόνον τὸ ὁμοούσιον ἀμφιβάλλοντας, χρὴ μὴ ὡς πρὸς ἐχθροὺς διακεῖσθαι· καὶ γὰρ καὶ ἡμεῖς οὐχ ὡς πρὸς Ἀρειομανίτας, οὐδ' ὡς μαχομένους πρὸς τοὺς πατέρας ἐνιστάμεθα, ἀλλ' ὡς ἀδελφοὶ πρὸς ἀδελφοὺς διαλεγόμεθα, τὴν αὐτὴν μὲν ἡμῖν διάνοιαν ἔχοντας, περὶ δὲ τό ὄνομα μόνον διστάζοντας. Athanasius does not seem to have put much confidence in the sincerity of Eusebius in subscribing the Nicene symbol, notwithstanding that he opposed the Arians so decidedly. In his Nicaenae fidei Defensio, Chap. II. § 3, he remarks: "And what is strange indeed, Eusebius of Caesarea in Palestine, who had denied the day before, but afterwards subscribed, sent to his church a letter, saying that this was the church's faith, and the tradition of the Fathers; and made a public profession that they were before in error, and were rashly contending against the truth. But though he was ashamed at that time to adopt these phrases, and excused himself to the church in his own way, yet he certainly means to imply all this in his letter, by his not denying the ὁμοούσιον, and the ἐκ τῆς οὐσίας. And in this way, he got into a difficulty; for while he was excusing himself, he went on to attack the Arians, as stating that 'the Son was not before his (temporal) generation.'" In § 4, Chap. II. of Nic. Def. (comp. also § 5), Athanasius says: "And supposing, even after subscription, the Eusebians did change again, and return like dogs to their vomit, do not the present gainsayers [the followers of Acacius, who had been a pupil of Eusebius] deserve still greater detestation?" Acacius's formula was ὅμοιος, simply.

held very exalted views of the Person of Christ, were the true representatives of Origen in this council. Others probably held low and latitudinarian views, and in reality desired that the council should dissolve without a distinct condemnation of Arianism. These mid-way statements were rejected by the council, and it was laid down as the scriptural doctrine to be universally received, that "the Son is begotten out of the essence of the Father, God of God, Light of Light, very God of very God (θεὸν ἀληθινὸν [ὁ θεὸς of Origen]), begotten not created (γεννηθέντα οὐ ποιηθέντα), *consubstantial with the Father* (ὁμοούσιον τῷ πατρί)."[1] This last important clause was added to the preceding statement that the Son is "God of God, *begotten* and not created," in order so to define the idea of eternal generation as to preclude the possibility of mistaking

---

[1] Πιστεύομεν ... εἰς ἕνα κύριον Ἰησοῦν Χριστὸν, τὸν υἱὸν τοῦ θεοῦ, γεννηθέντα ἐκ τοῦ πατρὸς μονογενῆ, τουτέστιν ἐκ τῆς οὐσίας τοῦ πατρὸς, θεὸν ἐκ θεοῦ, φῶς ἐκ φωτὸς, θεὸν ἀληθινὸν ἐκ θεοῦ ἀληθινοῦ, γεννηθέντα οὐ ποιηθέντα, ὁμοούσιον τῷ πατρί· ... Τοὺς δὲ λέγοντας ὅτι ἦν ποτὲ ὅτε οὐκ ἦν, καὶ πρὶν γεννηθῆναι οὐκ ἦν, καὶ ὅτι ἐξ οὐκ ὄντων ἐγένετο, ἢ ἐξ ἑτέρας ὑποστάσεως ἢ οὐσίας φάσκοντας εἶναι, ἢ κτιστὸν, τρεπτὸν ἢ ἀλλοιωτὸν τὸν υἱὸν τοῦ θεοῦ, ἀναθεματίζει ἡ καθολικὴ ἐκκλησία.—Three particulars are noteworthy in this statement. 1. The son is denominated θεὸν ἀληθινόν (equivalent to Origen's ὁ θεὸς), to preclude the notion of a secondary divinity. 2. Those are anathematized who assert that the Son did not exist *before* his generation; because this implies that his generation is in time, and that "there was a *when*, when he was not." 3. The term ὑπόστασις is employed as synonymous with οὐσία.—showing that at this time these two technical terms were not yet, as they afterwards were, strictly appropriated, the one to the personal distinction, and the other to the one Nature. This led to some misapprehension, particularly in the Oriental Church.

it, either for the creation of a substance confessedly temporal and finite, or the communication of a secondary substance midway between the finite and infinite. This clause contained the metaphysical kernel of the dogma, and was the crucial test of trinitarian orthodoxy and heterodoxy.

§ 3. *Nicene doctrine of Eternal Generation.*

The Nicene Symbol, while adopting from Monarchianism a conception and a term that had been vehemently opposed by Origen, at the same time adopted with Origen the idea of eternal generation. This idea, suggested by the Biblical terms "Son," "Only Begotten," and "First Begotten," all of which the Nicene theologians maintained to be literal and not metaphorical terms, and descriptive of the eternal and metaphysical relations of the second Person, they technically distinguished from that of creation, by the clause: "*begotten* not *created.*" In conducting the discussion of the doctrine of the trinity upon the side of the personal distinctions, it was necessary for the Nicene theologians to correct two errors that were current among their opponents. In the first place, the Essence of the Godhead was confounded with a personal distinction in that Essence. For those who were involved in this confusion of ideas, the "generation" of a Person would be the same as the generation of the Essence; and the "procession" of a Person would be the same as the procession of the Essence. And this would result in the destruction of the Divine Unity, and the multiplication of deities. The second error consisted in supposing that generation is the same as creation from nothing. For those who took this view, the "generation" of a Person would be the same as the origination of a creature; and since the definition of the term "procession" was inevitably determined by that of "generation," the "procession" of a Person would also be the same as making a creature *de nihilo*. And this would result in the degradation of the Son and Spirit to the rank of creatures. The Nicene trinitarians directed the best energies of their vigorous and metaphysical intellects to a correction of these two errors. They carefully discriminate the Divine Essence from a Divine Person. They are not the same. They are two distinct conceptions; to one of which unity relates, and to the other triunality. This being so, unity of Essence could be combined with the generation of a Person, or with the procession of a Person, without any self-contradiction. Athanasius and his co-adjutors did not pretend to explain either the eternal generation, or the eternal procession. They supposed that in these ineffable and immanent activities in the Godhead lies the heart of the trinitarian mystery. At the same time, however, they laid down certain positions for the purpose of precluding the *false inferences* which the Arians were drawing from the doctrine of eternal generation;

and these positions give some clue to the idea itself, as it lay in the Nicene mind.[1]

The Nicene theologians distinguish eternal generation from creation, by the following particulars: 1. Eternal generation is an offspring out of the eternal essence of God; creation is an origination of a new essence from nothing. 2. Eternal generation is the communication of an eternal essence; creation is the origination of a temporal essence. 3. That which is eternally generated is of one essence with the generator; but that which is created is of another essence from that of the creator. The substance of God the Son is one and identical with that of God the Father; but the substance of a creature is diverse from that of the creator. The Father and Son are one Nature, and one Being; God and the world are two Natures, and two Beings. 4. Eternal generation is necessary, but creation is optional. The filiation of the second Person in the trinity is grounded in the nature of deity; but the origination of the world depends entirely upon arbitrary will. It is as necessary that there should be Father and Son in the Godhead, as that the Godhead should be eternal, or self-existent; but there is no such necessity for creation.[2] 5. Eternal generation is an immanent perpetual activity in an

[1] Respecting generation and creation, compare WATERLAND'S First Defence, Queries XIII–XV.
[2] "I think it demonstrable, that one Infinite can never be from another by voluntary production, that it cannot by necessary emanation, I think not so." HOWE: I. 155 (New York Ed.). "The being of God is a kind of law to his

ever-existing essence; creation is an instantaneous act, and supposes no elements of the creature in existence.[1]

By these characteristics the eternal generation of the Son was differentiated from creation *de nihilo*, and raised entirely above the sphere of material and created existence. The idea of *time* is excluded, for it is an activity immanent and perpetual in the Divine Essence, and is therefore as strictly eternal as any activity of the Godhead. The idea of *contingency* is excluded, because the generation of the Son does not depend upon the optional will of either the first or the third Persons, but is a necessary act underlying a necessary relationship. Eternal gen-

---

working; for that perfection which God is, giveth perfection to that he doth. Those natural, necessary, and internal operations of God, the *generation* of the Son, the *proceeding* of the Spirit, are without the compass of my present intent; which is to touch only such operations as have their beginning and being by a voluntary purpose, wherewith God hath eternally decreed when and how they should be." HOOKER: Ecclesiastical Polity, Book I. ch. ii.

[1] At this point, we may also specify the difference between the Nicene "eternal generation," and the Oriental "emanation." 1. That which is eternally generated is infinite, and not finite; it is a divine and eternal Person, who is not the world, or any portion of it. In the Oriental schemes, emanation is a mode of accounting for the origin of the Finite. But in the Nicene trinitarianism, eternal generation still leaves the Finite to be originated. The begetting of the Son is the generation of an Infinite Person, who afterwards creates the finite universe *de nihilo*. 2. Eternal generation has for its result a *subsistence*, or personal hypostasis, totally distinct from the world; but emanation, in relation to the deity, yields only an impersonal, or at most a personified, *energy* or *effluence*, which is one of the powers or principles of nature,— a mere *anima mundi*.

eration, therefore, according to the Nicene theologians, is the *communication of the one eternal essence of deity* by the first Person to the second Person, in a manner ineffable, mysterious, and abstracted from all earthly and human peculiarities. And the peculiarity in the manner in which the communication takes place, in the instance of the second Person, constitutes "filiation;" and in the instance of the third Person constitutes "procession."[1]

In the Nicene trinitarianism, the terms Father

---

[1] PEARSON, who thoroughly understood the Nicene trinitarianism, and has stated it with great accuracy and acumen, remarks (Apostles' Creed, Art. II.) that, "the communication of the divine essence by the Father was the true and proper generation by which he hath begotten the Son." This communication of essence, however, he proceeds to say, is free from the imperfections and limitations of the finite. In human generation, though the son is begotten in the same nature with the father, yet the father necessarily precedes the son in time; but the Divine generation is not in time, and there is no temporal precedence. Human generation is corporeal, and by decission of substance; but Divine generation is incorporeal and by a total and plenary communication of the entire essence.

Pearson answers the objection, that if generation is the communication of essence, then the Holy Spirit is generated, and is consequently a Son, equally with the Son, by reference to the difference in the mode in which Eve and Seth were respectively produced from Adam. "Eve was produced out of Adam, and in the same nature with him, and yet was not born of him, nor was she truly the daughter of Adam; whereas Seth proceeding from the same person in the similitude of the same nature, was truly and properly the son of Adam. And this difference was not in the nature produced, but in the *manner of production*. . . . The Holy Ghost proceedeth from the Father in the same nature with him, the Word proceedeth from the same Person in the same similitude of nature also; but the Word proceeding is the Son, the Holy Ghost is not, because the first procession is by the way of generation, the other is not."

and Son are held as correlates; so that one has no meaning except in reference to the other, and the one hypostasis has no existence without the other. The Father is not, as in Origen's scheme, a Monad existing anterior in the order of nature to the Son, but is simply one member of the trinity. Though his relation to the Son implies an inequality in respect to the order and relative position of the hypostases, it implies no inequality in respect to their constituent substance or nature. The characteristic of Sonship is second to that of Paternity; but so far as concerns the *essence* of Father and Son, both alike, and in precisely the same degree, participate in the eternal and uncreated substance of the Godhead. An entire and perfect co-equality in respect to the constitutional being of both is affirmed. The Son does not belong to a grade of being inferior to that of the Father, for the Origenistic distinction of ϑεός and ὁ ϑεός is not allowed, but he is of the very same identical species: "*very* God of very God." But when we dismiss the conception of constituent essence, and take up that of *hypostatical character*, and *mutual relationship*, Athanasius and the Nicene trinitarians contend that subordination may be affirmed, without infringing upon the absolute deity of the Son. The filial *peculiarity* and *relation* is second and subordinate to the paternal, though the filial *essentiality* is equal and identical with the paternal.[1] As in the human sphere, father and son

[1] "When we speak simply of the Son, without reference to the

belong to the same grade of being, and so far as their constitutional *nature* is concerned, neither is superior to the other, both being alike and equally *human* beings, yet the latter is second in dignity to the former, so far as personal attitude and relationship are concerned; so in the sphere of the divine and uncreated, God the Father and God the Son are on the same common level of eternal and necessary existence, both alike being of one and the same essence or substance, while yet the latter stands second in the order, and relationships, of the three personal distinctions.[1]

In endeavouring to establish the consistency of the doctrine of eternal generation with the doctrine of the true deity of the Son, Athanasius relies much

---

Father, we truly and properly assert him to be self-existent, and therefore call him the sole first cause; but when we distinctly treat of the *relation* between him and the Father, we justly represent him as originating from the Father." CALVIN: Institutes, I. xiii. 19.

[1] "Your new reply to this query is that the word *God* when applied to the Father, denotes Him who alone has all perfections in and of Himself, *original, underived*, &c., but when applied to the Son, it denotes one who has not his perfections of Himself, but derived, and so the word *God* is used in different senses, *supreme* and *subordinate*. You might as well say that the word *man*, when applied to Adam denotes the person of Adam who was *unbegotten ;* but when applied to Seth it denotes the person of Seth who was *begotten ;* and therefore the word man does not signify the same thing, or carry the same idea in both cases, but is used in different senses. What I assert is, that the word God signifies or denotes *absolute perfection*, whether applied to Father or Son; and is therefore applied in the same sense to both. He that is possessed of *all perfection* (whether *originally* or *derivatively* [i. e., whether unbegotten or begotten]) is God." WATERLAND: Second Defence, Query III.

upon the phrases, ἐκ τῆς οὐσίας, and ὁμοοσύοις, as explanatory of the difference between generation and creation. "Let it be repeated," he says, "that a created thing is external to the nature of the being who creates; but a generation is the proper offspring of the nature.[1] The Son, not being a creation from nothing, but proper to the Father's substance, always is. For since the Father always is, whatever is proper to His substance must always be; and this is his Word and his Wisdom. And that creatures should not be in existence, does not disparage the Creator,—for He has the power of framing them out of nothing when he wills,—but for the Son not to be ever with the Father is a disparagement of the perfection of his substance."[2] In such statements as these, which, in these Discourses against the Arians, are repeated and enforced in a great variety of ways, and with great earnestness, Athanasius argues that as it is the very definition of the eternal Son to be *connatural* with the eternal Father, so is it the very definition of a creature to be from nothing, ἐξ οὐκ ὄντων; and that while it was not necessary from the *very nature of the Godhead*, that there should be eternally a Creator, and eternally a creation, it was necessary, from the very

---

[1] "It were madness to say, that a house is co-essential or consubstantial with the builder, or a ship with the shipwright; but it is proper to say, that every son is co-essential or consubstantial with his father." ATHANASIUS: Ep. ad Serapion.

[2] ATHANASIUS: Contra Arianos, I. viii.

nature of the Godhead, that there should be eternally a Father, and eternally a Son.

Hence the Nicene theologians harmonized the doctrine of eternal generation with that of unity of essence, by teaching the *necessity* of this generation. The Arians insisted that the generation of the Son must be dependent upon the arbitrary choice of the Father,—that it was optional with the first Person in the Godhead, whether the second Person should be, or not be. To this Athanasius replies, that because the being of the Son is in and of the eternal *substance* of the Deity, it cannot be a contingent being. Whatever necessity of existence attaches to the substance of the Godhead, attaches equally to the hypostatical distinctions in it, because these distinctions are in and of this substance. When, therefore, the Arians asserted that the Son is a pure product of the Father's will, and was consequently a creature, the Nicene trinitarian affirmed that the generation of the Son was as independent of an arbitrary volition of the Father, as is the existence of any one of the divine attributes, or even the divine existence itself. Athanasius, in his third Discourse against the Arians, argues as follows: "When the Arians themselves say that God is good and merciful, does this attribute attach to Him by optional will, or by nature? if by optional will, we must infer that He began to be good, and that his not being good is possible: for to counsel and choose implies an inclination two ways. But if it be too extravagant to maintain that God is good and merciful by optional will, then what the Arians have said themselves [in regard to the Nicene doctrine of eternal generation] must be retorted upon them [in regard to the attribute of divine goodness and mercy]: 'Therefore by external necessity, and not voluntarily, God is good,' and: 'Who is it that imposes this necessity upon Him?' But if it be extravagant to speak of compulsory necessity in the case of God, and therefore it is by *nature* that He is good, much more is He Father of the Son by nature and not by optional will. Moreover let the Arians answer us this: The Father himself, does He *exist*, first having counselled, and then being pleased to come into being? For they must know that their objections reach even to the existence of the Father himself. If, then, they shall say that the Father exists from optional will, what then was He before he counselled and willed, or what gained He after such counselling and option? But if such a question be extravagant, and absurd, in reference to the Father, will it not also be against reason to have parallel thoughts concerning God the Word, and to make pretences of optional will and pleasure in respect to his generation? For, as it is enough only to hear God's name, for us to know and understand that He is that He is [i. e., that His existence is necessary], so, in like manner, it is enough only to hear the name of the Word, to know and understand that He who is God not by optional will, has His proper Word, not by optional will, but by nature." In another place, Athanasius employs the following phraseology to teach a necessity of existence in the Son, that is equal to that of the Father: " The Son is the Father's All ; and nothing was in the Father before the Word."[1]

[1] ATHANASIUS: Contra Arianos, III. xxx. 6. 12.—The Nicene trinitarians did not hold that the generation of the Son is *against* the will of the Father. It was only when their opponents separated the will from the nature of God, that they denied that generation is by will. If the will be regarded as one with the nature, they granted that the generation of the Son, like any immanent activity in the Godhead, is according to will, and is not compulsory. It is in this sense, that those passages in Justin Martyr (*ante*, p. 271), and the earlier trinitarians, are to be taken, which speak of the generation of the Son, ἀπὸ τοῦ πατρὸς δυνάμει, καὶ βουλῇ αὐτοῦ (Dial. cont. Tryph. 353. D.). Some of the Post-Nicene writers make the distinction of a concurrent and a fore-going will,—ϑέλησις συνδρόμος and ϑέλησις προηγουμένη (Cyril. Trin. ii p. 56, Par. Ed.),— and say that the generation is by the former, and not the latter. Cyril also remarks that, " the Father wills his own subsistence, ϑελητής ἐστι; and yet he is not what he is, by any volition antecedent to his existence, ἐκ βουλήσεως τινός." (Thes. p. 56.) Athanasius does not make this distinction between a concurrent and an antecedent will, but says that the Son is generated by nature, and "nature transcends will and necessity also;" and that, " concerning His proper Word, begotten from Him by nature, God did not counsel beforehand ; for in Him, the Father makes other things whatever he counsels." Cont. Arianos, III. 61. Augustine (Trin. xv. 20) speaks of the Son, as " voluntas de voluntate."

WATERLAND, in reference to the internal acts of generation and procession distinguishes between will, and arbitrary will, and says that Dr. Clark's distinction between will of approbation and will of choice, is the same thing. (2d Defence, Qu. VIII. p. 314).

" Upon this ground or principle, of God having an arbitrary contingent free will to all things, did some of the Arian party endeavor to overthrow the divinity of the Son or Word. Because God must needs beget him unwillingly, unless he begot him by an arbitrary contingent free will, which would make him have a precarious existence, and to be destroyable at pleasure, and con-

In this way, the Nicene symbol sought to guard the doctrine of eternal generation, against those conceptions of creation, and contingent existence, which, we have seen, were latent in the scheme of Origen, and were developed in the scheme of Arius. When the ideas of consubstantiality and immanent necessity are combined with the idea of eternal generation, they so regulate and control it, as to preclude a degradation of the second Person in the trinity, either to the level of a secondary divinity, or of a creature. If, instead of holding that the Father communicates a *secondary* essence to the Son, Origen had maintained that the second Person participates in the absolute essence of the Godhead, just as fully as the first Person does, it would have been impossible for Arius to have derived the doctrine of a created Son of God from his scheme. For the absolute divine essence is confessedly uncreated, and eternal; and any personal hypostasis that pos-

---

sequently to be a creature. But Athanasius and the other catholic fathers in opposition hereunto, maintain that God the Father begot a Son not by arbitrary free will, but by way of natural emanation, incorporeal, and yet not therefore unwillingly, nor yet without will neither, *but his will and nature here concurring and being the same;* it being both a natural will and a willing nature. So that the Son begotten thus from eternity, by the essential foecundity of the Father, and his overflowing perfection (which is no necessity imposed upon him, nor yet a blind and stupid nature, as that of fire burning or the sun shining), this divine *apaugasma*, or outshining splendour of God the Father, hath no precarious, but a necessary existence, and is undestroyable." CUDWORTH: On Free Will, pp. 50, 51. London, 1838. Compare BILLROTH: Religionsphilosophie, § 80.

sesses it as the constituent substance of his own being is by this very fact, real deity, and "*very* God." It was because they so perceived, and so thought, that the Nicene theologians retained in the catholic creed of the Church that doctrine of eternal generation which was so prominent in the defective scheme of Origen, and which in later times, in some individual instances, has been misunderstood, and construed after the Origenistic, as distinguished from the Athanasian manner.

With respect to the explanation of the term "generation," suggested by the Biblical word "Son," and employed to denote the relation existing between the second and the first hypostasis in the trinity, the Nicene theologians are not full in their statements, and did not pretend to be. A complete definition of the term would, in their judgment, involve an explanation of the mystery of the trinity. They held that an exhaustive comprehension of the mode in which the Person subsists in the Essence is possible only to the Infinite Mind. The Trinal Unity is self-contemplative, and self-comprehending. Only God can comprehend the Godhead. Athanasius, in his Epistle to the Monks, written about 358, thus expresses himself respecting the mysteriousness of the trinity. "The more I desired to write, and endeavoured to force myself to understand the divinity of the Word, so much the more did the knowledge thereof withdraw itself from me; and in proportion as I thought that I apprehended it, I found myself to fail of doing so. Moreover, I was unable to express in writing, even what I seemed to myself to understand; and that which I wrote was unequal to the imperfect shadow of the truth which existed in my conceptions. Considering, therefore, how it is written in the book of Ecclesiastes: 'I said, I will be wise, but it was far from me; that which is far off, and exceeding deep, who shall find it out?' and what is said in the Psalms: 'The knowledge of Thee is too wonderful for me; it is high, I cannot attain unto it,' I frequently designed to stop, and to cease writing: believe me, I did. But lest I should be found to disappoint you, or by my silence to lead into impiety those who have made inquiry of you, and are given to disputation, I constrained myself to write briefly, what I have now sent to your piety. For although a perfect apprehension of the truth is at present far removed from us, by reason of the infirmity of the flesh; yet it is possible, as the Preacher himself has said, to perceive the madness of the impious, and having found it, to say that it is 'more bitter than death' (Eccles. vii. 26). Wherefore, for this reason, as perceiving this, and able to find it out, I have written, knowing that to the faithful, *the detection of error is a sufficient information wherein truth consists.*" The Patristic statements, consequently, respecting the meaning of the term "generation" are generally negative. Says Cyril, "How the Father begat the Son, we profess not to tell; only we insist upon its *not* being in this manner, or that."[1] Says Augustine, "If asked to define the trinity, we can only say, it is *not* this or that."[2] Says John of Damascus, "All we can know about the divine nature is, that it is *not* to be known."[3]

Yet the Nicene trinitarians did make some approximations to a positive statement, of which the two following particulars embrace the substance.

1. In the first place, they held that the term "Son" is employed in Scripture, to denote the *deity* of the second Person. The Logos is eternally, really, and naturally the Son of God, and not metaphorically or adoptively. For the term "Father," they argued, denotes the eternal and real, and not the temporal and metaphorical character of the first Person,—a position conceded by their opponents. But the term "Son" is correlative to the term "Father," and hence must have the same literal force. If the godhood of the first hypostasis is not invalidated by his being truly and properly the Father, neither is the godhood of the second hypostasis vitiated by his being truly and properly the Son. Furthermore, the Scripture texts which are relied upon to establish the divinity of the first and second Persons in the Godhead employ the terms Father and Son, by which to designate them. But

[1] CYRILLUS HIEROSOL.: Catecheses, XI. ii.
[2] AUGUSTINUS: Ennar. in Ps. xxvi. 8.
[3] JOHANNES DAMASCENUS: Expositio Fidei, I. iv.—Compare upon the general subject of eternal generation, PEARSON: On the Creed, Article II. pp. 203 sq. (Ed. Dobson).

if these terms denote only temporal and finite relationships, it is impossible to harmonize the subject with the predicates,—to justify the attribution of omnipotence, omnipresence, and infinity to a Person whose very name signifies limitation and finiteness. "Unto the *Son*, He saith, thy throne O *God* is forever and ever" (Heb. i. 8). Here the second Person in the trinity is denominated "Son," and *as so denominated* is addressed as Deity. This could not have been, they argued, unless Sonship in the Godhead is eternal. To a merely temporal hypostasis, it could not have been said: "Thy throne O God is forever and ever." Again, baptism was to be administered in the name of the "Son;" but this would have been impious, had filiation in the Godhead denoted only a finite and created relationship. The candidate would, in this case, have been baptized into a name that designated nothing eternal or divine; and, furthermore, a merely finite and temporal hypostasis would thereby have been associated, in a solemn sacramental act, in the eternal trinity. In the controversy respecting the validity of heretical baptism, the Church came to the decision that baptism in the name of Christ is not valid. It must be administered according to the Scriptural formula, in the name of the Eternal Three. But if baptism in the name of the God-man, solely, is not justifiable; still less would it be proper to baptize in the name of the "Son," if that term denoted a merely temporal and transitory distinction and relationship.

Hence, the Nicene trinitarians regarded Paternity and Filiation as *immanent and necessary relationships* in the Godhead, and the ineffable divine archetypes of all that corresponds to these relationships in the sphere of created existence. Sonship, in its abstract and generic definition, is participation in a common nature or essence. The manner in which this participation is brought about in the Godhead is spiritual, and in accordance with the transcendence of the Deity; while in the sphere of the creature it is material, and mediated by sex.[1] But in both spheres alike, Sonship implies *sameness of nature.* The eternal Son is consubstantial with the eternal Father; and the human son is consubstantial with the human father. For this reason, the Nicene trinitarians represent Sonship in the Godhead as the absolute Sonship, of which all created and finite sonship is only a faint and imperfect pattern; even as the finite individuality is only a faint and imperfect pattern of the Divine personality, and as human justice, mercy, and love, are merely shadows of the absolute justice, mercy, and love of God. Athanasius interprets the text: "I bow my knees unto the Father of our Lord Jesus Christ, *of whom the whole family in heaven and earth is named*" (Eph. iii. 14, 15), as teaching that

---

[1] This, however, is not absolutely necessary even in the human sphere. Eve was made to participate in the substance of Adam without the instrumentality of sex. Our Lord partook of human nature fully and completely, yet not by ordinary generation.

God the Father of the Son is the only absolute Father, in the same manner that he is the only absolute Good, and that all created paternity is only a shadow of the divine and uncreated. "It belongs," he says, "to the Godhead alone, that the Father is Father absolutely and in the highest sense (*κυρίως*); and the Son is Son absolutely and in the highest sense (*κυρίως*); for in them, and in them only, does it hold, that the Father is *ever* Father, and the Son is *ever* Son."[1] The *eternity* of the Divine Fatherhood and the *eternity* of the Divine Sonship, constitutes an absoluteness and perfection in the relationship such as cannot be found in the sphere of the creature. Paternity and filiation belong to the deity of *necessity*. God is not God without them. But in the sphere of the creature, paternity and filiation are only temporal and contingent. There is no such relation in the angelic world, and man may not be a father and yet be human, as was Adam at the moment of his creation.

The following train of reasoning, employed by Athanasius in his "Defence of the Nicene Faith," throws light upon the doctrine of the natural and eternal Sonship of the second Person, as held and maintained against the Arians, who denied it. There

---

[1] ATHANASIUS: Contra Arianos, I. xxiii, xxi. JEROME remarks, "As He who alone is good (Luke xviii. 19) makes men good, and who alone is immortal (1 Tim. vi. 16) bestows immortality, and who alone is true (Rom. iii. 4) imparts the name of truth; so, too, the only Father, in that He is the creator of all, and the cause of substance to all, gives to the rest to be called Father."

are two senses, in which the Scripture employs the word son. The first is found in passages like Deuteronomy, xiii. 18, and John, i. 12: "When thou shalt hearken to the voice of the Lord thy God ... ye shall be *children* of the Lord your God." "As many as received him, to them gave he power to become the *sons* of God." The other sense is that in which Isaac is the son of Abraham. If, now, the Son of God is a son only in the first sense, as the Arians assert, then he does not differ in his nature and grade of being from any creature, and could not be denominated the *Only*-Begotten. To the Arian answer, that the Son is called the Only-Begotten because he was brought into existence by God alone, while all other things were created by God through the Son, Athanasius replies that this certainly could not be because God had exhausted himself in creating the Son, and needed rest, and so devolved the creation of all other things upon him. But perhaps it was because all other creatures could not endure to be produced by the unapproachable and transcendent deity,—a reason assigned first by Asterius, and afterwards adopted by Arius. But if created things cannot be created directly by the deity, and must come into existence through a middle Being, then the Son (since he is a creature) would need a mediator to his creation. And this medium would also require a medium, and so on ad infinitum; and thus there could be no creation at all. The Son of God, is, therefore, so called, in the sense in which Isaac was the son of Abraham,— by nature and participation in the same substance. "What is naturally begotten from any one, and does not accrue to him from without, that, in the nature of things, is a *son*." But the generation of the Eternal Son differs from a human generation, in the following particulars. The offspring of men are portions of their progenitors; since their bodies are not uncompounded, but transitive. But God is without parts, and is Father of the Son without partition or passion. Again, men lose substance in generation, and gain substance again from the accession of food; and thus become the parents of many children. But God, being without parts, neither loses nor gains substance; and thus he is the Father of one Only-Begotten Son. "Let every corporeal thought be banished upon this subject, and, transcending every imagination of sense, let us, with the pure understanding and mind alone, apprehend the Son's genuine relation towards the Father, and the Word's individuality (ἰδιότητα) in reference to God, and the unvarying likeness of the radiance to the light. For, as the words 'Offspring' and 'Son' bear, and are meant to bear, no human sense, but one suitable to God, in like manner when we hear the phrase, 'one in substance,' let us not fall upon human senses, and imagine partitions and divisions of the Godhead; but as having our thoughts directed to things immaterial, let us preserve undivided the oneness of nature, and the identity of light. For this is the individuality, or hypostatical character, of the Son in relation to the Father; and in this is shown that God is truly the Father of the Word. Here, again, the illustration of light and its radiance is in point. Who will presume to say that the radiance is unlike, and foreign to, the sun? Rather, who thus considering the radiance relatively to the sun, and the identity of the light both in the sun and the sunbeam, would not say with confidence: 'Truly the light and the radiance are one, and the radiance is in the sun, so that whoever sees this sees the sun also?' But what should such a oneness and personal peculiarity (ἰδιότης) be called but 'Offspring,' 'one in substance'? And what should we fittingly consider God's Offspring, but the Divine Word, and Wisdom?"[1]

Similar arguments and illustrations are also set forth by Athanasius, in his singularly logical and powerful "Orations against the Arians." "We must not understand," he says, "those words, 'I am in the Father, and the Father in me,' as if the Father and the Son were two distinct essences or natures, blended or inlaid into one another; as if they had that property which philosophers call penetration of parts: that is to say, as if they were a vessel, supposed to be capable of being doubly filled at once; as if the Father occupied the same

[1] ATHANASIUS: Defensio Fidei Nicaenae, III. vi, vii, viii, x, xi, xxiv.

quantity or region of space with the Son, and the Son the same as the Father. The Father's personality is infinitely perfect and complete; and the Son's personality is the plenitude of his Father's substance. The Son has not his Sonship derived or communicated to him by any sort of intervention, or mediation. No; it is of the Son's very nature, of the Father's substance, and immediate from the Father..... There is an entire propriety and community of nature between the Son and the Father, in like manner as there is between brightness and light, between the stream and the fountain; and, consequently, he that sees the Son, sees in him the Father, and cannot but know that the Son is in the substance of the Father, as having his subsistence (ὑπόστασις) communicated to him out of that substance (οὐσία); and, again, that the Father is in the Son, as communicating his substance to the Son, as the nature of the solar substance is in the rays, the intellectual faculty in the rational soul, and the very substance of the fountain in the waters of the river..... The Son cannot be otherwise than begotten of the Father, and consequently, cannot be the Father; yet as being *begotten* of the Father, he cannot but be God; and as being God, he cannot but be one in essence with the Father: and therefore he and the Father are One,—one in propriety and community of nature, and one in unity of Godhead. Thus brightness is light; the splendour or radiance of the sun is coeval with the body of the sun. It is of its very substance. It is not a secondary flame kindled or borrowed from it, but it is the very offspring and issue of the sun's body. The sunbeams cannot be separated from that great fund of light. No man in his senses can suppose them subsisting, after their communication with the planet is cut off. And yet the sun and the brightness that flows from it are not one and the same thing. They are at once united, and yet individual, in the substance of that total light and heat which cherishes the world, and paints the face of nature. And this is an imperfect emblem of the all-glorious divinity of the Son of God, which is essentially one with that of his Father. They are one numerical substance. They are one God, and there are no other Gods besides that one. And both being one in essence and divinity, it follows that whatever can be affirmed of the Father may as truly and properly be affirmed of the Son, *except only the relation of Paternity.* . . . . That the Son is co-eternal with the Father is evinced by the *very nature of the relation of sonship.* For no one is father of a son, nor can in a physical sense be called so, until he has a son. The relationship of artist or workman does not necessarily imply a co-existence of mechanical works or productions with their maker; and therefore it does not follow that God could not be a Creator, before the existence of his creatures. *But he could not be a Father before he had a Son of his very substance; and therefore his Paternity must have been co-eternal with his Godhood.*"[1] From such reasonings as these, it is evident that the Nicene trinitarians regarded "generation" and "procession" as necessary and immanent activities in the Eternal Essence, and held that the Godhead cannot be conceived of without them, any more than without the activities of reason and will. Cyril of Alexandria, in answer to the inquiry whether the Son existed *before* his generation, says: "The generation of the Son did not *precede* his existence, but he always existed, and that by generation."[2]

---

[1] ATHANASIUS: Contra Arianos, III. i, iii, iv, vi.

[2] CYRILLUS ALEXANDRINUS: Thesaurus, V. p. 35.—We here throw into a note, some of the historical statements of WATERLAND, and BULL, respecting the Nicene doctrine of eternal generation.—According to WATERLAND (Second Defence, Qu. VIII.), there was some querying after the Nicene Council among orthodox Fathers, whether the idea of generation could apply to the eternal and immanent relation of the Son to the Father. "Whether," says Waterland, "the Logos might be rightly said to be begotten in respect of the state which was antecedent to the προέλευσις was the point in question. Athanasius argued strenuously for it, upon this principle, that whatever is *of another*, and *referred* to that other, as his Head (as the Logos, considered as such, plainly was), may and ought to be styled Son, and Begotten. Besides, the Arians had objected that there would be two unbegotten Persons, if the Logos always existed, and yet not in the capacity of Son. These considerations, besides the testimonies of elder Fathers who had admitted eternal generation, weighed with the generality of the Catholics; and so eternal generation came to be the more prevailing language, and has prevailed ever since." Waterland remarks, that those of this class who doubted respecting the eternal generation did not doubt concerning the eternal existence of the second Person. The only orthodox Fathers, however, whom he cites as doubtful are Hilary, "though he seems to have changed his language and sentiments too, afterward," Zeno Veron. (apud Bull, p. 200), Phaebadius (Contra Arianos), and Ambrose.

2. In the second place, the Nicene trinitarians rigorously confined the ideas of "Sonship" and "generation" to the hypostatical character. It is

These Fathers, he thinks, would confine the term generation, to the *oeconomical* mission and manifestation of the Son in Creation and Redemption,—the προέλευσις spoken of in the extract from Waterland above.

WATERLAND (First Defence, Qu. VIII.) finds three generations, in all, spoken of in the patristic writings. The *first* and most proper filiation and generation is the Son's eternally existing in and of the Father; the Eternal Logos of the Eternal Mind. In respect to this, chiefly, he is the *Only-Begotten*, and a distinct Person from the Father. His other generations were rather condescensions, first to creatures in general, and next to men in particular. His *second* generation was his condescension, manifestation, coming forth (προέλευσις), as it were, from the Father (though never separated or divided from him), to create the worlds; and in this respect properly he may be thought to be πρωτότοκος πάσης κτίσεως, first born of every creature, or before all creatures [The preposition in composition here governing the genitive]. His *third* generation or filiation was when he condescended to be born of a virgin, and to become man.

BULL'S theses are as follows: 1. That decree of the Nicene Council, in which it is decided that the Son of God is Θεὸν ἐκ Θεοῦ, was approved by those catholic doctors who wrote previously to the synod, as well as by those who wrote after it. For they all with one breath taught, that the Divine nature and perfections belong to the Father and Son, not collaterally, or co-ordinately, but subordinately; that is to say, that the Son has the same Divine nature in common with the Father, but *communicated* by the Father; so that the Father alone has this Divine nature from himself, or from no other, but the Son has it from the Father; and hence the Father is the fountain, origin, and principle (principium) of the divinity which is in the Son. 2. The catholic doctors, both before and after the Nicene council, unanimously affirm that God the Father is greater than God the Son even in regard to divinity; that is to say, not in respect to nature, or any essential perfection that is in the Father and not in the Son, but in respect to dignity only, or origin,—since the Son is from the Father, and not the Father from the Son. [Bull means, as is evident from his reasoning throughout his work, that the *Person* of God the Father is greater than the *Person* of God the Son. Fatherhood is primal,

not the essence of Deity that is generated, but a *distinction* in that essence. And, in like manner, the term "procession," applied to the Holy Spirit, pertains exclusively to the third hypostasis, and has no application to the substance of the Godhead.

The term "begotten," in the Nicene trinitarianism, is descriptive only of *that which is peculiar to the second Person, and confined to him.* The Son is generated with respect only to his Sonship, or, so to speak, his individuality (ἰδιότης), but is not generated with respect to his essence or nature. The term "generation," being thus rigorously confined to the *hypostatical character*, as distinguished from the unity and community of essence, denotes only a *relationship* between the first and second Persons.[1] It, consequently, no more implies

and Sonship secondary, ex vi terminorum. The *personal peculiarity* of the human father is superior to the *personal peculiarity* of the human son, though one is as truly human as the other.] 3. The ancient fathers regarded the doctrine of the subordination of the Son to the Father, as to his origin and principle, to be very useful and necessary; because, in this mode, the divinity of the Son can be affirmed, and yet the unity of God, and the Divine monarchy, be kept intact. For though there are two, viz., the Father and the Son, to whom the Divine name and nature are common, yet inasmuch as the former is the principle (principium) of the latter, from whom he is propagated (and that, too, by an interior and not exterior production), it is evident that God can properly be denominated one and only. And the same reasoning, these fathers believed to apply equally to the divinity of the Holy Spirit.

[1] "The truth is, the word *God* denotes all perfection, and the word *Father* denotes a *relation* of order, and a particular *manner of existing.*" WATERLAND: Second Defence, Query II.—The hypostatical character is *incommunicable* to the other Persons. The Father cannot possess the filial characteristic of the Son; the pa-

a subordination with respect to the *essence* of the second Person, than it does with respect to the essence of the first. For if the Son is the generated, the Father is the generator.[1] The idea of "genera-

ternal relation cannot belong to the Son; and neither paternity nor filiation can attach to the Holy Spirit. "The Persons of the trinity," says Hooker (Eccles. Polity, V. lvi.), "are not three particular substances to whom one general nature is common, but three that subsist by *one* substance, which itself is particular: yet they all three have it, and their *several ways of having it* are that which maketh their personal distinction." The Father possesses the Divine Essence by paternity, the Son by filiation, the Spirit by procession. The doctrine of the trinity is not that of one Nature *and* three Persons, but of one Nature *in* three Persons.

[1] Hence the Father was often denominated God Unbegotten, and the Son God Begotten. The term ἀγενητος, though etymologically a good one to apply to the first Person, in the sense of "ingenerate," was, however, not so applied by the catholic Fathers, because it was first applied to him by the Arian party in the sense of "*uncreated*." Athanasius himself accepts it in this sense, and consequently argues that the Son is not γενητός; because γενητός would mean "cre-

ated," if ἀγενητος means "uncreated." The Vatican manuscript, edited by Mai, reads μονογενής ϴεὸς in John i. 18,—a proof that this manuscript is of very early date; certainly before the Eutychian controversy, which rendered the orthodox shy of a phraseology that was quite current in the earlier ages. In the Apostolical Constitutions, III. 17, we find the following: πατὴρ, ὁ ἐπὶ πάντων ϴεὸς · Χριστὸς ὁ μονογενὴς ϴεὸς, ὁ ἀγαπητὸς υἱός, etc. The Peshito version renders the verse John i. 18, "the only God," showing that ϴεὸς was in the Greek manuscript from which this very early Syriac translation was made, and that μονογενής was imperfectly translated, or else that another word stood in its place. In the early trinitarian literature, the terms "Unbegotten" and "Begotten" merely denote a peculiar *modus existendi* in one and the same Eternal Essence. In the first Person, the divine Nature exists as "ingenerate;" in the second as "generate." The phrase "the Unbegotten God" expresses no more than the phrase 'God the Father;" and the phrase "the Begotten God" no more than "God the Son."

tion," consequently, has an application to the first Person as much as to the second; and if there is nothing in the fact of being a Father that infringes upon the essential deity of the first Person in the trinity, then there is nothing in the fact of being a Son, that infringes upon the essential deity of the second Person. Hence Athanasius represents filiation in the Son as the necessary and eternal antithesis to paternity in the Father, and argues that the passivity, or the being a Son, on the part of the second hypostasis, no more infringes upon his participation in the essence of the Godhead, than the activity, or the being a Father, on the part of the first hypostasis, infringes upon his participation in the same essence of the Deity. The Father and Son are of one and the same uncreated and infinite essence, even as the human father and son are of one and the same created and finite essence. The participation in the same identical nature or essence, or, in the Nicene phrase, the consubstantiality ($\dot{o}\mu oo\acute{v}\sigma\iota o\nu$), places the first and second persons in the Godhead in the same class or grade of being. Both are equally divine, because they share equally in the *substance* of deity; as, in the sphere of the finite, both father and son are equally human, because participating equally in the *substance* of humanity. The category of substance determines the grade of being. That which is of a divine substance is divine; and that which is of a human substance is human. And the mere relationship in each case,

—the mere being a father, and the mere being a son,—does not in the least affect the grade or *species* of being to which each belongs. The human son is as truly a *man* as is the human father; and the Divine Son is as truly God as is the Divine Father. " We men," says Athanasius, "consisting of a body and a soul, are all μίας φύσεως καὶ οὐσίας, of one nature or essence; but we are many persons." Again, when his Anomoean opponent compares the Father, Son, and Spirit, to a bishop, presbyter, and deacon, Athanasius directs his attention to the fact that these latter have all the same nature, being each of them man.[1]

In this way, the term "generation" was employed to discriminate the hypostatical character from the essential nature, in the triune Godhead, and in all use of the term, or criticism upon it, it should carefully be remembered that it is limited, in the Nicene trinitarianism, to the personal subsistence, and has no legitimate application to the eternal essence.[2] The trinity is not generated. The essence or substance of deity is not generated. The

[1] Howe: View of the late Considerations, &c.—It should be added to this illustration of Athanasius, that the *whole* Nature or Essence is in the divine Person; but the human person is only a *part* of the common human nature. Generation in the Godhead admits no abscission or division of substance; but generation in the instance of the creature implies separation or division of essence. A human person is an individualized *portion* of humanity.

[2] Ambrose preached a sermon upon the Incarnation before the emperor Gratian. The emperor " proposed to him an objection, upon which the Arians greatly depended; namely, that the Son being begotten could not be of the same nature with the Father who is unbegotten. He therefore

first and third hypostases are not generated. But the second hypostasis is generated, and is *alone*. The same, *mutatis mutandis*, is true of the term "procession." And with reference to the first hypostasis or Person, the agency on his part denoted by the term "beget," the correlate to "only-begotten," is *hypostatical* agency solely. It sustains no relation to the trinity as a whole. For God the Father does not generate the trinity. He is not the Father of the triune Godhead, or of the Divine Essence. Neither is he the Father of the third Person. He is only the Father of the Son.[1] So that the term "generate," or "beget,"—which is the necessary antithesis to the term "only-begotten," so often applied in the Scriptures to the second Per-

---

added the answer to this objection, which chiefly consists in showing that the distinction between *begotten* and *unbegotten* relates not to their nature, but to their personality." FLEURY: Eccl. Hist. B. xviii.

[1] "Non .... trinitatem natam de virgine Maria, et sub Pontio Pilato crucifixam et sepultam, tertio die resurrexisse, et coelum ascendisse, sed tantummodo Filium. Nec ..... trinitatem descendisse in specie columbae super Jesum baptizatum." AUGUSTINUS: De Trinitate, I. iv.—"The divine nature of the Son is no more begotten than the divine nature of the Father and of the Holy Ghost; the reason is, because it is the same divine nature which is common to, and possessed by all three. Hence it would follow, that if the divine nature of the Son was begotten, so would the divine nature of the Father and of the Holy Ghost be likewise. The divine essence neither begets nor is begotten. It is a divine *person* in the essence that begets, and a divine person is that essence that is begotten. Essence does not beget essence, but person begets person; otherwise there would be more than one essence; whereas, though there are more persons than one, yet there is no more than one essence." GILL: Doctrine of the Trinity, ch. vii.

son,—merely denotes the individuality of the first Person, or that which is peculiar to him, and confined to him, as the first in the series of three. Thus, from first to last, in the Nicene construction of the doctrine of the trinity, the terms "beget," "begotten," and "proceed," are confined to the hypostatical distinctions, and have no legitimate, or technical meaning when applied to the trinity as a whole, or, in other words, to the Essence in distinction from the hypostasis.[1]

[1] We condense the following statement of the relations of the Person to the Essence from TWESTEN's Dogmatik (§ 42). The entire section is a fine specimen of analysis. "Since God is pure act and life (actus purissimus); since by virtue of his absolute self-subsistence, and spontaneity, nothing dead, nothing given independent of his own act, nothing externally necessary, is in Him, those relations whereby the Divine Persons are distinguished from each other must rest upon the Divine *activity*,—viz: upon the two absolutely *immanent actions*, generation, and procession. These actions are 'opera ad intra,' because they have nothing but God himself for an Object; and are 'actus personales,' since, not the Divine Essence, in so far as it is common to the three Persons, but only in so far as it subsists in each of the hypostatical determinations (Bestimmungen), must be considered as their subject or principle. Hence, it follows that these 'actus personales' are not to be considered as the common action of all three Persons, but as the activities of definite individual Persons,—e. g.: of the Father, or Son, or both united, as in the procession of the Spirit.

But if the Father is unbegotten, does it not follow that He alone is the absolute Being of Beings? No, for there is no inequality of *Essence;* since this is in all three Persons equally and alike. The inequality can only refer to *subsistence;* and moreover, not to the notion of *necessity* of subsistence, but to the notion of *order* of subsistence, by virtue of which the Father is first, the Son second, and the Spirit is third. The inequality does not relate to *time*, for the three are equally eternal; nor to *nature*, for this is the same in all the Persons, since the Essence is identical in all; but to the *relations* of Paternity and Filiation, Mission

346   HISTORY OF THEOLOGY.

Perhaps the relationship of the Person to the Essence, in the Nicene scheme, has not been expressed more succinctly than by Hooker, in a sentence which condenses the whole reasoning of the Nicene controversy. "The substance of God, with this property, to be of none, doth make the person of the Father; the very self-same substance, with this property, to be of the Father, maketh the person of the Son; the same substance, having added to it the property of proceeding from the other two, maketh the person of the Holy Ghost. So that in every person, there is implied both the substance of God, which is one, and also that *property* which causeth the same person really and truly to differ from the other two. . . . Each person hath his own subsistence (ὑπόστασις) which no other person hath, although there be others besides that are of the same substance (οὐσία). As no man but Peter can be the person which Peter is, yet Paul hath the self-same nature which Peter hath. Again, angels have

and Procession, upon which relations the distinction of Persons rests. In this sense, the Athanasian symbol can assert, that, 'in trinitate nihil prius aut posterius (scil. tempore), nihil majus aut minus (scil. natura), sed tota tres personas coaeternas sibi et coequales (scil. propter ὁμοουσιότητα καὶ ταυτότητα τῆς οὐσίας),' and yet concede an inequality, if by it is meant that the Father is constituted the ground or principle of the subsistence of the Essence in the Son, and that the personality of the Spirit is grounded in the Father and Son.

But does it not follow from this that the Father alone is *absolute*? No, for absoluteness is an indispensable mark of the Divine *Essence*, and this belongs equally and necessarily to all. There is but one Essence, subsisting under a threefold τρόπος ὑπάρξεως."

every one of them the nature of pure and invisible spirits, but every angel is not that angel which appeared in a dream to Joseph."[1]

The nearest approximation to a *metaphysical* definition of the ideas of eternal generation, and procession, by the Nicene theologians, is found in the idea of "intercommunion," and "inter-agency." A common word employed by them, as a suggestive rather than exhaustive term, is περιχώρησις (circulatio[2]).

[1] HOOKER: Eccl. Pol. V. li. The term "property" in this extract must be taken in its etymological signification. Hooker means to denote by it, the individual peculiarity (ἰδιώτης), and not that the hypostasis is the *attribute* of the Essence. The following extract from ALCUIN (Quaestiones De Trinitate, in Augustini Opera, VIII. 473, Ed. Migne), throws light upon the distinction between the Person and the Nature. "If we may say that there are three persons, Father, Son, and Spirit, why may we not say there are three Gods, three Omnipotents, three Eternals, and three Infinites? Because the terms God, Omnipotent, Eternal, and Infinite, are names relating to the substance (substantialia nomina); hence they cannot be employed in the plural number, but only in the singular. Every term that denotes the substance or essence of God must always be used in the singular number. But the terms Father, Son, and Spirit are relative names, and therefore are rightly called three persons. What is meant by a relative name? Relative names refer one thing to another thing; as 'master' refers to 'slave,' and 'slave' to 'master;' 'father' refers to 'son' and 'son' to 'father.' When I speak of a 'father,' I imply a 'son;' for there cannot be a father unless there be a son in relation to whom he is a father."—Alcuin notices the following difference between the first and second persons as related to each other, and the third person as related to the first and second : "We may say, 'Father of the Son,' and 'Son of the Father.' We may say, 'Spirit of the Father,' but not 'Father of the Spirit,'—for this would imply two Fathers. We may say, 'Spirit of the Son,' but not 'Son of the Spirit,'—for this would imply two Sons."

[2] SHERLOCK (Vindication of the Trinity) translates it by *circumincession*. CUDWORTH (Intel. Syst. I. 737, Andover Ed.) employs the

Starting from the Scriptural idea and term of the "*living*" God, the trinitarian thinker endeavored to convey to the mind of the Arian the truth, that the one Essence is all in each of the Persons, so that the three Persons constitute but one Essence or Being, by representing this threefoldness as an immanent circulation (περιχώρησις) in the Divine Nature,—an unceasing and eternal *movement* in the Godhead, whereby each Person co-inheres in the others, and the others in each,—so that the Essence is equally the substance of all, while yet each Person preserves and maintains his own distinctive hypostatical character. The Father begets, but is not begotten. The Son begets not, but is begotten. The Spirit neither begets nor is begotten, but proceeds. Such is the phraseology employed to hint at, rather than explain, the mystery of the eternal interaction, and intercommunion, which was conceived to be going on in a Being whom the Nicene theologian was fond of contemplating under the idea of a living Unity, rather than under the notion of a lifeless Unit.[1] He

term. "These three hypostases, or persons, are truly and really one God. Not only because they have all essentially one and the same will (according to Origen, Cont. Cels. lib. viii. p. 386) . . . . but also because they are physically (if we may so speak) one also; and have a mutual περιχώ-ρησις, and ἐνύπαρξις, inbeing and permeation of one another,—according to that of our Saviour Christ: 'I am in the Father, and the Father in me; and the Father that dwelleth in me, he doeth the works.'" For a full discussion of the conception, see ATHANASIUS's third Discourse against the Arians.

[1] The distinction between a unit and a unity is real and valid. The former denotes mere singleness, and more properly pertains to an impersonal thing, than to a personal being. Self-consciousness supposes interior distinctions

employed this term περιχώρησις, to intimate that the Arian notion of *singleness* does not come up to the Scriptural idea of the Divine fullness and infinitude of being. God, he claimed, is a plural Unit. He is not "one" in the same sense in which an individual of a species in material nature is "one." The Deity is not a member of a species, and the term "individual" is inapplicable to him. And yet the Arian objections to the doctrine of the triunity of God proceeded upon the assumption that strict individuality, or singleness, is attributable to the Godhead, and consequently that the same modes of reasoning that apply to the finite, with its species, and individuals, apply equally to the Infinite. It was to correct this erroneous and shallow conception of that Eternal One who belongs to no species, but whose infinite plenitude of being sets him above finite modes of existence, that the Nicene theologians, when they were tempted as they sometimes were by the arithmetical rather than philosophical

in the self-conscious essence. There is a plenitude of existence in self-consciousness that is not exhausted by the notion of mere singleness, such as is attributable to a stone, or stick, or any pure unit in ma erial nature. It is noteworthy that the denominations of the opposing parties suggest this distinction. The Unitarian holds to the Arian unit; the Trinitarian believes in the trinal unity. Says AMBROSE (De fide, v. 1), "Singularitatem hanc dico, quod Graecè μονότης dicitur; singularitas ad personam pertinet, unitas ad naturam." CUDWORTH (Intellect. Syst. II. 445, Tegg's Ed.) marks this distinction, by the phrases "general essence," and "singular essence,"—the former of which is an essence that includes "subsistences," and the latter is a distinct and single "subsistence."

objections of the Arian to venture upon some positive statements and definitions, employed a term that hinted at the eternal and unchanging *circumincession* and *intercommunion* of the three Persons in the Godhead, whereby the Essence is all in each, and each is in the Essence; whereby the One is Three, and the Three are One.

But such endeavors to explain the incomprehensible mystery of the trinity were not carried any further than to this point and degree. The catholic mind followed out its thoughts in this direction just far enough to show, that the truth, though transcending reason, did not contradict reason,—in other words that the charge of palpable absurdity and self-contradiction, so often advanced by the Arian, could not be made good respecting one of the plainest doctrines of revelation, and most fundamental truths of Christianity; but that even before the bar of metaphysical reason something valid might be said in favour of it. But when this had been done, the mind of an Athanasius was disposed to stop, and allow speculation to pass over into worship.

The last and most comprehensive results of the controversy and investigation were embodied in a creed, which by its negative clauses denied, rejected, and in some instances anathematized, the false statements of the doctrine, because these were *known* to be unscriptural and untrue, and by its positive clauses endeavoured, though inadequately, to convey some distinct apprehension of the abysmal truth.

The so-called *Symbolum Quicumque*, falsely ascribed to Athanasius, and which probably originated in the school of Augustine, affords a fine specimen of this sort of dialectic statement.[1] It runs as follows:

'At this point, we throw into a note Augustine's explanation of certain difficult texts that were often quoted by the Arians, as casting light upon the general doctrine, and as specimens of the best patristic exegesis.—Augustine refers the words: "My Father is greater than I" to the human nature of Christ; and remarks that Christ in his estate of humiliation was inferior not only to the Father, but to *Himself* also. He might have said: "The Eternal *Word* is greater than I." For illustration he refers to Philippians ii. 6, 7, where Christ is represented as having the "form of God," and the "form of a servant." When in the form of a servant, and having respect to that, he could say that "the Father is greater than I," because this was merely saying that the "form of a servant" is inferior to the "form of God." The text 1 Cor. xv 28, Augustine refers to the Mediatorial character of Christ. When he has completed the work of recovering the elect, and bringing them into the beatific vision of God, he ceases to be Mediator any longer. Hence, says Augustine, we must not regard Christ as giving up the kingdom "to God and the Father," in such a sense as to take away the kingdom from God the Son. For the Father and Son, in respect to their nature and eternal relationship, are one. The text Mark xiii. 32, Augustine (as did Irenaeus before him) explains to mean, that the *disclosure* of the day and hour of judgment is the prerogative of the triune God, and is not a part of the Mediator's official work. "A man," says Augustine, "is said not to 'know' a thing, when he keeps others in ignorance by not revealing it. Thus God said to Abraham: 'Now I know that thou fearest God' (Gen. xxii. 12). God, in the strict sense, 'knew' that Abraham feared him before he tried him; but God did not know it in the sense of making Abraham know it, or of telling Abraham that it was a fact, until after the temptation." In like manner, Christ as the Eternal Word knew the day and the hour of judgment; but in his *Mediatorial* capacity he was not authorized to announce it, and as *Mediator* tells his disciples that he knows nothing about it, because it is a matter belonging to the eternal councils of the triune Godhead,—which in the order of nature are anterior to the council of redemption. "Christ," says

"1. Whoever would be saved, must first of all take care that he hold the catholic faith. 2. Which, except a man preserve whole and inviolate, he shall without doubt perish eternally. 3. But this is the catholic faith, that we worship one God in trinity, and trinity in unity. 4. Neither confounding the persons nor dividing the substance. 5. For the person of the Father is one; of the Son, another; of the Holy Spirit, another. 6. But the divinity (divinitas) of the Father, and of the Son, and of the Holy Spirit, is one, the glory equal, the majesty equal. 7. Such as is (qualis) the Father, such also is the Son, and such the Holy Spirit. 8. The Father is uncreated, the Son is uncreated, the Holy Spirit is uncreated. 9. The Father is infinite, the Son infinite, the Holy Spirit infinite. 10. The Father is eternal, the Son eternal, and the Holy Spirit eternal. 11. And yet, there are not three eternal Beings (aeterni), but one eternal Being.[1] 12. As also there are not three uncreated Beings (increati), nor three infinite Beings (infiniti), but one uncreated and one infinite Being. 13. In like manner, the Father is omnipotent, the Son omnipotent, and the Holy Spirit omnipotent. 14. And yet, there are not three omnipotent Beings, but

Augustine, " was not authorized at this time to give information to his disciples respecting the day of judgment, and this is called ignorance upon his part; just as a ditch is sometimes called 'blind,' not because it is really so, but because it is hidden from the sight of men." AUGUSTINUS: Opera VIII. 829-30, 857, (Ed. Migne).

[1] See note *ante*, p. 347.

one omnipotent Being. 15. Thus the Father is God, the Son, God, and the Holy Spirit, God. 16. And yet, there are not three Gods (dii), but one God only. 17. The Father is Lord, the Son, Lord, and the Holy Spirit, Lord. 18. And yet, there are not three Lords (domini), but one Lord only. 19. For as we are compelled by christian truth to confess each person distinctively to be both God and Lord, we are prohibited by the catholic religion to say that there are three Gods, or three Lords. 20. The Father is made by none, nor created, nor begotten. 21. The Son is from the Father alone, not made, not created, but begotten. 22. The Holy Spirit is not created by the Father and Son, nor begotten, but proceeds. 23. Therefore, there is one Father, not three Fathers; one Son, not three Sons; one Holy Spirit, not three Holy Spirits. 24. And in this trinity there is nothing prior or posterior, nothing greater or lesser, but all three persons are coeternal, and coequal to themselves. 25. So that through all (omnia), as was said above, both unity in trinity, and trinity in unity, is to be adored. 26. Whoever therefore would be saved, let him thus think concerning the trinity."

By this continual laying down of positions, and equally continual retraction of them, up to a certain point, in order to prevent their being pushed too far, the theological mind endeavored to keep clear of the two principal deviations from the exact truth, —Sabellianism and Arianism,—not denying the unity while asserting the trinity, nor denying the trinity while asserting the unity. It is the opinion of Hagenbach, that so far as the first two hypostases are concerned, the doctrine of the trinity has not received any clearer or fuller scientific statement than that which is contained in the *Nicene Symbol*, and the kindred *Symbolum Quicumque*, and he seems to intimate that it is impossible for anything more to be said in the way of dialectic and scientific statement, than is enunciated in these creeds. It appears to be his opinion, that the principal if not all the fundamental errors to which the human mind is liable in the construction of the doctrine of the trinity are specified, rejected, and condemned, in the negative side of the symbol; while, so far as concerns the positive definition and enunciation, the human mind has here gone as far in this direction as is possible for it. "Against this bulwark of the faith," he says, "all further attempts of the human understanding to reconcile the opposing antitheses in the statement of the doctrine, and to afford a full direct intuition that shall clear up all the mystery of the subject, must dash and break themselves, as do the waves of the sea against the inexorable cliffs and rocks."[1]

[1] HAGENBACH: Dogmengeschichte, § 97. 3d Auflage.

§ 4. *Nicene Doctrine of the Holy Spirit.*

The Nicene Symbol is remarkably reticent respecting the third Person in the trinity. It contains but a single clause respecting Him, in these words: "And we believe in the Holy Spirit." But so little was the theological mind occupied with the discrimination and definition of this hypostasis, that after this brief statement respecting the Holy Spirit, it immediately recurs again to the second Person, and affirms, that "those who say that there was once a time when the Son of God was not, or that before he was begotten, he was not in being,[1] or that he became existent out of nonentity, or that he is of another substance or essence [than that of Deity], or that he is created, or mutable, or changeable: all such, the catholic and apostolic Church anathematizes."

The controversy had been so deep and earnest, respecting the true nature and position of the Son that, although the views of Arius were as erroneous in respect to the Holy Spirit as in respect to the Logos, the Nicene theologians passed by his heresy on this point, without noticing it in their systematic symbol. Two reasons seems to have operated with them. First, they were not willing, unless com-

---

[1] The Arians meant by this to assert, that the Son was not before his *temporal* generation,—which was all the generation they would concede. To have said that he was not before his *eternal* generation would have been like saying that God did not exist before his eternal existence.

pelled to do so, to embarrass the already highly abstract and metaphysical discussion of the doctrine of the trinity with further matter and questions, at this time, preferring to leave the unsettled points for a future discussion, after the present subject had been fully disposed of. Secondly, it is possible that that considerably large body of Semi-Arian theologians, to whom we have alluded, would have hesitated to extend the doctrine of consubstantiality to the Holy Spirit. Hence the leading Nicene theologians, knowing that the doctrine of the equal deity of the second hypostasis would *logically* lead to the equal deity of the third, could afford to postpone the discussion of this part of the subject. The personality and hypostatical character of the Son had been brought to view, and insisted upon, in the Origenistic scheme, and in all the earlier Trinitarianism, while that of the Holy Ghost had been left comparatively without examination, or specification. The consequence was, that at the time of the Nicene Council the opinions of many theologians were vague and idefinite with respect to the third Person in the trinity.

The mind of the leading catholic theologians, however, was fully made up, even at this period. *Athanasius* distinctly affirms the hypostatical character, and proper deity of the third Person.[1] His

---

[1] The close of ATHANASIUS's Defence of the Nicene Symbol is as follows: "To God and the Father is due glory, honour, and worship, with his co-existent Son and Word, together with the All-Holy and Life-giving Spirit, now and unto endless ages of ages. Amen."

four Epistles to Serapion, bishop of Thmuis, were written to prove the consubstantiality of the Holy Spirit. In the fourth Epistle, he endeavours to show, in opposition to those who held that the Holy Spirit is a creature ($\varkappa\tau ίσμα$), that Arianism is not fully renounced, unless the fact is explicitly acknowledged that there is nothing in the Triad foreign to the essence of God,—no substance from without mingled in, that is not in harmony with the pure essence of Deity, and consubstantial with it. He refers to passages of Scripture, and also draws an argument from the Christian experience. "How can that," he says, "which is sanctified by nothing other than itself, and which is itself the source of all sanctification for all rational creatures, be of the same species of being and kind of essence, with that which is sanctified by another than itself?" In and by the Holy Spirit the creature obtains communion with God, and participation in a divine life; but this could not be the case if the Holy Spirit were himself a creature. So certainly as man through him becomes a partaker of the divine ($\vartheta εοποιεῖ$), so certainly must He himself be one with the divine Essence.

Basil the Great († 379) wrote a tract upon the divinity of the Holy Spirit, in which he denominates the Spirit, God, and refers to passages of Scripture in support of his view, and particularly to the baptismal formula, in which the Spirit forms the third in the series, with the Father and Son.

His brother *Gregory of Nyssa* († 394?), in the second chapter of his larger Catechism, employs the comparison suggested and warranted by the etymology of the word Spirit, and which had been much enlarged upon by earlier writers, particularly Lactantius,—the comparison of the Spirit to the breath. Unlike Lactantius, this writer, though not inclined to a strict and high trinitarianism, does not identify the Word and the Spirit, but marks the hypostatical distinction between them. *Gregory Nazianzen* († 390), also, agrees in opinion and in statement with Basil, and Gregory of Nyssa.

A portion of the Semi-Arians, however, in the further discussion of the general doctrine, would concede only a relative divinity to the Son (adopting the doctrine of resemblance or kindredness of essence, ὁμοιούσιον), and denied the divinity of the Holy Spirit, in any and every sense. The leading bishop in this party was Macedonius, and hence the name of *Macedonians* was given to it. Of this man, Sozomen[1] remarks, that he " taught that the Son is God,—in every respect, and according to essence, *like* the Father; and that the Holy Spirit is not a sharer in these prerogatives, but a minister and servant." Theodoret[2] states that Macedonius expressly denominated the Spirit a creature. Some of the

---

[1] Sozomen: Eccles. Hist. IV. xxvii.

[2] Theodoret: Eccles. Hist. II. vi. Theodoret remarks that Macedonius " taught that the Son of God is not of the *same* substance as the Father, but that he resembles Him in every particular."

objections which the Macedonians made to the doctrine of the deity and hypostatical character of the Holy Spirit were of a frivolous, as well as blasphemous nature. The following is a specimen of their argumentation. "The Holy Ghost is either begotten or unbegotten; if he is unbegotten, there are two unoriginated beings (δύο τὰ ἄναρχα), namely, the Father and the Spirit; if he is begotten, he must be either from the Father, or the Son; if he is from the Father, then there are two Sons in the Triad, and consequently brothers,—when the question arises, whether one is older than the other, or whether they are twins; but if on the other hand the Spirit is begotten from the Son, then there is a grandson of God."[1] Such objections as these betray a confusion of generation with creation, and show, also, that the mind of the objector is moving in the low range of finite existence, and is unable to rise to the transcendence of the Deity. Such a mind associates temporal attributes, and material qualities, with all the terms that are applied to the Godhead; and should it carry its mode of conception into all the discussions that relate to the Divine Nature, it could not stop short of an anthropomorphism that would be no higher than the grossest polytheism.

These Macedonian views, and similar ones, led to the calling of a second *Council at Constantinople*,

[1] GREGORIUS NAZ.: Oratio xxxi. 7. Compare ATHANASIUS: Ad Serapion, I. xv.

in 381, which, under the guidance and influence principally of Gregory Nazianzen, made more precise statements respecting the Holy Spirit. The term ὁμοούσιον did not appear, however, in the creed drawn up at this time, though the Holy Spirit is represented as proceeding from the Father, and being equal in honour and power to both the Father and the Son. The phraseology of the clause relating to the third Person runs thus: "And [we believe] in the Holy Spirit, the Lord, the Life-Giving, who proceeds from the Father, who is to be worshipped and glorified with the Father and the Son, and who spake through the prophets."

It was owing to this failure to expressly assert the consubstantiality of the Spirit with the Father and the Son, by the use of the technical term ὁμοούσιον, that the Constantinopolitan Symbol was not satisfactory to all parties. The position of the Holy Spirit in the trinity generally had indeed been established by it. He was acknowledged to be one of the Eternal Three, co-equal in power and glory; but his special relation to the Father and Son was left indefinite. While the creed asserted that the Spirit proceeds from the Father, it did not indeed expressly deny that He proceeds from the Son; and yet the omission of the Son seemed to look in this direction. The arguments for and against the procession of the third Person from the first and second were the following. On the one hand, the assertion that the Spirit proceeds from the Father *only*, and not from the Son, looked like an essential inferiority of the Son to the Father; while on the other hand the assertion that He proceeds from the Father *and* the Son seemed to place the Spirit in a more dependent attitude,—his hypostatical existence issuing from two hypostases instead of one. The endeavour to vindicate the deity of the Son, by asserting the procession of the Holy Spirit from Him as well as the Father, looked like infringement upon that of the Holy Spirit; and conversely the endeavour to give to the Spirit a greater independence, by disconnecting his procession from the second Person, endangered the dignity and deity of the Son. The Greek theologians, Athanasius, Basil, and Gregory Nyssa, asserted procession from the Father, *without, however, opposing the doctrine of procession from the Son.* Epiphanius, on the contrary, derived the Spirit from Father and Son, with whom Marcellus of Ancyra agreed, though holding to a Sabellian trinity.

The Western theologians, and among them Augustine, held the doctrine of procession from Father and Son, and this statement established itself so firmly and generally in the West, that at the third *Synod of Toledo*, in 589, the clause *filioque* was added to the Constantinopolitan Symbol. This formed one of the dogmatic grounds for the division between the Western and Eastern Churches,—the former of which to this day asserts, and the latter denies, that the Holy Spirit proceeds from the Father *and* Son.

§ 5. *Terminology of the Nicene Trinitarianism.*

The deity of the Son and Spirit having thus been enunciated in a creed form, the discussions among trinitarian theologians after the Councils of Nice and Constantinople had reference to the specific relations of the three Persons to each other, and especially to *fixing the terminology* of the subject. Certain terms had been employed during this controversy of two hundred years' duration, which it was important to define, and thereby establish their technicality, and scientific authority. The success and enduring influence of any systematic construction of truth, be it secular or sacred, depends as much upon an exact terminology, as upon close and deep thinking itself. Indeed, unless the results to which the human mind arrives are plainly stated, and firmly fixed in an exact phraseology, its thinking is to very little purpose in the end. "Terms," says Whewell, "record discoveries."[1] There may be the most thorough analysis, and the most comprehensive and combining synthesis; the truth in its deepest and most scientific form may be reached by the individual mind; and yet the public mind and after ages be none the wiser for it. That which was seen it may be with crystal clearness, and in

---

[1] WHEWELL: History of Inductive Sciences (Introduction). "Die Zierde,—und das äussere Merkmal,—einer endlich auf sichern Grund erbauten Wissenschaft, ist und bleibt doch eine bestimmte Terminologie." SCHELLING: Idealismus der Wissenschaftslehre (Phil. Schriften, 205).

bold outline, in the consciousness of an individual thinker, may fail to become the property and possession of mankind at large, because it is not transferred from the individual to the general mind, by means of a precise phraseology, and a rigorous terminology. Nothing is in its own nature more fugacious and shifting than thought; and particularly thought upon the mysteries of Christianity. A conception that is plain and accurate in the understanding of the first man becomes obscure and false in that of the second, because it was not grasped, and firmly held, in the form and proportions with which it first came up, and then handed over to other minds, a fixed and scientific quantity.

The following terms compose the scientific nomenclature employed in defining and fixing the oecumenical statement of the Doctrine of the Trinity: 1. Ὀυσία, with its equivalent φυσίς; to which the Latin correspondents are *substantia, essentia, natura*, and in some connections *res ;* and the corresponding English terms, *essence, substance, nature*, and *being*. 2. Ὑπόστασις, with its equivalents τὸ ὑποκείμενον, and πρόσωπον; to which correspond the Latin *hypostasis, substantia, aspectus,* and *persona*, and the English *hypostasis* and *person*. 3. The term ἰδιότης was employed to designate the individual peculiarity of the hypostasis,—the hypostatical character by which each divine Person is differentiated from the others. 4. Γέννησις, *generatio, generation*, as has been sufficiently explained, designates the eternal and immanent activity by which the first Person communicates the divine essence to the second. 5. Ἐκπόρευσις with its equivalent ἐκπεμψις; to which correspond the Latin *processio* and *missio*, and the English *procession* and *mission*.

Οὐσία, or *Essence*, denotes that which is common to Father, Son, and Spirit. It denominates the substance, or constitutional being, of the Deity, which is possessed alike, and equally, by each of the personal distinctions. The Essence is in its own nature one and indivisible, and hence the statement in the creed respecting it affirms simple unity, and warns against separation and division. The terms "generation" and "procession" do not apply to it.

Ὑπόστασις, or *Hypostasis*, is a term that was more subtile in its meaning, and use, than οὐσία. It denotes, not that which is common to the Three in One, but, that which is distinctive of and peculiar to them. The personal characteristic of the Hypostasis, or "subsistence" in the Essence, was denoted by the Greek word ἰδιότης, and if we use our English word "individuality" somewhat loosely, it will convey the idea sought to be attached to the Person in distinction from the Essence.

Inasmuch as the meaning of the term Person was more difficult to reach and state, than the meaning of the term Essence, more imperfection and indefiniteness appear in the terminology employed. The three-foldness is more difficult to grasp than the unity. The human mind quite readily apprehends the notion of substance, and of attributes. These two conceptions apply to all forms of created being, and are familiar to the reflection of the human understanding,—though when examined they baffle a perfectly metaphysical comprehension. But the doctrine of a "subsistence" in the substance of the Godhead brings to view a species of existence that is so anomalous, and unique, that the human mind derives little or no aid from those analogies which assist it in all other cases. The hypostasis is a real subsistence,—a solid essential form of existence, and not a mere emanation, or energy, or manifestation,—but it is intermediate between substance and attributes. It is not identical with the substance, for there are not three substances. It is not identical with attributes, for the three Persons each and equally possess all the divine attributes. "We know," says Howe, "that the hypostatical distinction cannot be less than is sufficient to sustain distinct predicates or attributions, nor can it be so great as to intrench upon the unity of the Godhead."[1] Hence the mind is called upon to grasp the notion of a species of existence that is totally *sui generis*, and not capable of illustration by any of the ordinary comparisons and analogies.[2]

[1] Howe: I. 137. (N. York Ed.)
[2] This remark is certainly true within the sphere of the impersonal material creation; but that the sphere of *self-conscious* existence may perhaps furnish an ana-

The consequence of this was, that the *term* ὑπόστασις was sometimes attended with ambiguity, though the meaning attached to the *idea* was uni-

logical illustration seems to be less and less doubted, as metaphysical psychology advances. Some of the Fathers, as Augustine for example, found a trinity in the human spirit. As a tentative effort in this direction, we subjoin the following positions in proof that the necessary conditions of self-consciousness in the finite spirit furnish an *analogue* to the doctrine of the trinity, and go to prove that trinity in unity is necessary to self-consciousness in the Godhead.

God is not "one" like a stone or tree, or any single thing in nature. He is "one" like a person. It may be presumed, therefore, that the same conditions which we find to exist in the instance of human personality, will be found in the instance of the Divine self-consciousness, only freed from the limitations of the finite. What, then, are these conditions?

In order to self-consciousness in man, the unity, viz.: the human spirit, must first become distinguished, but not divided, into two *distinctions;* one of which is the contemplating subject, and the other the contemplated object. The *I* must behold itself as an objective thing. In this first step in the process of becoming self-conscious, the finite spirit sets itself off over against itself, in order that it may see itself. That one essence, which, before this step, was an unreflecting and therefore unconscious unit, now becomes *two* definitudes, distinctions, hypostases, supposita. There is now a subject-ego, and an object-ego. There is a real distinction, but no *division* in the original being,—in the primitive unity.

But this is not the end of the process. We have not yet reached full self-consciousness. In order to the complete self-conscious intuition, the finite spirit must, yet further, perceive that this subject-ego and object-ego, this contemplant and contemplated, arrived at in the first step of the process, are one and the same *essence* or *being*. This second act of perception completes the circle of self-consciousness. For if the human spirit stopped with the first act of merely distinguishing, and never took the second step of reuniting; if the mind never became aware that the object contemplated in the first stage of the process is no other, as to essence, than the subject contemplating; it would not have *self*-knowledge at all. It would not perceive that it had been contemplating *self*. Stopping with the first act of dis-

form. The distinction between ὀυσία and ὑπόστασις, though made in fact, was not always made in form, by the first trinitarians. Some little time was

tinguishing, the object-ego would not differ, for the subject-ego, from any other object,—a tree or a stone e. g.; and the knowledge which the mind would have of itself as an object would not differ from that which it has of objects in nature, or of the *not me*, generally. It would not be *self-consciousness*, consequently, any more than the consciousness of any other thing is self-consciousness. The essence of the object must be seen to be the essence of the subject, or else *self*-knowledge is both incomplete and impossible.

There is then a *third* definitude, distinction, hypostasis, suppositum, in the one original unity of the human spirit, which, in a second act of perception, beholds the identity of the first and second determinations or distinctions —the essential oneness of the subject-ego and object-ego. There is now *full* self-consciousness. In and by the two acts of perception, and the three resulting *distinctions*, the human spirit has made itself its own object, and has perceived that it has done so. There is real triplicity in the unity. For the subject-ego, *as such*, is not the object-ego, *as such;* and the third distinction, which reunites these two in the perception of their identity of

essence and being, is, *as such*, neither the subject-ego nor the object-ego, yet is consubstantial with them both.

If it be asked, why a *fourth* factor is not needed to perceive the unity of essence between the third, and the first two distinctions, the answer is: that the third distinction has not, like the first one, posited an *object*, but has only perceived an *act*. It has simply witnessed and noticed that the first distinction has made the second distinction an object of contemplation. Hence there is no second *object* that requires to be reunited in the unity of essence.

These, then, are the necessary philosophical conditions of personality in the finite spirit. If a single one is lacking the circle is broken, and there is no self-consciousness. From what limitations, now, must they be freed, in order that they may be transferred to the Infinite Spirit? The answer is: from the two limitations of *time* and *degree*.

In the instance of the finite spirit, these acts of perception, which have been described, occur seriatim, and the unity comes to self-consciousness only *gradually*, and *intermittently*. Man is not self-conscious at every instant. He

required to set off each term to its own idea. Thus, the Nicene Symbol itself anathematizes those that teach that the Son is ἐξ ἑτέρας ὑποστάσεως ἢ οὐσίας. Athanasius employs the two terms as equivalents. "As to those who receive all else that was defined at Nice, but doubt about consubstantiality only, we must not feel as towards enemies.... for in con-

becomes so by voluntary reflection ; and the clearness and depth of his self-intuition is a thing of degrees. No man has ever yet attained to an absolutely perfect self-consciousness, as the baffled striving of the philosopher evinces.

But the Divine Essence is not included in such a process of gradually *becoming* self-conscious, instead of eternally *being* so. God is the same yesterday, to-day, and forever. The great vice of the modern pantheistic speculation consists in transferring the doctrine of gradual self-evolution from the sphere of the finite to that of the Infinite ; from the creature to the Creator. God, as the schoolmen define him, is "*actus purissimus sine ulla potentialitate.*" There never is nor can be anything potential and undeveloped in the Divine Essence. Hence, the above-mentioned conditions of self-consciousness must, in the instance of the Deity, be freed from the limitations of *time* and *degree.* That self-consciousness which in man is the result of a deliberate effort, and which continues only during the time of voluntary self-reflection, is ever present and ever existent in God. From eternity to eternity, the subject-ego (The Father) is perpetually beholding itself as the object ego (The Son), and the third distinction (The Holy Spirit) is unintermittently perceiving the essential unity and identity of the subject-ego and object-ego (Father and Son). Furthermore, the self-knowledge, in this instance, is an infinite, and fixed quantity. From the fathomless depths of the Divine Nature, there comes up at no moment during the eternal years of God, a yet profounder knowledge, a yet fuller self-intuition, than has before been gained ; but this Divine self-consciousness is the same exhaustive self-contemplation from everlasting to everlasting. The *eternity* and *immanency* of these activities in the Divine Essence are expressed in theological phraseology by the Nicene doctrine of the *eternal begetting* of the Father, the *eternal generation* of the Son, and the *eternal procession* of the Spirit.

fessing that the Son is from the substance of the Father, and not of other subsistence (ἐκ τῆς οὐσίας τοῦ πατρὸς εἶναι, καὶ μὴ ἐξ ἑτέρας ὑποστάσεως τὸν υἱόν), they are not far from receiving the phrase ὁμοούσιον also." Again, he remarks: "Hypostasis (ὑπόστασις) is substance (οὐσία), and means nothing else than simple being."[1] But Athanasius continually denies that there are three οὐσίαι, so that his use of ὑπόστασις must be determined in each instance from the connection in which he employs it. His object in asserting that "hypostasis is *substance*" was to deny that the personal distinction in the Godhead is merely an energy or effluence, such as the Nominal Trinitarians maintained it to be.[2]

---

[1] ATHANASIUS: De Synodis, xli; Ad Afros, iv.

[2] BULL and PETAVIUS differ with regard to the question whether the Nicene Council made a *technical* distinction between the two terms. BULL (Fid. Nic. II. ix. 11) contends that two different things were intended by the council to be designated by the terms οὐσία and ὑπόστασις, and that they desired to condemn *two* classes of errorists,—those, namely, who denied that the Son is from the Father's substance (οὐσία), but conceded that he was from the Father's hypostasis (ὑπόστασις); and those who denied that he was from either the Father's substance, or the Father's hypostasis. The latter class were the Arians, and the former were the Semi-Arians. The Semi-Arians, in Bull's opinion, would concede that the Son was begotten of the Father's *hypostasis* in a peculiar manner denoted by the term ὁμοιούσιος, and was not created from nothing like ordinary creatures; but would not concede that he was begotten of the same *substance* with the Father, or apply to him the term ὁμοούσιος. The Arians, on the other hand, would deny both that the Son was begotten of the Father's substance, and the Father's hypostasis, and assert that he was created de nihilo. PETAVIUS (De Trinitate, IV.) regards the word ὑπόστασις, in the nomenclature of the

Although the Latin trinitarians discriminated Person from Essence with full as much clearness as the Greek Nicene Fathers, yet there was some confusion of terms among them, owing to the poverty of the Latin language. One and the same word, *substantia*, was often employed in the Latin trinitarianism, to denote both the essentiality, and the personality. Had the term *essentia* been used from the very first, and invariably, to translate ὀυσία, and *substantia* to denote ὑπόστασις, the confusion would have been avoided. But the term *substantia*, in the Latin, was so commonly exchangeable, and entirely synonymous with *essentia*, (as the term substance, in English, is with essence,) that no term was left to denote that peculiar mode of existence which is intermediate between essence and attributes, unless these two synonymes should be distinguished from each other, and one rigorously confined to one conception, and the other to the other.[1]

This however was not done at first, and the

Nicene council, as only another term for ὀυσία, and contends that the two terms were not set off, each to its appropriate idea, until the council of Alexandria, in 362. " Vox *hypostasis*, non modo ante Nicaenum concilium, sed ne ab ipsis quidem Nicaenis Patribus aliter fere accepta sit, quam pro ὀυσία, et substantia, rarissime vero pro persona, et proprietate διακριτικῇ, ac numerum faciente." (De Trinitate, I. iii, 3).

[1] The following extract from ANSELM illustrates the later use of *substantia* and *essentia*. "Quod enim dixi summam trinitatem posse dici tres substantias, Graecos secutus sum, qui confitentur tres substantias in una essentia, eadem fide, qua nos tres personas in una substantia. Nam hoc significant in Deo per substantiam quod nos per personam." ANSELMUS: Monologium (Praefatio).

consequence was, that other terms came to be employed, occasionally, to hint at and suggest the meaning of the hypostatical distinction. Such a term is πρόσωπον. This corresponds to the Latin *persona*, from which the English "person" is derived. This term, it is obvious to remark, though the more common one in English, and perhaps in Protestant trinitarianism generally, is not so well adapted to express the conception intended, as the Greek ὑπόστασις. It has a Sabellian leaning, because it does not with sufficient plainness indicate the *subsistence* in the Essence. The Father Son and Spirit are more than mere aspects or appearances of the Essence. The Latin *persona* was the mask worn by the actor in the play, and was representative of his particular character for the particular time. Now, although those who employed these terms undoubtedly gave them as full and solid a meaning as they could, and were undoubtedly true trinitarians, yet the representation of the eternal and necessary hypostatical distinctions in the Godhead, by terms derived from transitory scenical exhibitions, was not the best for purposes of science, even though the poverty of human language should justify their employment for popular and illustrative statements.[1]

That the distinction between Essence and Hy-

[1] In the Semi-Arian controversy, which sprung up between the Nicene and Constantinopolitan Councils, the "Old Nicenes" would only acknowledge three πρόσωπα, while the "New Nicenes," who were the most accurate, contended for three ὑπόστασις.

postasis became a fixed one, and thus came down in the trinitarian nomenclature of the Modern Church, was owing, in a great measure, to the Western theologians Augustine and Hilary, whose treatises upon the doctrine of the trinity were the principal text-books for the Schoolmen in their speculations.

Ἐκπόρευσις and ἔκπεμψις were terms employed to denote the hypostatical character and relationship of the Holy Spirit. They were derived from John xv. 15, and kindred passages. "But when the Comforter is come, whom I will send (πέμψω) unto you from the Father, even the Spirit of truth, which proceedeth (ὁ ἐκπορεύεται) from the Father, he shall testify of me." The attempt to define the term "procession" was even less frequent than to define the term "generation." The same predicates, however, were applied to both. It was an *eternal* procession, out of the essence. It was a *necessary* procession grounded in the absolute nature of the Deity, and not dependent upon arbitrary and optional will.

§ 6. *Critical Estimate of the Nicene Controversy.*

We have now traced the history of this great doctrine of revelation through the period of its theoretic construction, and establishment. We have seen the theological mind, partly from its own impulse, and partly from the necessities of its position, first, *collate* from the written word the various and scattered data there given, then *combine* them into a general statement as in the Apostles' Creed, and then *expand* them into a more special form of doctrine, as in the Nicene and Athanasian Symbols. Collation, combination, and expansion are the parts of the scientific process. This process went on slowly, but continuously, for a period of five centuries,—as long a time as was required for pagan Rome to conquer and subjugate the Italian tribes, and lay the foundations of a nationality that was to last a millennium in its own particular form, and another millennium in mixture with still other nationalities,—as long a time as was required for the thorough mixing and fusion of British, Saxon, and Norman elements into that modern national character which in the Englishman and Anglo-American is, perhaps, destined to mould and rule the future more than even Rome has the past. These historic parallels are interesting and illustrative. Though the processes are totally unlike,—though the one is metaphysical, and relates to the mysterious nature and essence of the Ancient of Days, before whom all the nations and all the centuries of time are as nothing and vanity, while the other is political, and relates to the rise and formation of merely secular sovereignties, exceedingly impressive to the natural mind and dazzling to the carnal eye, constituting the very splendor and glory of secular history, yet, in comparison with the eternal years of God, passing away like a morning vapor,—though these processes are in their own nature so different; the mind is aided in forming a just estimate of the slowness and grandeur of their movement, by the comparison of one with the other. The theological controversies that resulted in forming and fixing the theoretic belief of Christendom in the Triune God appear unprofitable and valueless to the merely secular mind,—to the mind that is absorbed in the finite, and making no comparisons between time and eternity. The sneer that this whole contest of five centuries was merely about a single letter, merely whether the term should be ὁμοούσιον or ὁμοιούσιον, expresses the feeling of many a mind, for which, notwithstanding all its culture in other directions, the invisible is less august than the visible, and the temporal more impressive than the eternal.[1]

But he who feels a proper practical and philosophic interest in the paramount questions and problems of Christianity, and in their bearing upon the destiny of man as immortal and everlasting, will always look upon these centuries of intense metaphysical abstraction, and profound moral earnestness, with more veneration than upon any section of merely pagan and secular history, however striking or imposing. These bloodless meta-

[1] The value of a letter in an algebraic problem, or a formula of the calculus, is not greater than in this trinitarian technical term.

physical victories secured to the Church Universal a correct faith, and obtained for her all those benefits that flow perennially from the possession of the real and exact truth,—from the revealed idea and definition of the Triune God.

CHAPTER IV.

POST-NICENE TRINITARIANISM.

§ 1. *Mediaeval and Papal Trinitarianism.*

THE history of the Doctrine of the Trinity in the Scholastic and Modern Churches can be compressed into a brief statement, the more readily, because this doctrine, more than is the case with any other, reached its approximately full developement in the first stages of its history. After the year 600, expansion in theory, and technical accuracy in statement, can be detected much more plainly in Soteriology, and even in Anthropology, than in Theology. The Scholastic and Protestant systems have unfolded the doctrines of sin and redemption, far more than they have the doctrine of the trinity.

In the Middle Ages, the character of the investigation of the doctrine of the trinity was determined by the general bent of the individual mind, or of his school. Men like Anselm, Bernard, and

Aquinas joined on upon the views of the past. The writings of the Western Latin trinitarians, particularly Hilary and Augustine, as we have already remarked, were resorted to, and their general type of doctrine prevailed among thinkers of this class. The Greek language was but little cultivated, and hence the speculations of the Greek Fathers exerted comparatively little direct influence. In regard to the opinions of the leading theologians of the Mediaeval Church, it may be summarily remarked, that the trinitarianism that had been formed and authoritatively established during the first six centuries was adopted and defended.

In that class of speculative minds, to which we had occasion to allude in the history of Apologies, we find more or less deviation from the catholic creed and faith. That adventurous thinker of the ninth century, Scotus Erigena, whose philosophizing upon the general doctrine of the Deity was pantheistic, presented views of the trinity that were Sabellian. Abelard was charged with the same tendency. Roscellin was accused of tritheism, and Gilbert of Poictiers of Damian's old heresy of tetratheism.[1] But such opinions were regarded by those who controlled the public sentiment of the church, and by the church itself as represented in councils, as heterodox. The Anselms, Bernards, and Aquinases

---

[1] Damian of Alexandria was accused of holding the theory of a Monad (the αὐτόθεος, or generic one), and three persons, or individualizations, in *addition*,—Three *and* One, instead of Three *in* One.

of the Mediaeval Church were one in sentiment upon this doctrine, with the Athanasiuses, Basils, Gregories, Augustines, and Hilaries of the Ancient Church.

§ 2. *Trinitarianism of the Continental and English Reformers.*

At the Reformation, the Roman and Protestant churches adopted the same dogmatic statement of the doctrine of the Trinity. This is the only cardinal truth of revelation in respect to which, both parties stood upon the same ground. The anthropology, soteriology, and eschatology, of the *Council of Trent* are different from those of the Reformers; but its theology is the same. The Tridentine scheme presents Semi-Pelagian views of sin, teaches the doctrine of justification in part by works, and nullifies the doctrine of endless punishment by its purgatorial fires. But it adopts the trinitarian symbols of the Ancient Church, not so much from any vital interest in them, as because they have come down from the past, and there is no motive for alteration, and no intellectual adventurousness prompting to the formation of new theories. That the Roman Church is trinitarianly orthodox, because it has no motive to be otherwise, is proved by the fact that a doctrine which lies so near the heart of Christianity as the doctrine of the trinity, and which appeals even more directly to the heart of the Christian,—the doctrine of forgiveness solely through the atonement of Christ,—has been remorselessly mutilated, and in effect annihilated by it.

The *Augsburg Confession*, the chief Lutheran symbol, adopts the decisions of the Nicene Council respecting the unity of the divine Essence, and the three Persons, in its statement that there is "one divine Essence which both is, and is called God, eternal, incorporeal, indivisible, infinite in power wisdom and goodness, the Creator and Preserver of all things visible and invisible; and yet, there are three Persons, of the same essence and power, co-eternal, Father, Son, and Holy Spirit."[1]

The *Second Helvetic Confession*, drawn up by Bullinger in 1564, is as fair an expression of the Reformed or Calvinistic doctrine as any. Its teaching upon the doctrine of the trinity is as follows: "We believe that God, one and indivisible in Essence, is without division or confusion distinct in three Persons, Father, Son, and Holy Spirit, so that the Father generates the Son from eternity, the Son is begotten by an ineffable generation, but the Holy Spirit proceeds from each and that from eternity, and is to be adored together with each; so that there are not three Gods, but three Persons, consubstantial, coeternal, and coequal, distinct as hypostases, and one having precedence of another as to order, but with no unequality as to essence."[2]

---

[1] HASE: Libri Symbolici, p. 9. [2] NIEMEYER: Confessiones, pp. 470, 471.

The trinitarianism of *Calvin*, as enunciated in his Institutes, is a very clear exhibition of the Nicene type of doctrine, under the additional light that had been thrown upon the subject by the thinking of Hilary and Augustine, and by his own profound and patient study of the Scriptures. "What I denominate a Person," he says,[1] "is a subsistence in the Divine essence, which is related to the others, and yet distinguished from them by an incommunicable property. By the word *subsistence* we mean something different from the word *essence*. For if the Word were simply God, and had no peculiar property, John had been guilty of impropriety in saying that he was always *with* God. When he immediately adds that the Word also *was* God, he reminds us of the unity of the essence. But, because he could not be *with* God without subsisting in the Father, hence arises that subsistence, which, although inseparably connected with the essence, has a peculiar mark, by which it is distinguished from it. Now, I say that each of the three subsistences has a relation to the others, but is distinguished from them by a peculiar property. We particularly use the word *relation* (or *comparison*) here, because when mention is made simply and indefinitely of God, this name pertains no less to the Son and Spirit, than to the Father. But whenever the Father is *compared* with the Son, the property peculiar to each distinguishes him from the other.

[1] CALVIN: Institutes, I. xiii. 6.

Thirdly, whatever is proper to each of them, I assert to be *incommunicable*, because whatever is ascribed to the Father as a character of distinction, cannot be applied or transferred to the Son."

Calvin, as did the Nicene theologians, carefully confined the term "generation" to the hypostatical character. "We teach," he says, "according to the Scriptures, that there is essentially but one God; and therefore, that the *essence* of both the Son and the Spirit is unbegotten. But since the Father is first in order, and hath of himself begotten his Wisdom, therefore, as has before been observed, he is justly esteemed the original and fountain of the whole Divinity.[1] Thus God, indefinitely [i. e. the Godhead, the Essence in distinction from the Persons], is unbegotten; and the Father also is unbegotten with regard to his Person..... The Deity [the Essence] is absolutely self-existent; whence we confess, also, that the Son, as God, independently of the consideration of Person is self-existent; but as the Son, we say, that he is of the Father. Thus his essence is unoriginated; but the origin of his Person is God himself."[2]

---

[1] By this Calvin means, that the Father is "the original and fountain of the whole Divinity," considered *hypostatically*, not *essentially*; for he expressly says that the *essence* is unbegotten. He means that the Father is that *hypostasis* from whom the second and third hypostases issue. That this is the correct interpretation of his language, is proved by the fact, that in the section following (§ 26) that from which the above statement is taken, Calvin remarks that "the Father is the fountain of the Deity, *not with regard to essence*, but in respect to order."

[2] CALVIN: Institutes, I. xiii. 25.

Notwithstanding the clearness and explicitness of Calvin's views, he was accused by Caroli of both Arianism and Sabellianism. He defended himself before the synod of Lausanne. Caroli held it to be heresy that Calvin, in his confession there presented, affirmed that Christ is that Jehovah who of himself, alone, is always self-existent. "Certainly," said Calvin in reply, "if the *distinction* between the Father and the Word be attentively considered, we shall say that the one is from the other. If however the *essential quality* of the Word be considered, in so far as He is one God with the Father, whatever can be said concerning God may also be applied to Him, the second person in the glorious Trinity..... We teach, certainly, that Christ is the true and natural Son of God, who has possessed the like essential deity with the Father from all eternity."[1]

The Nicene trinitarianism passed also into the symbols of the English Churches; both the Established and the Non-Conforming. The *Thirty-Nine Articles* teach that "in the unity of the Godhead there be three Persons, of one substance, power, and eternity;" and that the Son "is begotten from eternity of the Father, very and eternal God, of one substance with the Father."[2] The *Westminster Confession* teaches that "in the unity of the Godhead there be three Persons, of one substance, power, and eter-

[1] CALVIN: Letters, Vol. II. pp. 30, 31. Edinburgh Translation. [2] Articles I. II.

nity; God the Father, God the Son, and God the Holy Ghost. The Father is of none, neither begotten, nor proceeding; the Son is eternally begotten of the Father; the Holy Ghost eternally proceeding from the Father and the Son."[1]

§ 3. *Unitarianism.*

In the 16th century, an opposition to the church doctrine of the trinity arose in the modern Unitarianism. The two brothers *Socini* (Laelius and

---

[1] WESTMINSTER CONFESSION: Chapter II.—The Nicene trinitarianism came with the English and Continental colonists into the American churches. The Episcopalian Church adopts it, in adopting the Thirty-Nine Articles. The Presbyterian Church receives it in the Westminster Confession; as did also the early Congregational churches. The churches of New England, represented in the Synod at Boston in 1680, made their statement in the following phraseology: "In the unity of the God-head there be three persons, of one substance, power, and eternity; God the Father, God the Son, and God the Holy Ghost. The Father is of none, neither begotten, nor proceeding; the Son is eternally begotten of the Father; the Holy Ghost eternally proceeding from the Father and Son." (Boston Confession, Chap. II). An earnest defender of the Nicene doctrine of "eternal generation" is SAMUEL HOPKINS (Works, I. 293 sq.), the leader of one of the later New England schools. The elder EDWARDS is also supposed to have left in manuscript reflections upon the doctrine of the trinity, in the line of the Nicene trinitarianism. During the present century, some opposition to the doctrine of the Eternal Sonship has shown itself in a few New England writers. The opposition, however, is founded upon an inadequate dogmatico-historical knowledge,—the Origenistic theory of eternal generation, as revived in England in the last century by SAMUEL CLARKE, being mistaken for the historical doctrine of Athanasius and the Nicene theologians.

Faustus), by their writings and endeavours in other ways, associated and centralized those in the midst of Protestantism who agreed in their rejection of the doctrine of the trinity, and gave the party an external form and position. The growing spirit of toleration in the Protestant Church favoured them, and permitted the Socini to do what was forbidden to their predecessor *Servetus*, at the time of the Reformation, and for attempting which he lost his life at the stake,—a measure, it should be observed, that was approved in that age by theologians of all parties, both Roman and Protestant, and was by no means a distinctively Calvinistic procedure. One of the Polish Palatines afforded this party an asylum, and encouraged it in many ways. It flourished to such an extent as to produce a body of theologians, and to construct a creed. The writings of the *Fratres Poloni* are to this day the ablest in the Unitarian theology, and the Racovian Creed and Catechism, drawn up by them, contain an explicit and logical announcement of the Unitarian scheme, which it would be for the interest of their modern successors to adopt, and of their modern opposers to examine. The only statement of Unitarianism that has any interest for the scientific theologian must be sought for in that period of its history when it had both a creed and a catechism.[1]

This scheme of doctrine did not, however, attract

[1] Schomann in 1591, Faustus Socinus in 1618, and Moscoro-vius in 1625, published catechisms.

any very considerable attention on the part of the church. It was a less profound form of error, than that Sabellianism and Arianism which in the first centuries had compelled the theologian to employ his most extensive learning, and his subtlest thinking. As a consequence, it has been, and still is, confined to but a small portion of the Protestant world. Had Unitarianism adopted into its conception of Christ those more elevated views of his nature and person which clung to Sabellianism, and even to Arianism, it would have been a more influential system. But merely reproducing that low humanitarian view of Christ which we found in the third class of Anti-Trinitarians of the 2d and 3d centuries,—the Ebionites, Artemonites, Theodotians, and Alogi,—the Unitarian Christ possessed nothing that could lift the mind above the sphere of the merely human, and nothing that could inspire the religious affections of veneration and worship.

§ 4. *Latitudinarian Trinitarianism in the English and German Churches.*

In the 18th and 19th centuries, the history of the Doctrine of the Trinity presents little that is new. The English Church during the 18th century was called upon to defend the catholic faith from the attacks of Socinians and Arians,—the former mostly in the Dissenting Churches, and the latter within its own communion. The opinions and statements of *Priestley* were reviewed and refuted in a superior manner, by *Horsley*, bishop of St. Asaph. Those of *Samuel Clarke*, who was court preacher to Queen Anne, and by her deposed from his office, were examined by *Waterland*, Master of Magdalen College.

Clarke's views were, in reality, a reproduction of the Origenistic and High-Arian doctrine of subordination, as distinguished from the Athanasian. His positions were the following. The supreme and only God is the Father, the sole origin of all being, power, and authority. " Concerning the Father, it would be the highest blasphemy to affirm that he could possibly have become man; or that he could possibly have suffered in any sense, in any supposition, in any capacity, in any circumstance, in any state, or in any nature whatsoever."[1] With the Father, there has existed "from the beginning" a second divine Person, who is called his Word or Son, who derives his being or essence, and all his attributes, from the Father, *not by mere necessity of nature, but by an act of the Father's optional will.* It is not certain whether the Son existed from all eternity, or only before all worlds; neither is it certain whether the Son was begotten from the same essence with the Father, or made out of nothing. " Both are worthy of censure, who, on the one hand, affirm that the Son was made out of nothing; or, on the other, affirm that he is the self-existent sub-

---

[1] CLARKE: On the Trinity, Ch. II. § v.

stance." Clarke will not be positive upon these points, because of the danger of presuming to be able to define the particular metaphysical manner of the Son's deriving his essence from the Father. With the Father, a third Person has also existed, deriving his essence from him through the Son; this Person has higher titles ascribed to him than to any angel, or other created being whatsoever, but is nowhere called God in Scripture, being subordinate to the Son, both by *nature*, and by the *will* of the Father.[1]

The error of Clarke originated in his failure to discriminate carefully between the essence and the hypostasis. Hence, in quoting from the Scriptures, and the Fathers, he refers to the *essential nature* phraseology that implies subordination, and which was intended by those employing it, to apply only to the *hypostatical character*.[2] He even cites such high trinitarians as Athanasius and Hilary, as holding and teaching that the subordination of the Son to the Father relates to the Son's *essence*. The

---

[1] NELSON: Life of Bull, p. 276.
[2] CLARKE, in his reply to Nelson (p. 4), in answering the complaint of Nelson that he (Clarke) had cited Bull to prove sentiments directly contrary to those which Bull held, says: "This objection, you are sensible, I had endeavored to prevent; by declaring beforehand, that I cited modern authors, and the Fathers too, not with any intention to show what was *on the whole* the opinion of those authors. . . . but only to show what *important concessions* they were obliged to make; even such concessions, as of necessity and in strictness of argument *inferred my conclusion*, whether the authors themselves made any such inference or no."

term "unbegotten" he also held, as did the Arians, to be a synonyme with "uncreated," so that the term "begotten" must necessarily signify "created."[1] Thus misconceiving the Nicene use of these two terms, he endeavours to prove that the Nicene trinitarians taught that the Father alone possesses necessary existence, while the Son exists contingently. But both of these terms, as we have seen, were limited by the council of Nice to the Person, and have no relation to the Essence. The Essence, as such, neither begets, nor is begotten. They merely indicate the peculiar manner in which the first and second hypostases participate in one and the same eternal substance or nature. In this use of the terms, consequently, "begotten" signifies "uncreated" as much as does "unbegotten." The Begotten Son is as necessarily existent as the Unbegotten Father, because the Essence is the seat and source of necessary existence, and this is possessed alike by both,—in the instance of the first Person by paternity, and of the second by filiation.

In the controversy between Clarke and Waterland, a distinction was made by the latter between self-existence, and necessary existence, which it is important to notice. Waterland attributes necessary existence to the Son, but denies self-existence to him. The second Person, he maintains, is *necessarily* existent, because he participates in the one

---

[1] CLARKE: On the Trinity, Pt. I. ch. ii. § 5; Pt. II. §11, 12.

substance of the Godhead; but he is not *self*-existent, because he participates in it, not by and from himself, but by communication from the Father. The first Person is both necessarily existent and self-existent, because he not only participates in the Divine Essence, but does so without any communication of it to him by either of the other two Persons in the trinity. According to this distinction and discrimination, "self-existent" simply means "unbegotten." "I suppose," says Waterland, "the Father to be *Father* of his Son; which expresses a relation of *order*, and mode of existence; not any difference in any *essential* perfection. Neither is there any greater perfection in being a Father, in this case, than in being a Son; both are equally perfect, equally necessary, in respect of existence,— all things being common, but the personal characters. And *self*-existence, as distinct from *necessary* existence, is expressive only of the *order* and *manner* in which the perfections are in the Father, and not of any distinct perfection. With this answer the catholic Fathers baffled the Arians and Eunomians."[1] Waterland thus sums up the difference between himself and his opponent. "We say the Son is not self-existent, meaning that he is not *unoriginate* [or unbegotten]. You not only say the same, but contend for it, meaning not *necessarily existing*. We say, not unoriginate, meaning that

[1] WATERLAND: Second Defence, Question III.

he is not the head or fountain, not the *first Person* of the trinity. You take up the very same word, and zealously contend that the Son is not unoriginate, understanding it in respect to *time* or *duration*. We say the Son is subordinate, meaning it of a subordination of *order*, as is just and proper. You also lay hold of the word subordinate, and seem wonderfully pleased with it, but understanding by it an inferiority of *nature*. We say, that the Son is not absolutely supreme or independent, intimating thereby that he is *second* in order as a Son, and has no separate, independent existence from the Father, being coessentially, and coeternally one with him. You also take up the same words, interpret them in a low sense, and make the Son an inferior dependent *Being*,—depending at first on the *will* of the Father for his existence, and afterwards for the continuance of it."[1]

On the Continent, the doctrine of the trinity has been most discussed, during the present century, within the German Church. The Rationalists have rejected trinitarianism altogether, and have adopted the Deistical conception of God,—substantially that of Socinianism. So far as the Orthodox theology has been affected by the pantheistic systems of philosophy, it is easy to see a leaning in it towards the Sabellian construction of the trinity. The attempt of Schleiermacher to evince the substantial accord-

[1] WATERLAND: Vindication, Question XIII.

ance of the Sabellian with the catholic scheme, while unsuccessful before the bar of science, had the effect to modify the views of his school. Some of the essays upon the trinity that are occasionally appearing in German periodical literature, betoken an inclination towards the theory of a modal trinity. At the same time, it is worthy of notice, that the learned and logical histories of the Doctrine of the Trinity that have been produced in Germany, within the last half century, whether proceeding from a friend or an enemy of the orthodox creed, from a Dorner or a Baur, show very conclusively, by their manner of construing the historical facts, that it is the received opinion that, whether true or false, the Nicaeno-Constantinopolitan symbol contains the historical trinitarianism adopted by the Ancient, the Mediaeval, and the Modern Church.

CHAPTER V.

DOCTRINE OF THE PERSON OF CHRIST.

§ 1. *Principal Heresies in Christology.*

FOUR factors are necessary in order to the complete conception of Christ's Person: 1. True and proper deity; 2. True and proper humanity; 3. The union of deity and humanity in one Person; 4. The distinction of deity from humanity, in the one Person, so that there be no mixture of natures. If either of these is wanting, the dogmatic statement is an erroneous one. The heresies which originated in the Ancient Church took their rise, in the failure to combine all these elements in the doctrinal statement. Some one or more of these integral parts of the subject were adopted, while the others were rejected. The classification of the ancient errors in Christology will, therefore, very naturally follow the above enumeration.[1]

[1] Compare GUERICKE: Church History, § 87-90; HOOKER: Ecclesiastical Polity, Book V. Ch. li-lv.

I. The *Arians* would not concede the existence of a truly and properly divine nature in the Person of Jesus Christ. Even the Semi-Arians, who allowed that the Son of God, or the Logos, was of a nature *similar* to that of God, yet not identical with it, could not attribute absolute divinity to the Redeemer of the world. That exalted and pre-existent being who became incarnate in Christ, even upon the Semi-Arian theory could not be called *God*-man with technical accuracy. But the Arian Christ was confessedly lacking in a divine nature, in every sense of the term. Though the Son of God was united with human nature, in the birth of Jesus, yet that Son of God was a κτίσμα. He indeed existed long before that birth, but not from eternity. The only element, consequently, in the Arian construction of Christ's Person that was preserved intact and pure was the humanity. Upon this point the Arians were orthodox.

Into the same class with the Arians, fall the earlier *Nominal Trinitarians*. Inasmuch as, in their construction of the doctrine of the trinity, the Son is not a *subsistence* (ὑπόστασις) in the Essence, but only an *effluence* (δύναμις) or energy issuing from it, they could not logically assert the union of the divine *nature*, or the very substance of the Godhead, with the humanity of Jesus. A merely effluent energy proceeding from the deity, and entering the humanity of Christ, would be nothing more than an indwelling inspiration kindred to that of the prophets. The element of true essential deity, in union with true essential humanity, in the Person of Christ, was, consequently, wanting in the Christology of the Nominal Trinitarians.

II. The *Monarchians*, or *Patripassians*, went to the opposite extreme of error. They asserted the true and proper deity in Christ's Person, but denied his humanity. According to them, the one single Person of the Godhead, the true and absolute deity, united itself with a human *body*, but not with a human rational soul. The humanity in Christ's Person was thus incomplete. It lacked the rational part,—the spirit as distinguished from the flesh.

This Patripassian Christology received a slight modification from Apollinaris bishop of Laodicea († 382), who has given the name of *Apollinarism* to the scheme. The threefold division of human nature, into body ($\sigma\tilde{\omega}\mu\alpha$), soul ($\psi v \chi \acute{\eta}$), and spirit ($\pi v \varepsilon \tilde{v} \mu \alpha$), had become current, and Apollinaris supposed that it would be easier to conceive of, and explain Christ's Person, if the Logos were regarded as taking the place of the higher rational principle in the ordinary threefold nature of man, and thereby becoming an integral portion of the humanity.[1] But upon this scheme, the Divine did not take to itself a complete and *entire* human nature, any more

---

[1] According to Suidas (sub voce 'Απολλινάριος), Apollinaris thought the human reason would be a superfluity in union with the Divine Reason: Μηδὲ γὰρ δεηϑῆναί φησὶ τὴν σάρκα ἐκείνην ἀνϑρωπίνου νοὸς, ἡγεμονευομένην ὑπό τοῦ αὐτὴν ἐνδεδυκότος ϑεοῦ.

than in the original Patripassian theory. The material body, with the *animal* soul, or the vital principle, is by no means the whole of man. The Logos, upon this theory, was united with a fundamentally defective and mutilated humanity. For if the rational part be subtracted from man, he becomes either an idiot or a brute. It is true that Apollinarism supplies the deficiency with the Divine Reason; but it is no less true, that at the instant of the union of the two natures, the human part is merely the body ($σῶμα$), with its vital principle ($ψυχή$). It is irrational, and God assumes into personal union with himself a merely brutal nature. The human factor, consequently, was defective in the Apollinarian Christology.

III. The third general error in Christology, that arose in the Ancient Church, is the *Nestorian*.[1] By this we mean the theory that was finally eliminated by the controversies between Nestorius and his opponents. Whether it was a theory which Nestorius himself would have accepted in the opening of the controversy, or one that he intended to construct, is certainly open to debate. But Nestorian*ism* was a definite scheme, when ultimately formed, and is wanting in some essential elements and features.

The defect in the Nestorian Christology relates not to the distinction of the two natures, but to the

[1] Compare WALCH: Ketzerhistorie; and DOLLINGER: Church History, II. 150, 152 sq.

union of the two in one Person. A true and proper deity and a true and proper humanity are conceded. But they are not *united* in a single self-conscious personality. The Nestorian Christ is two persons, —one divine, and one human. The important distinction between a "nature" and a "person" is not observed, and the consequence is that there are two separate and diverse selves in Jesus Christ.[1] Instead of a blending of the two natures into only one self, the Nestorian scheme places two selves side by side, and allows only a moral and sympathetic union between them. The result is that the acts of each nature derive no character from the qualities of the other. There is no divine humiliation, because the humanity is confessedly the seat of the humiliation, and the humanity is by itself, unblended in the unity of a common self-consciousness. And there is no exaltation of the humanity, because the divinity is confessedly the source of the exaltation, and this also is insulated and isolated for the same reason.

---

[1] "Between Nestorius and the church of God, there was no difference, saving only that Nestorius imagined in Christ as well a personal human subsistence, as a divine; the church acknowledging a *substance* both divine and human, but no other personal *subsistence* [i. e. personal ego] than divine, because the Son of God took not to himself a man's *person*, but the *nature*, only, of a man." HOOKER: Eccles. Polity, Book V. Ch. liii. The anathemas which Nestorius uttered against the doctrine of Cyril separate the two natures very plainly. He appears to regard the union, or rather, the association of deity with humanity as occurring at birth, and represents the humanity as laid aside again after Christ's death and resurrection. MILMAN: Book II. Ch. iii.

There is God, and there is man; but there is no God-Man.

IV. The fourth of the ancient heresies in Christology is the *Eutychian* or *Monophysite*. This is the opposite error to Nestorianism. It asserts the unity of self-consciousness in the Person of Christ, but loses the duality of the natures. Eutyches taught that in the incarnation the human nature was *transmuted* into the divine; so that the resultant was one person and one nature. For this reason, the Eutychians held that it was accurate and proper to say that "God suffered,"—meaning thereby that He suffered in God's nature. When the Catholics employed this phrase, as they sometimes did, it was with the meaning that God suffered in man's nature. "When the apostle," remarks Hooker, "saith of the Jews that they crucified the Lord of Glory (1 Cor. ii. 8), we must needs understand the whole person of Christ, who, being Lord of Glory, was indeed crucified, *but not in that nature* for which he is termed the Lord of Glory. In like manner, when the Son of Man, being on earth, affirmeth, that the Son of Man was in heaven at the same instant (John iii. 13), by the Son of Man must necessarily be meant, the whole person of Christ, who being man upon earth, filled heaven with his glorious presence, *but not according to that nature* for which the title of Man is given him."[1]

---

[1] HOOKER: Eccl. Pol. Book V. Ch. liv.

The councils of Nice and Constantinople, in determining the true statement of the doctrine of the Trinity, assisted to settle the doctrine of Christ's Person, indirectly. So far as his deity was concerned, the Nicaeno-Constantinopolitan creed furnished material that must necessarily go into a scriptural Christology. But it did not come within the purpose of these councils to make statements respecting Christ's humanity, or to determine the relations of the two natures to each other. It was for this reason, among others, that the subject of Christology was less developed than that of the Trinity; and that men like Apollinaris, who were correct in their Trinitarian views, should embody an error in their Christological theory. These various errors and deficiencies in the statement of the doctrine of Christ's Person were finally corrected and filled out, in the creed drawn up by the *Council of Chalcedon*, in 451. The *Council of Ephesus*, in 431, had made some beginning towards the settlement of the questions involved; but this, though summoned as such, was not strictly an oecumenical council, and was too much under the influence of the then Monophysitizing Cyril[1] to yield a comprehensive and impartial result.

---

[1] Cyril's anathematizing positions, which he succeeded in forcing upon the Council of Ephesus, in 431, asserted that after the incarnation, the distinction between the two natures no longer existed. This he afterwards tacitly retracted, though not formally.

§ 2. *The Chalcedon Christology.*

The Chalcedon Symbol[1] defines the Person of Christ as follows. "We teach that Jesus Christ is perfect as respects godhood, and perfect as respects manhood; that he is truly God, and truly a man consisting of a rational soul and a body; that he is consubstantial (ὁμοούσιον) with the Father as to his divinity, and consubstantial (ὁμοούσιον) with us as to his humanity, and like us in all respects sin excepted. He was begotten of the Father, before creation (πρὸ αἰώνων), as to his deity; but in these last days he was born of Mary the mother of God (Θεοτόκος),[2] as to his humanity. He is one Christ,

---

[1] See Mansi, VII. 108; Guericke's Church History, § 89; Gieseler's Church History, I. § 89.

[2] The Catholics were tenacious of this word as applied to the "person" in distinction from the "natures." The mother, they maintained, is the mother of the *whole* person, although the soul, as the immaterial nature. is not conceived,—the theory of Creationism being adopted. As the human mother gives birth, not merely to the body, but to the whole person, which consists of a real and essential union of body and soul, so the Virgin Mary, although she did not give birth to the divine nature, as such, is nevertheless the mother of the God-Man, who is a Person composed of deity and humanity. And as the God-Man may be properly denominated God, Mary was, *in this sense*, Θεοτόκος. That she was not the "Mother of God," in the sense that the divine nature was conceived and born of her, is proved by the guarding clause in the creed statement,— " he was born of Mary the mother of God, *as to his humanity.*" The object of the Chalcedon divines, in the use of the term Θεοτόκος, was to teach, that Mary was not the mother of a mere and ordinary man, as the Nestorian doctrine would imply. For, according to Nestorianism, Christ was the second Person in the Trinity associated, by a merely moral union, with a distinct human person,—of which distinct and sepa-

existing in two natures without mixture (ἀσυγχύ-τως), without change (ἀτρέπτως), without division (ἀδιαιρέτως), without separation (ἀχωρίστως),—the diversity of the two natures not being at all destroyed by their union in the person, but the peculiar properties (ἰδιότης) of each nature being preserved, and concurring to one person (πρόσωπον), and one subsistence (ὑπόστασιν)."

This statement not only asserts that there are two natures in Christ's Person, but also adjusts their relation to each other.

1. In the first place, according to the Chalcedon symbol, the uniting of the two natures in one personality does not confuse or mix them, in such a manner as to destroy their distinctive properties. The deity of Christ is just as pure and simple deity, after the incarnation, as before it. And the humanity of Christ is just as pure and simple human nature as that of Mary his mother, or any other human individual, sin being excluded. The unifying act, by which the nature of God, and the nature of man, are blended into one personal subsistence, does not in the least alter their constituent properties. The

rate human person *alone*, Mary was the mother. The Chalcedon position was that the union of the two natures was *embryonic*, in and by the miraculous conception in the womb of the Virgin, so that "that holy thing born" of her (Luke i 35) was theanthropic. It was not a mere man, but a God-Man that was conceived, and not a mere man, but a God-Man that was born. And in denominating Mary ϑεοτόκος, as the Catholic Church did, they meant that she was the mother of the entire Divine-human *Person*,— she was the mother of Jesus Christ.

human nature is not transmuted into the divine; the divine nature is not transmuted into the human; neither is there a *tertium quid* formed by mixing the two,—a third Divine-human nature that is neither human nor divine.

2. In the second place, the Chalcedon statement prohibits the division of Christ into two selves or persons. The incarnating act, while it makes no changes in the properties of the two united natures, gives as a resultant a Person that is a *tertium quid*, a resultant that is neither a human person, nor a divine person, but a theanthropic person. For, if we have reference merely to his *self-consciousness*, or personality, Jesus Christ is neither human, nor divine, but is Divine-human. Contemplating him as the resultant of the *union* of God and man, he is not to be denominated God, and he is not to be denominated man; but he is to be denominated *God-Man*. The "person" of Jesus Christ, as distinguished from the "natures" that compose it, is a *theanthropic* person. Says Leo the Great: "Two natures met together in our Redeemer, and while the properties of each remained, so great a unity was made of either substance, that from the time that the Word was made flesh in the virgin's womb, we may neither think of Him as God without this which is man, nor as man without this which is God. Each nature certifies its own reality under distinct actions, but neither disjoins itself from connexion with the other. Nothing is wanting from either

towards the other; there is entire littleness in majesty, entire majesty in littleness; unity does not introduce confusion, nor does propriety divide unity. There is one thing passible, another impassible, yet his is the contumely whose is the glory. He is in infirmity who is in power; the self-same Person is both capable, and conqueror, of death. God did then take on Him whole man, and so knit Himself into him, and him into Himself, in pity and in power, that either nature was in the other, and neither in the other lost its own property."[1]

This union of two natures in one self-conscious Ego may be illustrated by reference to man's personal constitution. An individual man is one person. But this one person consists of two natures,— a material nature, and a mental nature. The personality, the self-consciousness, is the resultant of the *union* of the two. Neither one of itself makes the person. Both body and soul are requisite in order to a complete individuality. The two natures do not make two individuals. The material nature, taken by itself, is not the man; and the mental part, taken by itself, is not the man. But only the *union* of the two is. Yet, in this intimate union of two such diverse substances as matter and mind, body and soul, there is not the slightest alteration of the properties of each substance or nature. The

[1] Leo Magnus: Sermo LII. ii. II. 706 sq.; Hooker: Eccl. Pol. Compare Dorner: Person Christi, Book V. Ch. li. sq.

body of a man is as truly and purely material, as a piece of granite; and the immortal mind of a man is as truly and purely spiritual and immaterial, as the Godhead itself. Neither the material part, nor the mental part, taken by itself, and in separation, constitutes the personality; otherwise, every human individual would be two persons in juxtaposition. There is, therefore, a material "nature," but no material "person;" and there is a mental "nature," but no mental "person." The person is the *union* of these two natures, and is not to be denominated either material or mental, but *human*. In like manner the Person of Christ takes its denomination of *theanthropic*, or *Divine-human*, neither from the Divine nature alone, nor the human nature alone, but from the *union* of both natures.

One very important consequence of this statement of the Council of Chalcedon is, that *the properties of both natures may be attributed to the one Person*. If the Person be called Jesus Christ, then it is proper to say, that Jesus Christ wept, and Jesus Christ is the same yesterday to-day and forever. The first statement denotes a characteristic of humanity, which is attributable to the Person; the last statement a characteristic of deity which is attributable to the Person; and both alike are characteristic of one and the same theanthropic Person. If, again, the Person be called the God-Man, then it is accurate to say that the God-Man existed before Abraham and the God-Man was born in the reign of Augustus Caesar; that He was David's son, and David's Lord. The characteristics of the finite nature, and of the infinite nature, belong equally to that Ego, that conscious self, which is constituted of them both.[1]

Another equally important consequence of this Chalcedon adjustment of the relations of the two natures was, that *the suffering of the God-Man was truly and really infinite*, while yet the Divine nature is impassible.[2] The God-Man suffered in his human nature, and not in his divine. For, although the properties of each nature may be attributed to the one Person, the properties of the one nature cannot be attributed to the other nature. The *seat* of the suffering, therefore, must be the humanity, and not the divinity, in the Person. But the Person suffering is the God-Man; and his personality is as truly infinite as it is truly finite. Jesus Christ really suffered; not in his Divine nature, for that

---

[1] "By reason not of two persons linked in amity, but of two natures, human and divine, conjoined in one and the same person, the God of glory may be said as well to have suffered death, as to have raised the dead from their graves; the Son of Man as well to have made as redeemed the world." HOOKER: Eccl. Pol. Book V. Ch. liii. "A man is called tall, fair, and healthy, from the state of his body; and learned, wise, and good, from the qualities of his mind. So Christ is called holy, harmless, and undefiled; is said to have died, risen, and ascended up to heaven, with relation to his human nature. He is also said to be in the form of God, to have created all things, to be the brightness of the Father's glory, and the express image of his person, with relation to his Divine nature." BURNET: On the Thirty-Nine Articles (Article II).

[2] Compare PEARSON: On the Creed (Article IV).

cannot be the seat of suffering, but in his human nature, which he had assumed so that he might suffer. The passion, therefore, is infinite because the Person is infinite; although the nature which is the medium through which the Person suffers is finite.

Here, again, the analogies of finite existence furnish illustrations. A man suffers the sensation of heat from a coal of fire; and a brute suffers the same sensation from the same coal. The seat of the sensation, the *sensorium*, in each instance is a physical nature. For the mental and immaterial nature of the man is not burned by the fire. The point of contact, and the medium of suffering, in each instance, is a material and fleshly substance. But the character and value of the suffering, in one instance, is vastly higher than in the other, by reason of the difference in the subject, the Ego. The painful sensation, in the case of the man, is the suffering of a rational and immortal person; in that of the brute, it is the suffering of an unreasoning and perishing creature. The former is *human* agony; the latter is *brutish* agony. One is high up the scale, and the other low down, not because of the sensorium, or "nature," in which it is seated (for this is the same thing in both), but because of the person or subject to which it runs and refers back.

Now the entire humanity of Christ,—the "true body and reasonable soul,"—sustained the same relation to his Divinity, that the fleshly part of a man does to his rational part. It was the sensorium, the passible medium or "nature," by and through which it was possible for the self-conscious EGO, the theanthropic Person, to suffer.[1] And as, in the instance of an ordinary man, the mere fleshly agony is converted into a truly human and rational suffering, by reason of the humanity that is united with the animal soul and body, so, in the instance of Jesus Christ, the mere human agony is converted into a truly divine suffering, by reason of the divinity that is united with the human soul and body, in the unity of one self-consciousness.

Another important implication in the Chalcedon Christology is, that *it is the Divinity, and not the humanity, which constitutes the root and basis of Christ's personality.* The incarnation is the humanizing of deity, and not the deification of humanity. The second subsistence in the Divine Essence assumes human nature to itself; so that it is the Godhood, and not the manhood, which is prior and determining in the new complex-person that results. The redemption of mankind is accomplished, not

---

[1] Or more strictly, perhaps, to be *conscious* of suffering. In the instance of an ordinary human suffering that arises from a *physical* source, the immaterial part of man does not, properly speaking, itself suffer a sensation, but is *conscious* of a painful sensation occurring in the material part. In like manner, the deity in Christ's Person does not itself suffer, but is conscious of a suffering that occurs in the humanity. The consciousness itself is in the divinity, which is the root of the personality of the God-Man; but the *material* of the consciousness is in the humanity.

by the elevation of the finite to the infinite, but by the humiliation of the infinite to the finite.[1]

It is further to be noticed, that, according to the Chalcedon doctrine, *the Logos did not unite Himself with a distinct individual, but with a human nature.* An individual man was not first conceived and born, with whom the second Person in the Godhead then associated himself, but the union was effected with the substance of humanity in the womb of a Virgin: Says Hooker: "'He took not angels, but the seed of Abraham.' If the Son of God had taken to himself a man *now made and already perfected*, it would of necessity follow, that there are in Christ two persons, the one assuming, and the other assumed; whereas the Son of God did not assume a man's *person* into his own [person], but a man's *nature* to his own person; and therefore took *semen*, the seed of Abraham, the very first original element of our nature, before it was come to have any personal human subsistence. The flesh and the conjunction of the flesh with God, began both at one instant; his making and taking to himself our flesh was but one act, so that in Christ there is no personal subsistence but one, and that from everlasting."[2] The distinction between a "nature" and a "person" is of as great consequence

---

[1] "What strikes us first of all, in comparing the greatness of Jesus with that of the heroes of antiquity, is, that the source of His greatness is not His ascending, but His condescending; not rising above men, but letting Himself down to them." ULLMANN: Sinlessness of Jesus, p. 60.

[2] HOOKER: Eccl. Pol. B. V. Ch.

in Christology, as in Trinitarianism; and the Chalcedon divines were enabled, by carefully observing it, to combine all the Scripture data relating to the Incarnation, into a form of statement that has been accepted by the church universal ever since, and beyond which it is probable the human mind is unable to go, in the endeavor to unfold the mystery of Christ's complex Person, which in some of its aspects is even more baffling than the mystery of the Trinity.

liii. An American writer seems to have had this statement of Hooker in his eye. "The personality of Jesus Christ," says HOPKINS: (Works I. 283), "is in his divine nature, and not in the human. Jesus Christ existed a distinct, divine person from eternity, the second person in the adorable Trinity. The human nature which this divine person, the Word, assumed into a personal union with himself, *is not, and never was, a distinct person by itself, and personality cannot be ascribed to it, and does not belong to it, any otherwise than as united to the Logos, the Word of God.* The Word assumed the human *nature*, not a human *person*, into a personal union with himself, by which the complex person exists, God-man. Had the second person in the Trinity taken a human *person*, into union with himself, and were this possible, Jesus Christ, God and man, would be *two* persons, not one. Hence, when Jesus Christ is spoken of as being a man, 'the Son of Man, the man Christ Jesus,' etc., these terms *do not express the personality of the manhood, or of the human nature of Jesus Christ;* but these personal terms are used with respect to the human nature, *as united* to a divine person, and not as a mere man. For the personal terms, He, I, and Thou, cannot, with propriety or truth, be used by, or of, the human nature, *considered as distinct* from the divine nature of Jesus Christ."

END OF VOL I.

www.ingramcontent.com/pod-product-compliance
Lightning Source LLC
Chambersburg PA
CBHW022109290426
44112CB00008B/600